The Best of COUNTRY COOKING
2003

Editor: Jean Steiner
Art Director: Lori Arndt
Food Editor: Janaan Cunningham
Associate Editors: Julie Schnittka, Heidi Reuter Lloyd
Food Photography: Dan Roberts, Rob Hagen
Senior Food Photography Artist: Stephanie Marchese
Food Photography Artist: Julie Ferron
Photo Studio Manager: Anne Schimmel
Graphic Art Associates: Ellen Lloyd, Catherine Fletcher
Chairman and Founder: Roy Reiman
President: Tom Curl

©2003 Reiman Media Group, Inc.
5400 S. 60th St., Greendale WI 53129
International Standard Book Number: 0-89821-358-4
International Standard Serial Number: 1097-8321
All rights reserved.
Printed in U.S.A.

For additional copies of this book or information on other books, write *Taste of Home* Books,
P.O. Box 908, Greendale WI 53129, call toll-free 1-800/344-2560 to order with a credit card
or visit our Web site at **www.reimanpub.com**.

PICTURED ON COVER AND ABOVE. From the top: Butternut Squash Layer Cake (p. 117), Oven-Roasted Carrots (p. 73) and Pork Chops with Onions and Apples (p. 37).

358 Country Favorites in One Convenient Recipe Collection

IF DOWN-HOME COOKING is the order of the day at your house, *The Best of Country Cooking 2003* will fill the bill. It's the sixth in our popular cookbook series, and it's serving up 358 country favorites.

This giant collection includes the very best recipes from recent issues of *Country Woman, Country, Country EXTRA, Reminisce* and *Reminisce EXTRA* magazines. All are hearty, wholesome and proven favorites of a family just like yours.

You see, these recipes weren't developed in some high-tech industrial "kitchen". Instead, they're from the personal recipe files of hundreds of everyday cooks across the country. Each and every dish has been sampled and approved by the toughest critic around—a hungry family!

What's more, every recipe in this book was tested—many of them twice—by us as well. So you can be doubly confident each and every dish is a "keeper" that doesn't require a tryout first.

So go ahead *today* and take your pick of this beautiful book's 67 Main Dishes, including Country-Style Ribs (a surefire company pleaser for Annette McCullough of Pahrump, Nevada), Busy Day Beef Stew (Beth Wyatt of Paris, Kentucky lets it simmer all day in her slow cooker) and Cheesy Tuna Noodles (O'Fallon, Missouri cook Tamara Duggan serves this comforting casserole once a month).

There's also a Side Dishes & Condiments chapter filled with 34 country-style complements like Loaded Mashed Potatoes from Dawn Rueter of Oxford, Wisconsin. And turn to Breads & Rolls for fresh-baked goodies such as Buttermilk Pan Rolls shared by Patricia Young of Bella Vista, Arkansas—they go well with just about any meal.

Everyone will save room for dessert when any of this book's 82 scrumptious cakes, pies, cookies and more will be the sweet conclusion. Kathy Kittell of Lenexa, Kansas says people who eat her Creamy Candy Bar Dessert smile like kids in a candy store, no matter what their age. And Betty Ferrell of Jasper, Georgia likes to serve Crispy Butter Cookies with a cold glass of milk.

In addition, this tried-and-true treasury contains a savory selection of 47 Soups & Salads, and an appealing assortment of Snacks & Beverages. You'll also enjoy some extra-special features most other cookbooks overlook:

Thirty-Minute Meals—Six complete meals (18 recipes in all) that are ready to eat in *less than half an hour*.

Memorable Meals—Six complete meals featuring 24 favorite recipes from home cooks.

Cooking for Two—A separate chapter with 48 recipes all properly proportioned to serve two people.

Want more? *The Best of Country Cooking 2003* offers individual sections on cooking quick-and-easy fare that you can whip up for your hungry family with little effort.

As you page through *The Best of Country Cooking 2003*, watch for the special symbol at right. It signifies a "best of the best" recipe—a winner of a coast-to-coast cooking contest one of our magazines sponsored.

Finally, throughout this colorful collection are lots of helpful kitchen tips from everyday cooks plus dozens of "restricted diet" recipes marked with this check ✓ that use less fat, sugar or salt.

See why we call this book "The Best"? Now, wait 'til you and your family *taste* why!

CONTENTS

Snacks & Beverages...4

Main Dishes...12

Soups & Salads...46

Side Dishes &
Condiments...66

Breads & Rolls...80

Cookies, Bars &
Candies...90

Cakes, Pies
& Desserts...108

Cooking for Two...132

Meals in Minutes...152

Our Most
Memorable Meals...164

Index begins on page 176

WHEN *mid-day munchies or late-night hunger strikes, turn to these satisfying snacks and beverages.*

SNACK ATTACK. From top: Citrus Quencher, Herbed Garlic Cheese Spread and Cheesy Sausage Nachos (all recipes on p. 5).

Snacks & Beverages

CHEESY SAUSAGE NACHOS
(Pictured at left)

Jane Sodergren, Red Wing, Minnesota

This dish is very versatile. It can be used as an entree or appetizer. It gets rave reviews either way.

- 3/4 pound bulk pork sausage
- 1/4 cup chopped onion
- 3 cups diced fresh tomatoes, *divided*
- 3/4 cup picante sauce
- 4 cups tortilla chips
- 3 cups (12 ounces) shredded Monterey Jack cheese, *divided*
- 1 medium ripe avocado, diced

In a skillet, cook sausage and onion over medium heat until meat is no longer pink; drain well. Add 2 cups tomatoes and picante sauce. Bring to a boil. Reduce heat; simmer, uncovered, for 20 minutes or until most of the liquid has evaporated.

Sprinkle tortilla chips over a 12-in. pizza pan. Top with 2 cups cheese and the sausage mixture; sprinkle with remaining cheese. Bake at 350° for 8-10 minutes or until cheese is melted. Sprinkle with avocado and remaining tomatoes. **Yield:** 8-10 servings.

HERBED GARLIC CHEESE SPREAD
(Pictured at left)

Christine Duffy, Concord, New Hampshire

I've taken this creamy spread to many holiday gatherings and parties—and there's never any left to bring home! Well-seasoned with a blend of herb flavors, this cheesy treat tastes great on slices of French bread, too.

- 2 packages (8 ounces *each*) cream cheese, softened
- 1 cup butter (no substitutes), softened
- 1/2 teaspoon *each* dried basil, marjoram, oregano, thyme, dill weed, garlic powder and pepper

Assorted crackers

In a mixing bowl, beat the cream cheese, butter and seasonings until well blended. Cover and refrigerate for at least 2 hours. Serve with crackers. **Yield:** about 3 cups.

CITRUS QUENCHER
(Pictured at left)

Romaine Wetzel, Lancaster, Pennsylvania

Here's a refreshing beverage that's perfect on a hot summer day. It's a great complement to any chicken dish.

- 1 cup lemon juice
- 1 cup lime juice
- 1 cup sugar
- 1 carton (64 ounces) orange juice
- 2 cups chilled club soda

Lime slices, optional

In a large pitcher or container, combine the lemon juice, lime juice and sugar; stir until sugar is dissolved. Stir in orange juice. Refrigerate until serving. Add soda and ice cubes. Garnish with lime if desired. **Yield:** 3 quarts.

PICNIC STUFFED EGGS

Rebecca Register, Tallahassee, Florida

My dad loves these stuffed eggs, which are a Southern favorite. I've been cooking since I became a teenager, and this is one of my original recipes.

- 12 hard-cooked eggs
- 1/2 cup mayonnaise
- 1/4 cup sweet pickle relish, drained
- 1 tablespoon honey mustard
- 1 teaspoon garlic salt
- 1/2 teaspoon Worcestershire sauce
- 1/4 teaspoon pepper

Fresh parsley sprigs, optional

Slice eggs in half lengthwise; remove yolks and set whites aside. In a small bowl, mash yolks with a fork. Add the mayonnaise, pickle relish, mustard, garlic salt, Worcestershire sauce and pepper; mix well. Stuff or pipe into the egg whites. Refrigerate until serving. Garnish with parsley if desired. **Yield:** 2 dozen.

CURRY CARROT DIP

Louise Weyer, Marietta, Georgia

The flavors of mustard and curry blend deliciously in this appetizing dip. It's great with an assortment of vegetables.

✓ **Uses less fat, sugar or salt. Includes Nutritional Analysis and Diabetic Exchanges.**

- 1 small onion, chopped
- 2 teaspoons canola oil
- 4 medium carrots, sliced
- 1/3 cup water
- 1/4 teaspoon salt
- 1/4 teaspoon pepper
- 1/4 teaspoon curry powder
- 2 tablespoons reduced-fat mayonnaise
- 2 teaspoons prepared mustard
- Assorted raw vegetables

In a nonstick skillet, saute onion in oil. Add the carrots, water, salt, pepper and curry. Bring to a boil. Reduce heat; cover and simmer for 6 minutes or until vegetables are tender. Uncover; cook for 8 minutes or until liquid has evaporated. Cool. Transfer to a food processor or blender; cover and process until smooth. Add mayonnaise and mustard; mix well. Serve with vegetables. **Yield:** 1 cup.

Nutritional Analysis: One serving (2 tablespoons dip) equals 45 calories, 2 g fat (trace saturated fat), 1 mg cholesterol, 140 mg sodium, 5 g carbohydrate, 1 g fiber, 1 g protein. **Diabetic Exchange:** 1/2 starch.

July Fourth Fare

NEED bang-up holiday fare that's a snap to make? Pop this Independence Day treat in the oven and friends will be flagging you down for the recipe!

The Fourth of July Pizza requires only four ready-to-use ingredients so it can be assembled in no time, says Flo Burtnett of Gage, Oklahoma.

"I just unroll refrigerated pizza dough for the crust and spread on a jar of sauce," she explains.

Putting the pizza together can even spark some family fun. Kids will get a charge out of adding the American cheese stars and string cheese stripes to the red "flag".

But the real enjoyment comes when you bite into this patriotic pie. Serve large slices as a meatless main dish or cut small squares to snack on before your holiday barbecue. Either way, it's a blast!

FOURTH OF JULY PIZZA

(Pictured below left)

- 1 tube (10 ounces) refrigerated pizza crust
- 2 slices process American cheese
- 8 strips string cheese
- 1 jar (15 ounces) pizza sauce

Unroll pizza dough and press onto the bottom and 1/2 in. up the sides of a greased 15-in. x 10-in. x 1-in. baking pan. Bake at 425° for 8-10 minutes or until golden brown.

Using a 1-in. star cookie cutter, cut eight stars from the American cheese. Cut each strip of string cheese in half lengthwise. Spread pizza sauce over crust. Arrange stars in the upper left corner. For stripes, arrange 15 pieces of string cheese over sauce (save remaining piece for another use). Bake 5-8 minutes longer or until cheese is melted. **Yield:** 16 slices.

GARDEN SALSA

(Pictured at right)

Barbara Mundy, Radford, Virginia

I grow almost all of these ingredients in my garden. This recipe makes a large batch, but it's always gone in no time.

    4 to 5 medium tomatoes, chopped
    1 medium onion, chopped
    1 medium green pepper, chopped
    2 jalapeno peppers, seeded and chopped*
    2 to 3 tablespoons chopped stuffed olives
    2 tablespoons minced fresh basil
    2 tablespoons minced fresh parsley
    1 can (8 ounces) tomato sauce
    2 tablespoons olive *or* vegetable oil
    4 teaspoons lime juice
1-1/2 teaspoons garlic salt
    1/2 teaspoon pepper
Tortilla chips

In a bowl, combine the first seven ingredients. In another bowl, combine the tomato sauce, oil, lime juice, garlic salt and pepper. Pour over vegetable mixture and mix well. Cover and refrigerate until serving. Serve with tortilla chips. **Yield:** 7 cups.

***Editor's Note:** When cutting or seeding hot peppers, use rubber or plastic gloves to protect your hands. Avoid touching your face.

CRANBERRY APPLE CIDER

(Pictured below)

Jennifer Naboka, North Plainfield, New Jersey

I love to start this soothing cider in the slow cooker on nights before my husband goes hunting. Then he can

fill his thermos and take it with him out into the cold. The cider has a terrific fruit flavor we both enjoy.

    4 cups water
    4 cups apple juice
    1 can (12 ounces) frozen apple juice
        concentrate, thawed
    1 medium apple, peeled and sliced
    1 cup fresh *or* frozen cranberries
    1 medium orange, peeled and sectioned
    1 cinnamon stick

In a slow cooker, combine all ingredients; mix well. Cover and cook on low for 2 hours or until cider reaches desired temperature. Discard cinnamon stick. If desired, remove fruit with a slotted spoon before serving. **Yield:** 10 servings (about 2-1/2 quarts).

MINT ICED TEA COOLER

Debbie Terenzini Wilkerson, Lusby, Maryland

This cool rose-colored tea quenches your thirst in the most delightful way. It's a pleasant blend of fruit and mint flavors. It's very easy to make, but more special than traditional iced tea.

    3 peppermint-flavored tea bags
    7 cups boiling water
    1 cup cranberry juice
    3/4 cup pink lemonade concentrate

Steep tea bags in boiling water for 5-10 minutes. Discard tea bags. Pour tea into a pitcher or large bowl; stir in cranberry juice and lemonade concentrate. Cover and refrigerate overnight. Serve over ice. **Yield:** 8 servings.

1 teaspoon ground nutmeg
1 teaspoon vanilla extract
1/8 teaspoon salt, optional
1 cup whipping cream
Additional nutmeg, optional

In a mixing bowl, beat milk and pudding mix on low speed for 2 minutes. Beat in the sugar, nutmeg, vanilla and salt if desired. In another mixing bowl, beat cream until thickened, about 3 minutes. Stir into pudding mixture. Refrigerate until serving. Sprinkle with additional nutmeg if desired. **Yield:** about 2-1/2 quarts.

BLACK BEAN SALSA
(Pictured above)

Charlene Denges, Elgin, Texas

My husband, son and I think this colorful salsa is great as a dip or with burritos or chimichangas.

>   2 cans (15 ounces *each*) black beans, rinsed and drained
>   1 can (15-1/4 ounces) whole kernel corn, drained
>   1 can (10 ounces) diced tomatoes and green chilies, undrained
>   1 jar (7-1/2 ounces) roasted red peppers, drained and diced
>   2 plum tomatoes, chopped
>   1 medium red onion, finely chopped
>   4 green onions, finely chopped
> 2/3 cup minced fresh cilantro *or* parsley
>   2 garlic cloves, minced
> 1/3 cup orange juice
>   1 teaspoon ground cumin
>   1 teaspoon grated orange peel
> 1/8 teaspoon coarsely ground pepper

Tortilla chips

In a large bowl, combine the first 13 ingredients. Cover and refrigerate for at least 2 hours. Serve with tortilla chips. **Yield:** 8 cups.

MOCK EGGNOG

Susannah Wayman, South Jordan, Utah

I found a mock eggnog recipe in a newspaper, made a few changes and this is the result.

>   2 quarts cold milk
>   1 package (3.4 ounces) instant French vanilla *or* vanilla pudding mix
> 1/4 cup sugar

SALMON CHEESE SPREAD
(Pictured below)

Raymonde Bernier, St. Hyacinthe, Quebec

Here's a delightful hors d'oeuvre that's excellent for any occasion.

>   2 packages (3 ounces *each*) cream cheese, softened
>   3 tablespoons mayonnaise
>   1 tablespoon lemon juice
> 1/2 teaspoon salt
> 1/2 teaspoon curry powder
> 1/4 teaspoon dried basil
> 1/8 teaspoon pepper
>   1 can (7-1/2 ounces) salmon, drained, bones and skin removed
>   2 green onions, thinly sliced

Crackers

In a mixing bowl, combine the cream cheese, mayonnaise and lemon juice. Add the salt, curry powder, basil and pepper; mix well. Gently stir in salmon and onions. Cover and refrigerate for at least 1 hour. Serve with crackers. **Yield:** 1-1/2 cups.

Snacks & Beverages

EMERALD ISLE DIP

Nancy Citro, Cape Coral, Florida

Friends joke that they won't go to St. Patrick's Day parties unless I bring my dip. And I've lost count of how many times I've given the recipe to people! I like to serve this snack with extra bread for dipping.

- 2 cups mayonnaise
- 2 cups (16 ounces) sour cream
- 1 package (2-1/2 ounces) cooked corned beef, finely chopped
- 2 tablespoons dried minced onion
- 2 tablespoons dried parsley flakes
- 2 tablespoons dill weed, *divided*
- 1/2 to 1 teaspoon seasoned salt
- 1 round unsliced loaf (1 pound) sourdough *or* rye bread

Assorted vegetables and crackers

In a bowl, combine mayonnaise, sour cream, corned beef, onion, parsley, 1 tablespoon dill and seasoned salt. Cover and refrigerate overnight.

Draw a large shamrock onto a piece of waxed paper; cut out. Place on loaf. Carefully cut out and remove shamrock; set aside. Hollow out loaf, leaving a 1/2-in. shell. Cut removed bread and cutout shamrock into cubes.

Fill shell with dip; sprinkle with remaining dill. Serve with bread cubes, vegetables and crackers. **Yield:** 4 cups.

You'll Dig This Snack

IF YOU "carrot" all about serving up a good time for your guests, plant this playful appetizer on your party menu.

"I make this delicious appetizer for parties, and it catches everyone's eye," reports Pam Goodlet of Washington Island, Wisconsin.

With its "14-carrot" good looks, you'd think it would be time-consuming to make. But the tasty spread blends together in a jiffy.

CHEDDAR CHEESE CARROT

(Pictured below left)

- 1 package (3 ounces) cream cheese, softened
- 2 cups (8 ounces) shredded cheddar cheese
- 1/2 cup finely shredded carrot
- 1/2 cup finely chopped peanuts
- 2 tablespoons finely chopped onion
- 1/4 teaspoon dill weed

Fresh parsley sprigs
Assorted crackers

In a small mixing bowl, beat cream cheese and cheddar cheese for 1 minute. Add carrot, peanuts, onion and dill; mix well.

On a serving platter, shape mixture into an 8-in. log, tapering one end to form a carrot shape. Cover and refrigerate for 2 hours or until serving. Place parsley at wide end for carrot top. Serve with crackers. **Yield:** 2 cups.

FIESTA CHEESE BALL
(Pictured below)

Virginia Horst, Mesa, Washington

Whenever I bring this zippy cheese ball to church functions, showers or parties, folks always ask for the recipe. A deliciously different appetizer, it makes even a plain plate of crackers seem festive.

> 1 package (8 ounces) cream cheese, softened
> 1/4 cup shredded Colby-Monterey Jack cheese
> 3 to 4 tablespoons minced fresh cilantro *or* parsley
> 2 to 3 tablespoons grated onion
> 1 tablespoon chili powder
> 1 teaspoon dried minced garlic
> 1/2 teaspoon garlic salt
> 1/4 teaspoon dried oregano
> 1/4 teaspoon crushed red pepper flakes
> 1/8 teaspoon ground cumin
> 1/8 to 1/4 teaspoon hot pepper sauce
> 1/4 cup minced fresh parsley

Assorted crackers

In a mixing bowl, beat cream cheese. Add the next 10 ingredients and mix well. Cover and refrigerate for at least 1 hour. Shape into a ball. Roll in parsley. Cover and refrigerate for 8 hours or overnight. Serve with crackers. **Yield:** 1 cheese ball.

NEW HAVEN CLAM PIZZA
(Pictured above)

Susan Seymour, Valatie, New York

This appetizer is the perfect start to any meal. It's always been a big hit with our family and friends.

> 1 package (1/4 ounce) active dry yeast
> 1 cup warm water (110° to 115°)
> 1 teaspoon sugar
> 2-1/2 cups all-purpose flour
> 1 teaspoon salt
> 2 tablespoons vegetable oil
> 2 cans (6-1/2 ounces *each*) chopped clams, drained
> 4 bacon strips, cooked and crumbled
> 3 garlic cloves, minced
> 2 tablespoons grated Romano *or* Parmesan cheese
> 1 teaspoon dried oregano
> 1 cup (4 ounces) shredded mozzarella cheese

In a mixing bowl, dissolve yeast in water. Add sugar; let stand for 5 minutes. Add the flour, salt and oil; beat until smooth. Cover and let rise in a warm place until doubled, about 15-20 minutes.

Punch dough down. Press onto the bottom and up the sides of a greased 14-in. pizza pan; build up edges slightly. Prick dough several times with a fork.

Bake at 425° for 6-8 minutes. Sprinkle remaining ingredients over crust in order listed. Bake for 13-15 minutes or until crust is golden and cheese is melted. Cut into wedges. **Yield:** 8 servings.

CITRUS GRAPE DRINK

Sylvia Murphy, River Ranch, Florida

My mom made this often while I was growing up and I loved it. When I got married, I requested that it be served at the reception.

    4 cups water
    1 cup sugar
    2 cups red grape juice, chilled
    1/3 cup lemon juice, chilled
    1/3 cup orange juice, chilled

In a saucepan, heat water and sugar until sugar is dissolved. Cool. Pour into a large pitcher or punch bowl; stir in the juices. Serve over ice. **Yield:** about 2 quarts.

PEPPERMINT HOT CHOCOLATE

More than a hint of cool mint makes this delicious sipper a special switch from traditional hot chocolate. Our Test Kitchen staff came up with the rich beverage that's quick to fix. A dollop of whipped cream with crushed candy tops each mug lusciously.

3-1/2 cups milk
    8 squares (1 ounce *each*) white baking
      chocolate, chopped
1/4 to 1/2 teaspoon peppermint extract
    2/3 cup whipping cream
    8 peppermint candies, crushed
Additional crushed peppermint candies,
    optional

In a saucepan, heat milk over medium heat until steaming. Add chocolate; whisk until smooth. Stir in peppermint extract. In a mixing bowl, beat cream until stiff peaks form. Fold in the crushed candies. Ladle hot chocolate into mugs; dollop with whipped cream. Sprinkle with additional candies if desired. **Yield:** 4 servings.

FRUIT 'N' NUT TRAIL MIX
(Pictured below)

Pat Habiger, Spearville, Kansas

This snack recipe has a good mix of fruit and nuts. The mild cinnamon flavor adds a nice touch.

    1/4 cup sunflower kernels
      2 tablespoons butter *or* margarine
      4 cups old-fashioned oats
    1/2 cup vegetable oil
    3/4 cup cashew halves
    2/3 cup slivered almonds, toasted
    1/2 cup sesame seeds, toasted
    1/2 cup packed brown sugar
    1/2 cup honey
      1 teaspoon ground cinnamon
1-1/4 cups assorted bite-size dried fruit
      (raisins, apricots, dates, apples, bananas)

In a large skillet over medium heat, lightly toast sunflower kernels in butter; remove and set aside. In the same skillet, lightly toast oats in oil. Add the sunflower kernels, cashews, almonds and sesame seeds. Combine the brown sugar, honey and cinnamon; add to oat mixture. Cook and stir for 5 minutes.

Spread in two ungreased 15-in. x 10-in. x 1-in. baking pans. Bake at 350° for 15-20 minutes or until golden brown, stirring every 5 minutes. Cool, stirring occasionally. Stir in dried fruit. Store in an airtight container. **Yield:** 10 cups.

WHETHER *your family is partial to pork, fish, poultry or beef, these hearty main dishes will satisfy their taste buds.*

ROASTS TO RELISH. Clockwise from top left: Glazed Holiday Pork Roast, Busy Day Beef Stew and Sweet 'n' Sour Pot Roast (all recipes on p. 13).

Main Dishes

Main Dishes

GLAZED HOLIDAY PORK ROAST
(Pictured at left)

Sherry Kreiger, York, Pennsylvania

With its sweet and tangy fruit glaze, this pretty pork roast is perfect for a holiday meal.

    1 pork rib roast (4 to 4-1/2 pounds)
    1 cup mixed dried fruit, *divided*
  2/3 cup water
  2/3 cup honey
    1 envelope onion soup mix
  1/4 cup ketchup
    2 tablespoons lemon juice
    2 teaspoons grated lemon peel

Make 15-20 slits, about 1 to 1-1/2 in. deep, in the roast; place some fruit in each slit. In a bowl, combine the water, honey, soup mix, ketchup, lemon juice, peel and remaining fruit; mix well.

Place roast fat side up in a roasting pan. Pour fruit mixture over the top. Cover and bake at 325° for 3 to 3-1/2 hours or until a meat thermometer reads 160°. Let stand for 10-15 minutes before carving. **Yield:** 6-8 servings.

SWEET 'N' SOUR POT ROAST
(Pictured at left)

Taryn Daniels, Maple City, Michigan

Just a whiff of this pot roast reminds me of my grandmother—she's been making this family favorite for over 40 years.

      1 teaspoon garlic salt
    1/2 teaspoon ground mustard
    1/4 teaspoon pepper
      1 boneless beef chuck roast (4-1/2 to 5 pounds)
      2 tablespoons vegetable oil
      2 cups water
    1/2 cup soy sauce
      2 tablespoons white vinegar
      2 tablespoons honey
      1 tablespoon celery seed
  1-1/2 teaspoons ground ginger
      6 tablespoons cornstarch
    1/2 cup cold water

Combine garlic salt, mustard and pepper; rub over entire roast. In a Dutch oven, brown roast on all sides in oil over medium-high heat; drain. Combine the water, soy sauce, vinegar, honey, celery seed and ginger; pour over roast. Bring to a boil. Reduce heat; cover and simmer for 3 to 3-1/2 hours or until meat is tender.

Remove roast from pan and keep warm. Pour pan drippings and loosened brown bits into a measuring cup. Skim fat, reserving drippings. Add enough water, if needed, to measure 5 cups. Return to Dutch oven. Combine cornstarch and cold water until smooth; gradually add to drippings. Bring to a boil; cook and stir for 2 minutes or until thickened. Slice roast; serve with gravy. **Yield:** 12-16 servings.

BUSY DAY BEEF STEW
(Pictured at left)

Beth Wyatt, Paris, Kentucky

Here's a classic old-fashioned beef stew that simmers for hours in the slow cooker. I call it my "lazy" stew.

    1 boneless beef chuck roast (1 to 1-1/2 pounds)
    1 envelope onion soup mix
    2 teaspoons browning sauce, optional
  1/2 teaspoon salt
  1/2 teaspoon pepper
    6 cups water
    2 cups cubed peeled potatoes
    6 to 8 medium carrots, cut into chunks
    1 medium onion, chopped
    1 cup frozen peas, thawed
    1 cup frozen corn, thawed, optional
    5 tablespoons cornstarch
    6 tablespoons cold water

Place roast in a slow cooker; sprinkle with soup mix, browning sauce if desired, salt and pepper. Pour water over meat. Cover and cook on low for 8 hours.

Remove roast to a cutting board; let stand for 5 minutes. Add vegetables to slow cooker. Cube beef and return to slow cooker. Cover and cook on low for 1-1/2 hours or until vegetables are tender. Combine cornstarch and cold water until smooth; stir into stew. Cover and cook on high for 30-45 minutes or until thickened. **Yield:** 8-10 servings.

ungreased 13-in. x 9-in. x 2-in. baking dish. Bake, uncovered, at 350° for 20-25 minutes or until chicken juices run clear.

Meanwhile, drain cherries, reserving juice. Add enough water to juice to measure 1 cup. In a saucepan, combine sugar and cornstarch. Stir in cherry juice until smooth. Add cherries. Bring to a boil; cook and stir for 2 minutes or until thickened. Remove from the heat. Stir in lemon juice, extract and food coloring if desired.

Discard toothpicks from roll-ups; serve with cherry sauce. **Yield:** 8 servings.

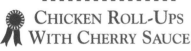

SALMON STUFFED PEPPERS
(Pictured below)

Kathleen Bowman, Sun Valley, Nevada

I used to make these stuffed peppers often for my large family. They're a nice change from the usual beef stuffed peppers.

```
    6 medium green, sweet yellow or red
      peppers
1-1/4 pounds salmon fillets or steaks
  3/4 cup chicken broth
    1 medium leek (white portion only),
      chopped or 1/2 cup chopped green
      onions
    1 to 3 medium jalapeno peppers, minced*
    2 tablespoons minced fresh cilantro or
      parsley
```

CHICKEN ROLL-UPS WITH CHERRY SAUCE
(Pictured on page 18)

Margaret Scott, Traverse City, Michigan

Since I grew up on a cherry farm, I have many recipes featuring that delightful fruit. This one is a delicious way to use chicken.

```
    8 boneless skinless chicken breast halves
    8 slices Swiss or Brie cheese
    1 egg
    1 tablespoon water
    1 tablespoon Dijon mustard
  3/4 cup dry bread crumbs
  1/2 teaspoon dried thyme
  1/4 teaspoon salt
Dash pepper
  1/4 cup all-purpose flour
  1/4 cup vegetable oil
CHERRY SAUCE:
    2 cups canned pitted tart red cherries
  3/4 cup sugar
    2 tablespoons cornstarch
    1 teaspoon lemon juice
  1/4 teaspoon almond extract
    3 drops red food coloring, optional
```

Flatten chicken breasts to 1/4-in. thickness. Place a slice of cheese on each; roll up and secure with toothpicks. In a shallow dish, beat egg, water and mustard. In another shallow dish, combine bread crumbs, thyme, salt and pepper. Lightly coat chicken with flour, then dip in egg mixture and roll in bread crumb mixture.

In a large skillet, heat oil. Add roll-ups; cook until golden brown, turning often. Transfer to an

1 teaspoon Worcestershire sauce
1/2 teaspoon dried tarragon
1/2 teaspoon dried oregano
1/4 teaspoon salt
1/8 teaspoon pepper
2 cups hot cooked rice
1/2 cup tartar sauce
1/2 cup sour cream
2 tablespoons shredded Parmesan cheese

Cut tops off peppers and remove seeds. Cook peppers in boiling water for 3-5 minutes or until tender. Drain and rinse in cold water; set aside.

Broil salmon 4-6 in. from the heat for 4-5 minutes on each side or until fish flakes easily with a fork. Discard bones and skin. Flake fish with a fork; set aside.

In a large skillet, combine the broth, leek, jalapenos, cilantro, Worcestershire sauce, tarragon, oregano, salt and pepper. Bring to a boil. Reduce heat; simmer, uncovered, for 10 minutes or until the liquid has evaporated.

Stir in hot rice, tartar sauce and sour cream. Fold in salmon. Spoon into peppers. Place in an ungreased shallow baking dish. Sprinkle with Parmesan cheese. Cover and bake at 350° for 25-30 minutes or until peppers are tender and filling is hot. **Yield:** 6 servings.

*Editor's Note: When cutting or seeding hot peppers, use rubber or plastic gloves to protect your hands. Avoid touching your face.

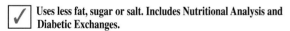

DOWN-HOME POT ROAST

(Pictured above right)

Lenore Rein, Kelliher, Saskatchewan

My mother often made pot roasts, and the aroma wafting through the house made our mouths water. Through the years, I've tried different variations, but this is a favorite.

✓ Uses less fat, sugar or salt. Includes Nutritional Analysis and Diabetic Exchanges.

1 boneless beef sirloin tip roast (3 pounds)
1 tablespoon canola oil
1 can (14-1/2 ounces) reduced-sodium beef broth
3 tablespoons cider vinegar
2 garlic cloves, minced
1/2 teaspoon dried basil
1/4 teaspoon dried thyme
1 small head cabbage, cut into wedges
4 medium potatoes, quartered
2 medium onions, cut into wedges
3 medium carrots, cut into chunks
1 medium sweet red pepper, cut into 1-inch pieces
1/2 teaspoon salt
1/2 teaspoon pepper
1/4 cup all-purpose flour
1/4 cup cold water

In a Dutch oven, brown roast on all sides in oil over medium-high heat; drain. Add broth. Pour vinegar over roast. Sprinkle with garlic, basil and thyme. Bring to a boil. Reduce heat; cover and simmer for 2 hours, turning roast occasionally. Add water if needed. Spoon off fat.

Add vegetables to pan. Sprinkle with salt and pepper. Cover and simmer for 35-45 minutes or until vegetables and meat are tender. Remove meat to a serving platter and keep warm.

For gravy, pour drippings and loosened browned bits into a measuring cup. Skim fat, reserving 2 cups drippings. Return drippings to pan. Combine flour and cold water until smooth; gradually stir into drippings. Bring to a boil; cook and stir for 2 minutes or until thickened. Serve with meat and vegetables. **Yield:** 12 servings.

Nutritional Analysis: One serving (with 2 tablespoons gravy) equals 238 calories, 6 g fat (2 g saturated fat), 68 mg cholesterol, 305 mg sodium, 20 g carbohydrate, 4 g fiber, 28 g protein.
Diabetic Exchanges: 3 lean meat, 2 vegetable, 1/2 starch.

simmer for 15 minutes or until vegetables are tender. Remove from the heat. Stir in the turkey, soup, sour cream, Worcestershire sauce, salt and pepper. Spoon into a greased 2-qt. baking dish.

In a bowl, combine the flour, baking powder and salt. Combine milk, eggs, 3/4 cup cheese, green pepper and pimientos; stir into the flour mixture until combined. Drop by tablespoonfuls over the hot turkey mixture.

Bake, uncovered, at 350° for 40-45 minutes or until golden brown. Sprinkle with remaining cheese. Bake 3 minutes longer or until cheese is melted. **Yield:** 4-5 servings.

ROAST PORK WITH RASPBERRY SAUCE

(Pictured on page 18)

Carolyn Zimmerman, Fairbury, Illinois

Want to treat your guests to a spectacular meal? Plan this pork as the centerpiece of your menu. The fruity sauce enhances the meat's flavor and looks so pretty! I decorate the platter with red spiced apples and fresh parsley.

    1 teaspoon salt
    1 teaspoon rubbed sage
    1 teaspoon pepper
    1 boneless pork loin roast (3-1/2 to 4
      pounds)
SAUCE:
    1 package (10 ounces) frozen sweetened
      raspberries, thawed
1-1/2 cups sugar
    1/4 cup white vinegar
    1/4 teaspoon *each* ground ginger, nutmeg
      and cloves
    1/4 cup cornstarch
    1 tablespoon butter *or* margarine, melted
    1 tablespoon lemon juice
    3 to 4 drops red food coloring,
      optional

Combine the salt, sage and pepper; rub over entire roast. Place roast fat side up on a rack in a shallow roasting pan. Bake, uncovered, at 350° for 70-80 minutes or until a meat thermometer reads 160°.

For the sauce, drain raspberries, reserving liquid. Set berries aside. Add enough water to juice to measure 3/4 cup. In a saucepan, combine the sugar, vinegar, spices and 1/2 cup raspberry juice. Bring to a boil. Reduce heat; simmer, uncovered, for 10 minutes.

Combine cornstarch and remaining raspberry juice until smooth; stir into the saucepan. Bring

TURKEY POTPIE

(Pictured above)

Debi Engelhard, Donnybrook, North Dakota

The best part of a turkey dinner is the leftovers—especially when they're baked into this comforting potpie! Relatives who visit husband Curt and me and our three children always leave with this recipe. It's a super second-time-around supper.

    1 cup diced carrots
    3/4 cup chopped onion
    1/2 cup chopped celery
    1/4 cup chicken broth
    3 cups cubed cooked turkey
    1 can (10-3/4 ounces) condensed cream
      of chicken soup, undiluted
    1 cup (8 ounces) sour cream
    1 teaspoon Worcestershire sauce
    1/2 teaspoon salt
    1/8 teaspoon pepper
TOPPING:
    1 cup all-purpose flour
    2 teaspoons baking powder
    1/2 teaspoon salt
    1/2 cup milk
    2 eggs
    1 cup (4 ounces) shredded cheddar
      cheese, *divided*
    3 tablespoons chopped green pepper
    2 tablespoons chopped pimientos

In a large saucepan, bring the carrots, onion, celery and broth to a boil. Reduce heat; cover and

to a boil; cook and stir for 2 minutes or until thickened. Remove from the heat. Stir in the butter, lemon juice, food coloring if desired and reserved raspberries.

Let roast stand for 10-15 minutes before slicing. Serve with raspberry sauce. **Yield:** 8-10 servings.

MARINATED BEEF TENDERLOIN
(Pictured on page 19)

Connie Scheffer, Salina, Kansas

My three grown children and grandkids enjoy this tempting tenderloin. Leftovers make wonderful sandwiches with oven-fresh bread and Dijon mustard. I sometimes substitute a marinated eye of round roast...and it turns out fine.

    1 cup soy sauce
  3/4 cup beef broth
  1/2 cup olive *or* vegetable oil
    2 tablespoons red wine vinegar *or* cider
      vinegar
    4 to 5 garlic cloves, minced
    1 teaspoon coarsely ground pepper
    1 teaspoon dried thyme
  1/2 teaspoon salt
  1/2 teaspoon hot pepper sauce
    1 bay leaf
    1 whole beef tenderloin (3-1/2 to 4
      pounds)

In a bowl, combine the first nine ingredients; mix well. Cover and refrigerate 1 cup for basting. Pour remaining marinade into a large resealable plastic bag; add bay leaf and tenderloin. Seal bag and turn to coat; refrigerate overnight.

Drain and discard marinade and bay leaf. Place tenderloin on a rack in a shallow roasting pan. Bake, uncovered, at 425° for 55-60 minutes or until meat reaches desired doneness (for rare, a meat thermometer should read 140°; medium, 160°; well-done, 170°), basting often with reserved marinade. Let stand for 15 minutes before slicing. **Yield:** 6-8 servings.

SHRIMP PATTY SANDWICHES
(Pictured at right)

Tina Jacobs, Hurlock, Maryland

Quite often when we eat at a restaurant, my husband will try something and tell me that I could make it better at home. That was the case with this shrimp patty. It had very few shrimp and needed more flavor. I made some improvements and now it's one of my husband's favorites.

    4 eggs
    4 cans (6 ounces *each*) shrimp, rinsed
      and drained *or* 2 cups medium cooked
      shrimp, peeled and deveined
    8 ounces haddock, cooked and flaked
    1 cup plus 3 tablespoons pancake mix
    2 tablespoons cornmeal
  1/2 teaspoon dried parsley flakes
  1/2 teaspoon celery salt
  1/4 teaspoon ground mustard
  1/4 teaspoon paprika
  1/2 cup dry bread crumbs
    3 to 4 tablespoons vegetable oil
    8 hamburger buns
Lettuce leaves, tomato slices and onion slices, optional

In a large bowl, beat the eggs. Add the shrimp, haddock, pancake mix, cornmeal, parsley, celery salt, mustard and paprika; mix well. Shape into eight patties. Coat with bread crumbs.

In a skillet over medium-high heat, cook patties in oil for 2 minutes on each side or until golden brown. Serve on buns with lettuce, tomato and onion if desired. **Yield:** 8 servings.

IF YOU'RE HUNGRY *for a hearty main dish, now you can "roast easy". Few meats are as tender, juicy and flavorful!*

PRIMED FOR PLATES. Clockwise from top left: Roast Pork with Raspberry Sauce (p. 16), Marinated Beef Tenderloin (p. 17), Stuffed Pork Tenderloin (p. 21), Slow-Cooked Rump Roast (p. 20) and Italian Beef Sandwiches (p. 20).

SLOW-COOKED RUMP ROAST
(Pictured on page 18)

Mimi Walker, Palmyra, Pennsylvania

I enjoy a good pot roast, but I was tired of the same old thing…so I started experimenting. Cooking the beef in horseradish sauce gives it a tangy flavor. Even my young kids love this roast with its tender veggies and gravy.

- 1 boneless beef rump roast (3 to 3-1/2 pounds)
- 2 tablespoons vegetable oil
- 4 medium carrots, halved lengthwise and cut into 2-inch pieces
- 3 medium potatoes, peeled and cut into chunks
- 2 small onions, sliced
- 1/2 cup water
- 6 to 8 tablespoons horseradish sauce
- 1/4 cup red wine vinegar *or* cider vinegar
- 1/4 cup Worcestershire sauce
- 2 garlic cloves, minced
- 1-1/2 to 2 teaspoons celery salt
- 3 tablespoons cornstarch
- 1/3 cup cold water

Cut roast in half. In a large skillet, brown meat on all sides in oil over medium-high heat; drain. Place carrots and potatoes in a 5-qt. slow cooker. Top with meat and onions. Combine the water, horseradish sauce, vinegar, Worcestershire sauce, garlic and celery salt. Pour over meat. Cover and cook on low for 10-11 hours or until meat and vegetables are tender.

Combine cornstarch and cold water until smooth; stir into slow cooker. Cover and cook on high for 30 minutes or until gravy is thickened. **Yield:** 6-8 servings.

ITALIAN BEEF SANDWICHES
(Pictured on page 18)

Kristen Swihart, Perrysburg, Ohio

I'm a paramedic/firefighter, and slow-cooked recipes like this one suit my unpredictable schedule. My husband and children and the hungry bunch at the firehouse love these robust sandwiches that have a little zip.

- 1 jar (11-1/2 ounces) pepperoncinis*
- 1 boneless beef chuck roast (3-1/2 to 4 pounds)
- 1/4 cup water
- 1-3/4 teaspoons dried basil
- 1-1/2 teaspoons garlic powder
- 1-1/2 teaspoons dried oregano
- 1-1/4 teaspoons salt
- 1/4 teaspoon pepper
- 1 large onion, sliced and quartered
- 10 to 12 hard rolls, split

Drain pepperoncinis, reserving liquid. Remove and discard stems of peppers; set peppers aside. Cut roast into large chunks; place a third of the meat in a 5-qt. slow cooker. Add water.

In a small bowl, combine the basil, garlic powder, oregano, salt and pepper; sprinkle half over beef. Layer with half of the remaining meat, then onion, reserved peppers and liquid. Top with remaining meat and herb mixture.

Cover and cook on low for 8-9 hours or until meat is tender. Shred beef with two forks. Using a slotted spoon, serve beef and peppers on rolls. **Yield:** 10-12 servings.

*Editor's Note: Look for pepperoncinis (pickled peppers) in the pickle and olive section of your grocery store.

CHICKEN FRENCH BREAD PIZZA
(Pictured at left)

Laura Mahaffey, Annapolis, Maryland

This delicious and easy recipe is great for casual get-togethers. It's always gobbled up very quickly!

- 1 loaf (1 pound) French bread
- 1/2 cup butter *or* margarine, softened
- 1/2 cup shredded cheddar cheese
- 1/3 cup grated Parmesan cheese
- 1 garlic clove, minced
- 1/4 teaspoon Italian seasoning
- 1 can (10 ounces) chunk white chicken, drained and flaked
- 1 cup (4 ounces) shredded mozzarella cheese

1/2 cup chopped sweet red pepper
1/2 cup chopped green onions

Cut bread in half lengthwise, then in half widthwise. Combine the butter, cheddar, Parmesan, garlic and Italian seasoning; spread over bread. Top with the remaining ingredients. Place on a baking sheet. Bake at 350° for 10-12 minutes or until cheese is melted. Cut into smaller pieces if desired. **Yield:** 4 servings.

STUFFED PORK TENDERLOIN

(Pictured on page 19)

Dale Ann Glover, Strathroy, Ontario

I combined part of one recipe and another to come up with this extra-special roast.

2 pork tenderloins (1 pound *each*)
2 tablespoons vegetable oil
2 tablespoons soy sauce
2 tablespoons lemon juice
1/4 cup finely chopped celery
2 tablespoons finely chopped onion
2 tablespoons butter *or* margarine
2 cups soft bread crumbs
1/2 cup chopped apple
2 tablespoons raisins
2 tablespoons red currant *or* raspberry jelly
3/4 teaspoon salt
1/4 teaspoon poultry seasoning
Dash pepper
Dash dried rosemary, crushed
6 bacon strips

Cut a lengthwise slit down the center of each tenderloin to within 1/2 in. of bottom; open tenderloins so they lie flat. Cover with plastic wrap; pound to flatten to 3/4-in. thickness. Remove plastic wrap. In a large resealable plastic bag, combine the oil, soy sauce and lemon juice; add tenderloins. Seal bag and turn to coat; refrigerate for 8 hours or overnight.

In a skillet, saute celery and onion in butter until tender. Remove from the heat. Stir in bread crumbs, apple, raisins, jelly, salt, poultry seasoning, pepper and rosemary. Remove tenderloins from marinade; discard marinade. Spread stuffing down the center of one tenderloin; top with second tenderloin. Tie several times with kitchen string and secure ends with toothpicks. Arrange bacon over the top.

Place on a rack in a shallow roasting pan. Bake, uncovered, at 350° for 1 hour or until a meat thermometer reads 160°. Broil 4-6 in. from the heat for 4-5 minutes or until bacon is browned and crisp. Let stand for 10-15 minutes before slicing. **Yield:** 4-6 servings.

PASTA JAMBALAYA

(Pictured above)

Evelyn O'Connor, Bolton, Connecticut

This nicely spiced dish is loaded with vegetables. My family really loves it...and I bet yours will, too.

1/4 pound bulk hot pork sausage
1 small onion, chopped
2 to 3 garlic cloves, minced
1 boneless skinless chicken breast, cut into cubes
1 can (14-1/2 ounces) Cajun stewed tomatoes
1 can (8 ounces) tomato sauce
1/3 cup salsa
1 medium carrot, julienned
1 small yellow summer squash, sliced and quartered
1 small zucchini, sliced and quartered
1 tablespoon minced fresh parsley
1 teaspoon salt
1/2 teaspoon Italian seasoning
1/2 teaspoon dried thyme
1/8 teaspoon pepper
1 cup frozen cooked shrimp, thawed, peeled and deveined
Hot cooked pasta
3 bacon strips, cooked and crumbled

In a large skillet, cook the sausage, onion and garlic over medium heat until sausage is no longer pink; drain. Add the chicken; cook until chicken is no longer pink.

Add the tomatoes, tomato sauce, salsa, carrot, squash and seasonings. Bring to a boil. Reduce heat; cover and simmer for 15-20 minutes or until vegetables are tender. Stir in shrimp; heat through. Serve over pasta; sprinkle with bacon. **Yield:** 4 servings.

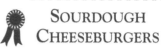

SOURDOUGH CHEESEBURGERS

(Pictured below)

Michelle Dommel, Quakertown, Pennsylvania

Here's a mouth-watering cheeseburger that's easy and quick. I came up with it one night when I realized I'd run out of hamburger buns. My husband loved the tang and toasty crunch of the sourdough bread.

    3 tablespoons mayonnaise
    1 tablespoon ketchup
    1 tablespoon sweet pickle relish
1/2 pound ground beef
Salt and pepper to taste
    1 small onion, sliced and separated into
        rings
    4 tablespoons butter *or* margarine,
        divided
    4 slices sourdough bread
    4 slices Swiss cheese

In a small bowl, combine the mayonnaise, ketchup and relish; cover and refrigerate. Shape beef into two oval patties. In a large skillet, fry burgers over medium heat for 4-5 minutes on each side or until a meat thermometer reads 160°. Season with salt and pepper; remove and keep warm. In the same skillet, saute onion in 1 tablespoon butter until tender. Remove and keep warm.

Using 2 tablespoons of butter, butter one side of each slice of bread. Melt remaining butter in the skillet. Place bread, buttered side up, in skillet; cook for 2-3 minutes or until golden brown. Turn; top two pieces of bread with two slices of cheese. Cook 2 minutes longer or until cheese is melted.

To serve, place toast, cheese side up, on a plate. Top with a burger, relish mixture, onion and remaining toast. **Yield:** 2 servings.

JALAPENO GRILLED CHICKEN

(Pictured above)

Cheryl Kvintus, Altus, Oklahoma

I've had this recipe for years, so it's long been a family favorite. The jalapeno stuffing adds some spice to ordinary grilled chicken.

    4 to 8 jalapeno peppers, seeded and
        chopped* *or* 1 can (4 ounces) chopped
        green chilies
2/3 cup lemon juice, *divided*
1/4 cup minced fresh parsley *or* 1
        tablespoon dried parsley flakes
    6 to 10 garlic cloves, minced
    2 teaspoons dried rosemary, crushed
    2 teaspoons dried thyme
    8 bone-in chicken breast halves
2/3 cup chicken broth
    2 teaspoons pepper
1/2 teaspoon grated lemon peel

In a bowl, combine the peppers, 1/3 cup lemon juice, parsley, garlic, rosemary and thyme. Gently stuff pepper mixture under the skin of each chicken breast. Place in a greased 13-in. x 9-in. x 2-in. baking dish. Combine the broth, pepper, lemon peel and remaining lemon juice; pour over chicken. Cover and refrigerate for at least 6 hours.

Drain and discard marinade. Place chicken skin side up on grill. Grill, covered, over medium heat for 45 minutes or until juices run clear, turning once. **Yield:** 8 servings.

*Editor's Note: When cutting or seeding hot peppers, use rubber or plastic gloves to protect your hands. Avoid touching your face.

22

Main Dishes

COUNTRY-STYLE RIBS

(Pictured at right)

Annette McCullough, Pahrump, Nevada

Whenever I need a surefire company pleaser, I cook up these scrumptious ribs. Usually, I double or triple the recipe, since the ribs freeze well and keep their flavor when reheated. The meat's tender and tasty every time.

- 1/3 cup all-purpose flour
- 2 teaspoons salt
- 1/4 teaspoon pepper
- 4 to 4-1/2 pounds bone-in country-style pork ribs
- 3 tablespoons vegetable oil
- 1 medium onion, chopped
- 1 can (14-1/2 ounces) beef broth
- 1/4 cup ketchup
- 3 tablespoons Worcestershire sauce
- 2 tablespoons cider vinegar
- 3 whole cloves
- 3 whole allspice
- 1 garlic clove, minced
- 1 bay leaf
- 1/2 teaspoon celery salt
- 1/8 teaspoon cayenne pepper

In a large resealable plastic bag, combine the flour, salt and pepper. Add ribs, a few pieces at a time, and shake to coat. In a large skillet, brown ribs in oil; transfer to a greased 13-in. x 9-in. x 2-in. baking dish. Sprinkle with onion. Combine the remaining ingredients; pour over ribs.

Cover and bake at 350° for 1-1/4 hours or until meat is tender. Remove ribs to a serving platter; keep warm. Strain liquid; skim fat. Serve sauce with ribs. **Yield:** 6 servings.

CHICKEN LASAGNA

Marilynn Hieronymus, Sedalia, Missouri

Give this good-for-you lasagna a try. It's a great change of pace from the more traditional lasagnas featuring ground beef.

✓ Uses less fat, sugar or salt. Includes Nutritional Analysis and Diabetic Exchanges.

- 1 medium onion, chopped
- 1/2 cup chopped green pepper
- 3 tablespoons butter *or* margarine, melted
- 6 ounces fresh mushrooms, sliced
- 1 can (10-3/4 ounces) condensed reduced-fat reduced-sodium cream of mushroom soup, undiluted
- 1/3 cup fat-free milk

- 1 jar (2 ounces) diced pimientos, drained
- 1/2 teaspoon dried basil
- 2-1/2 cups cubed cooked chicken
- 8 ounces reduced-fat process American cheese, cubed
- 1-1/2 cups fat-free cream-style cottage cheese
- 1/2 cup grated Parmesan cheese, *divided*
- 9 lasagna noodles, cooked and drained
- 2 teaspoons minced fresh parsley

In a saucepan, saute onion and green pepper in butter until tender. Add mushrooms; cook until tender. Remove from the heat; stir in soup, milk, pimientos and basil. In a bowl, combine the chicken, American cheese, cottage cheese and 1/4 cup Parmesan cheese.

Spread a fourth of the mushroom sauce in a 13-in. x 9-in. x 2-in. baking dish coated with nonstick cooking spray. Top with three noodles, half of the chicken mixture and a fourth of the mushroom sauce. Repeat layers of noodles, chicken and mushroom sauce. Top with the remaining noodles and mushroom sauce.

Sprinkle with parsley and remaining Parmesan. Cover and bake at 350° for 30 minutes. Uncover; bake 15-20 minutes longer or until hot and bubbly. Let stand for 15 minutes before cutting. **Yield:** 12 servings.

Nutritional Analysis: One serving equals 196 calories, 7 g fat (3 g saturated fat), 31 mg cholesterol, 696 mg sodium, 130 g carbohydrate, 7 g fiber, 9 g protein. **Diabetic Exchanges:** 2 lean meat, 1-1/2 fat, 1 starch, 1 vegetable.

ROAST BEEF SANDWICH ROLL

(Pictured below)

Shonda Haught, Wichita, Kansas

I'm a teacher and am always looking for quick and delicious recipes. I like how easy this sandwich roll can be put together.

    2 loaves (1 pound *each*) frozen bread
       dough, thawed
  3/4 cup chopped sweet red pepper
  1/2 cup chopped red onion
    1 teaspoon garlic salt
    1 teaspoon Italian seasoning
    8 to 10 ounces thinly sliced deli roast
       beef, julienned
    2 cups (8 ounces) finely shredded
       cheddar cheese
    1 egg white
    1 tablespoon water

Combine loaves of dough and shape into one ball. Place in a greased bowl, turning once to grease top. Cover and let rise in a warm place for 90 minutes.

In a microwave-safe bowl, combine the red pepper, onion, garlic salt and Italian seasoning. Cover and microwave on high for 1 minute or until vegetables are tender.

Punch dough down. On a lightly floured surface, roll into a 15-in. x 12-in. rectangle. Combine the beef, cheese and red pepper mixture; spread over the dough to within 1/2 in. of edges. Roll up jelly-roll style, starting with a long edge; pinch seams and ends to seal. Place seam side down on a lightly greased baking sheet.

In a small bowl, beat egg white and water; brush over dough. Cut a slit with a sharp knife in top of dough. Bake at 400° for 30-35 minutes or until golden brown. Let stand for 10 minutes before slicing. **Yield:** 8 servings.

BROCCOLI HAM QUICHE

(Pictured above)

Marilyn Day, North Fort Myers, Florida

This rich quiche recipe is featured in a family cookbook I compiled. It's attractive enough to serve for a company brunch...and it tastes terrific. My husband is proof that quiche can satisfy even a man-sized appetite!

    1 unbaked deep-dish pastry shell (9
       inches)
    1 cup water
  1/2 cup chopped fresh broccoli
    1 cup (4 ounces) shredded Swiss cheese
    1 cup (4 ounces) shredded mozzarella
       cheese
    2 tablespoons all-purpose flour
    4 eggs
1-1/4 cups milk
    2 tablespoons chopped green onion
  1/4 teaspoon salt
  1/8 teaspoon pepper
  1/8 teaspoon dried thyme
  1/8 teaspoon dried rosemary, crushed
  1/2 cup diced fully cooked ham

Line unpricked pastry shell with a double thickness of heavy-duty foil. Bake at 450° for 8 minutes. Remove foil; bake 5 minutes longer. Cool on a wire rack. Meanwhile, in a saucepan, bring water to a boil. Add broccoli; cover and cook for 2 minutes. Drain and immediately place broccoli in ice water. Drain and pat dry with paper towels.

Toss cheeses with flour; set aside. In a bowl, beat the eggs. Add the milk, onion and seasonings; mix well. Stir in the ham, broccoli and cheese mixture. Pour into prepared crust. Bake at 350° for 40-45 minutes or until a knife inserted near the center comes out clean. Let stand for 10 minutes before cutting. **Yield:** 6-8 servings.

SOUTHWESTERN PORK ROAST

Jenell Sommers, Alexandria, Minnesota

I saw this recipe in our local newspaper and thought it sounded delicious. I tried it, and it's now a favorite. It has just the right amount of zip.

 Uses less fat, sugar or salt. Includes Nutritional Analysis and Diabetic Exchanges.

    5 teaspoons chili powder
    1 tablespoon olive *or* canola oil
    2 garlic cloves, minced
    1 teaspoon dried oregano
  3/4 teaspoon ground cumin
  1/2 teaspoon dried rosemary, crushed
    1 boneless pork loin roast (3 pounds)

Combine the first six ingredients; rub over the roast. Cover and refrigerate overnight. Place roast fat side up on a rack in a shallow roasting pan. Bake, uncovered, at 350° for 1-1/4 to 1-1/2 hours or until a meat thermometer reads 160°. Let stand for 10 minutes before slicing. **Yield:** 12 servings.

Nutritional Analysis: One serving equals 174 calories, 7 g fat (2 g saturated fat), 62 mg cholesterol, 62 mg sodium, 1 g carbohydrate, trace fiber, 25 g protein. **Diabetic Exchange:** 3 lean meat.

CHEESE-STUFFED PORK ROAST

Kara Holtkamp, West Point, Iowa

I first served this roast for a Christmas dinner a few years ago. My family raved about it! The spices create a unique flavor.

    1 tablespoon all-purpose flour
  1/4 teaspoon lemon-pepper seasoning
    2 tablespoons butter *or* margarine, melted
    2 tablespoons whipping cream
    1 cup (4 ounces) shredded Swiss cheese
    1 boneless pork loin roast (2 to 2-1/2 pounds), trimmed
    6 ounces thinly sliced deli ham
    1 teaspoon paprika
  1/2 teaspoon *each* dried marjoram, oregano and basil

CREAM SAUCE:
    1 small onion, finely chopped
    1 tablespoon butter *or* margarine
    1 tablespoon cornstarch
    1 cup whipping cream
  1/4 cup chicken broth
    1 teaspoon sour cream
Salt to taste

In a bowl, combine the flour, lemon-pepper, butter and cream until smooth. Stir in the cheese; set aside. Cut a lengthwise slit down the center of the roast to within 1/2 in. of the bottom. Open roast so it lies flat; cover with plastic wrap. Flatten to 3/4-in. thickness. Remove plastic; place ham slices over roast. Spread cheese mixture lengthwise down the center of one side of roast to within 1-1/2 in. of ends. Roll up, jelly-roll style, starting with the long side with cheese filling. Tie several times with kitchen string; secure ends with toothpicks. Combine paprika, marjoram, oregano and basil; rub over roast.

Place on a rack in a shallow roasting pan. Bake, uncovered, at 325° for 1-1/4 to 1-1/2 hours or until a meat thermometer reads 160°. Let stand for 10 minutes. Meanwhile, in a skillet, saute onion in butter until tender. Stir in the cornstarch until blended. Whisk in cream and broth. Bring to a boil; cook and stir for 2 minutes or until thickened. Remove from the heat; stir in sour cream and salt. Slice roast; serve with cream sauce. **Yield:** 8-10 servings.

stir-fry for 5 minutes. Combine cornstarch and reserved juice mixture until smooth; add to skillet. Bring to a boil; cook and stir for 1 minute. Add onions, beef and the reserved pineapple; heat through. Serve over rice. **Yield:** 4 servings.

CORNISH HENS WITH VEGGIES

(Pictured below)

Arlene Lauritzen, Genoa, Illinois

It's easy to serve an elegant dinner when these nicely seasoned game hens with roasted vegetables are on the menu. This bountiful platter makes such a pretty presentation for a special occasion.

        4 **Cornish game hens (22 ounces *each*)**
    1/3 **cup butter *or* margarine, melted**
1-1/2 **teaspoons minced fresh rosemary**
        ***or* 1/2 teaspoon dried rosemary, crushed**
        1 **tablespoon minced fresh parsley**
        1 **teaspoon salt**
    1/2 **teaspoon pepper**
        2 **pounds small red potatoes**
        1 **pound carrots, cut into 2-inch slices,**
        optional

Place the hens, breast side up, on a rack in a roasting pan; tie drumsticks together. Combine butter, rosemary, parsley, salt and pepper; spoon over hens. Bake, uncovered, at 375° for 1 hour. Meanwhile, peel a 1-in. strip around the center of each potato. Place potatoes and carrots if desired in a saucepan; cover with water. Bring to a boil. Reduce heat; cover and simmer for 15 minutes. Drain; add to roasting pan.

Baste hens and vegetables with pan drippings. Bake for 15-20 minutes or until a meat thermometer reads 180° and vegetables are tender. Strain pan drippings and thicken for gravy if desired. **Yield:** 4 servings.

PINEAPPLE BEEF STIR-FRY

(Pictured above)

Helen Vail, Glenside, Pennsylvania

A zippy marinade sparks the flavor of this change-of-pace steak specialty. Chock-full of veggies, seasonings and pineapple chunks, this stir-fry makes a colorful presentation when I serve it to relatives and friends.

        1 **can (20 ounces) pineapple chunks**
    1/2 **cup minced fresh parsley *or* cilantro**
    1/4 **cup soy sauce**
        1 **tablespoon ground ginger**
        1 **pound boneless beef round steak, sliced**
        2 **teaspoons vegetable oil**
        1 **medium sweet red pepper, thinly sliced**
    1/2 **cup cut fresh green beans**
        1 **tablespoon chopped green chilies**
        2 **garlic cloves, minced**
        1 **teaspoon cornstarch**
        2 **green onions, sliced**
Hot cooked rice

Drain the pineapple, reserving 1 cup pineapple and 3/4 cup juice (save remaining pineapple and juice for another use). In a bowl, combine parsley, soy sauce, ginger and reserved pineapple juice; mix well. Remove 3/4 cup; cover and refrigerate.

Place beef in a large resealable plastic bag; add remaining marinade. Seal bag and turn to coat; refrigerate for 30 minutes. Drain and discard marinade.

In a skillet, stir-fry beef in oil for 5-6 minutes. Remove beef with a slotted spoon and keep warm. Add red pepper, beans, chilies and garlic to skillet;

FRUIT-STUFFED PORK ROAST

(Pictured at right)

Theresa McIlveen, Turner Valley, Alberta

This moist flavorful roast, with its fruity filling and tangy glaze, has become a tradition at our family events. It's not tricky to prepare and is so impressive on the table.

    3/4 cup diced dried pitted prunes
    3/4 cup diced dried apricots
    3/4 teaspoon ground ginger *or* 1 tablespoon
        minced fresh gingerroot
1-1/2 teaspoons ground cumin, *divided*
      1 teaspoon grated orange peel
    1/2 teaspoon ground cinnamon
    1/4 teaspoon salt
    1/8 teaspoon pepper
      1 boneless pork loin roast (3 to 4 pounds)
    1/4 cup packed brown sugar
      2 teaspoons all-purpose flour
      1 teaspoon cornstarch
      1 teaspoon ground mustard
      2 teaspoons cider vinegar

In a bowl, combine the prunes, apricots, ginger, 3/4 teaspoon cumin, orange peel, cinnamon, salt and pepper; set aside. Untie roast and separate pieces. Spoon fruit mixture onto one piece. Top with the second piece; retie with kitchen string. Place on a rack in a shallow roasting pan.

Combine the brown sugar, flour, cornstarch, mustard, vinegar and remaining cumin until smooth; rub over roast. Bake, uncovered, at 350° for 1-1/4 hours or until a meat thermometer reads 160°. Let stand for 10 minutes before slicing. **Yield:** 12-14 servings.

CHEESY TUNA NOODLES

Tamara Duggan, O'Fallon, Missouri

Not only is this dish delicious, it's economical, too! I serve it once a month.

2-1/2 cups uncooked wide egg noodles
      1 medium onion, chopped
      2 tablespoons butter *or* margarine
      1 can (10-3/4 ounces) condensed cream
        of celery soup, undiluted
    1/3 cup milk
      1 can (6 ounces) tuna, drained and flaked
      1 cup (4 ounces) shredded cheddar
        cheese
    1/4 cup grated Parmesan cheese

Cook noodles according to package directions. Meanwhile, place onion in a greased microwave-safe 11-in. x 7-in. x 2-in. dish; dot with butter.

Microwave, uncovered, on high for 1 minute; stir. Microwave 1-1/2 to 2 minutes longer, stirring every 30 seconds.

In a bowl, combine soup and milk; stir in tuna and cheeses. Pour over onion. Drain noodles; add to tuna mixture and mix well. Cover and microwave on high for 4-5 minutes or until heated through and cheese is melted. **Yield:** 4-5 servings.

Editor's Note: This recipe was tested in an 850-watt microwave.

BOW TIE TURKEY BAKE

Betty Aiken, Bradenton, Florida

This convenient casserole can be assembled the night before and refrigerated to cook the next day. It's so easy to make.

2-1/2 cups uncooked bow tie pasta
      8 ounces turkey Italian sausage links,
        casings removed
      1 jar (26 ounces) spaghetti sauce
    3/4 cup cottage cheese, drained
    1/4 cup grated Parmesan cheese
      1 package (10 ounces) frozen chopped
        spinach, thawed and squeezed dry
      1 tablespoon shredded Parmesan cheese

Cook pasta according to package directions. Meanwhile, in a skillet, cook sausage over medium heat until no longer pink; drain. Drain the noodles. Spread 1/4 cup spaghetti sauce in a greased 2-qt. microwave-safe dish. Layer with half of the noodles, a third of the remaining sauce and half of the cottage cheese, sausage and grated Parmesan.

Top with spinach. Repeat layers of noodles, sauce, cottage cheese and grated Parmesan. Top with remaining sauce. Sprinkle with shredded Parmesan. Cover and microwave on high for 8 minutes or until heated through. **Yield:** 4-6 servings.

Editor's Note: This recipe was tested in an 850-watt microwave.

HAM LOAF WITH MUSTARD SAUCE
(Pictured below)

Betty Saelhof, Edmonton, Alberta

Brown sugar, mustard, herbs and spices season this hearty ham loaf. I like to make several loaves to serve to our retirement club. To speed things up, I use my food processor's chopper blade to grind the ham and pork.

```
    1 cup dry bread crumbs
    1 cup milk
    2 eggs, beaten
    2 pounds ground fully cooked ham
1-1/2 pounds ground pork
  3/4 cup packed brown sugar
  1/2 teaspoon ground cloves
  1/2 teaspoon ground mustard
```
MUSTARD SAUCE:
```
    2 egg yolks, beaten
    3 tablespoons prepared mustard
    2 tablespoons white vinegar
    1 tablespoon sugar
    1 tablespoon water
  3/4 teaspoon salt
    1 tablespoon butter (no substitutes)
    1 tablespoon prepared horseradish
  1/2 cup whipping cream, whipped
```

In a large bowl, combine the bread crumbs, milk and eggs. Crumble meat over mixture and mix well. In a small bowl, combine brown sugar, cloves and mustard. Spread in two greased 9-in. x 5-in. x 3-in. loaf pans. Press meat mixture on top. Bake,

uncovered, at 350° for 1-1/2 hours or until a meat thermometer reads 160°. Let stand for 10 minutes before inverting onto serving platters.

For sauce, combine egg yolks, mustard, vinegar, sugar, water and salt in a heavy saucepan. Cook and stir over low heat until mixture is thickened and reaches 160°, about 5 minutes. Remove from the heat. Stir in butter and horseradish. Cool. Fold in cream. Serve with ham loaves. **Yield:** 2 ham loaves (6-8 servings each).

BARBECUED PORK CHOP SUPPER
(Pictured above)

Jacqueline Jones, Round Lake Beach, Illinois

I start this barbecued pork chop recipe in the morning in the slow cooker and enjoy a tasty supper later without any last-minute work.

```
    6 small red potatoes, cut into quarters
    6 medium carrots, cut into 1-inch pieces
    8 bone-in pork loin or rib chops (1/2 inch
      thick)
    1 teaspoon salt
  1/4 teaspoon pepper
    1 bottle (28 ounces) barbecue sauce
    1 cup ketchup
    1 cup cola
    2 tablespoons Worcestershire sauce
```

Place potatoes and carrots in a 5-qt. slow cooker. Top with pork chops. Sprinkle with salt and pepper. Combine the barbecue sauce, ketchup, cola and Worcestershire sauce; pour over chops. Cover and cook on low for 8-9 hours or until meat and vegetables are tender. **Yield:** 8 servings.

SLOW-COOKED CABBAGE ROLLS

Rosemary Jarvis, Sparta, Tennessee

I've worked full-time for more than 30 years, and this super slow-cooker recipe has been a lifesaver. It cooks while I'm away and smells heavenly when I walk in the door in the evening.

   1 large head cabbage
   1 egg, beaten
   1 can (8 ounces) tomato sauce
3/4 cup quick-cooking rice
1/2 cup chopped green pepper
1/2 cup crushed saltines (about 15 crackers)
   1 envelope onion soup mix
1-1/2 pounds lean ground beef
   1 can (46 ounces) V8 juice
Salt to taste
Grated Parmesan cheese, optional

Remove core from cabbage. Steam 12 large outer leaves until limp; drain well. In a bowl, combine the egg, tomato sauce, rice, green pepper, cracker crumbs and soup mix. Crumble beef over mixture and mix well. Place about 1/3 cup meat mixture on each cabbage leaf. Fold in sides, starting at an unfolded edge, and roll up completely to enclose the filling. Secure with toothpicks if desired.

Place cabbage rolls in a slow cooker. Pour V8 juice over rolls. Cover and cook on low for 6-7 hours or until filling reaches 160°. Just before serving, sprinkle with salt and cheese if desired. **Yield:** 6 servings.

CREAMY FETTUCCINE

Cheryl Ross, Grand Forks, British Columbia

This recipe has been a family favorite for years. It's special enough for holiday celebrations but simple enough for weeknight meals.

   1 package (8 ounces) fettuccine
   1 small onion, chopped
   2 garlic cloves, minced
1/2 cup butter *or* margarine, *divided*
   4 ounces cream cheese, cubed
1/2 cup whipping cream
   2 plum tomatoes, chopped
3/4 cup frozen peas, thawed
   1 tablespoon minced fresh parsley
Salt and pepper to taste
Shredded Parmesan cheese

Cook fettuccine according to package directions. Meanwhile, in a skillet, saute onion and garlic in 2 tablespoons butter until tender. Add the cream cheese, cream and remaining butter;

cook and stir until cheese is melted. Add tomatoes, peas, parsley, salt and pepper. Cook for 8-10 minutes or until heated through. Drain fettuccine; top with cream sauce and Parmesan cheese. **Yield:** 4 servings.

FRUITED CHICKEN

(Pictured below)

Mirien Church, Aurora, Colorado

With three young children, I appreciate the ease of preparing entrees like this with my slow cooker. The combination of fruity flavors in this chicken dish is unique and tasty. My husband loves having home-cooked meals each night…and this one is always a hit!

   1 large onion, sliced
   6 boneless skinless chicken breast halves
1/3 cup orange juice
   2 tablespoons soy sauce
   2 tablespoons Worcestershire sauce
   2 tablespoons Dijon mustard
   1 tablespoon grated orange peel
   2 garlic cloves, minced
1/2 cup chopped dried apricots
1/2 cup dried cranberries
Hot cooked rice

Place onion and chicken in a 5-qt. slow cooker. Combine the orange juice, soy sauce, Worcestershire sauce, mustard, orange peel and garlic; pour over chicken. Sprinkle with apricots and cranberries. Cover and cook on low for 7-8 hours or until chicken juices run clear. Serve over rice. **Yield:** 6 servings.

TROPICAL GLAZED CHICKEN STRIPS
(Pictured below)
Kris Marquart, Escondido, California

This recipe was given to me by our pastor's wife. We live on a 65-acre avocado ranch and have many varieties of avocados to choose from. With our children grown and gone, my husband and I keep quite busy ranching.

  4 boneless skinless chicken breast halves, cut in half lengthwise
  2 tablespoons vegetable oil
3/4 cup pineapple-orange juice concentrate
1/4 cup butter *or* margarine
  1 teaspoon ground ginger
  1 teaspoon soy sauce
  1 medium ripe avocado, peeled and sliced
  1 tablespoon lime juice
1/2 cup macadamia nuts
Hot cooked brown rice

In a skillet, brown chicken in oil. Transfer to a greased 11-in. x 7-in. x 2-in. baking dish. In a saucepan, combine the juice concentrate, butter, ginger and soy sauce. Bring to a boil. Reduce heat; simmer, uncovered, for 15 minutes.

Spoon sauce over chicken. Bake, uncovered, at 350° for 25-30 minutes, basting occasionally. Brush avocado slices with lime juice. Arrange chicken, avocado and nuts over rice. **Yield:** 4 servings.

 ## SPICY CHICKEN LINGUINE
(Pictured above)
Tracy Haroldson, Aztec, New Mexico

Our state is famous for its green chilies. Naturally, my husband and I included them in this linguine dish we invented. The sauce is also excellent with spaghetti or fettuccine noodles. All of our five children absolutely love it.

   1/4 cup butter *or* margarine
     3 tablespoons all-purpose flour
     2 teaspoons garlic powder
     1 teaspoon pepper
2-1/2 cups milk
     1 package (8 ounces) cream cheese, cubed
     1 cup (4 ounces) shredded Parmesan cheese
    12 ounces uncooked linguine
     3 cups cubed cooked chicken
     1 can (4 ounces) diced green chilies

In a saucepan, melt butter. Stir in flour, garlic powder and pepper until smooth. Gradually add milk. Bring to a boil; cook and stir for 2 minutes or until thickened. Reduce heat; add cream cheese and Parmesan cheese. Cook and stir for 8-10 minutes or until cheese is melted.

Meanwhile, cook linguine according to package directions. Add chicken and chilies to cheese sauce; cook 5 minutes longer or until heated through. Drain linguine; top with chicken mixture. **Yield:** 6 servings.

CHEESY TURKEY BURGERS

Margaret Pache, Mesa, Arizona

If you're tired of traditional hamburgers, give these tasty turkey burgers a try!

✓ **Uses less fat, sugar or salt. Includes Nutritional Analysis and Diabetic Exchanges.**

      3 ounces reduced-fat cream cheese
  1/2 cup shredded reduced-fat Mexican
          cheese blend
      1 small onion, grated
      3 tablespoons old-fashioned oats
      2 tablespoons minced chives
      1 garlic clove, minced
  1/2 to 1 teaspoon caraway seeds
  1/2 teaspoon salt
1-1/2 pounds lean ground turkey
      8 onion rolls, split
      8 lettuce leaves
      8 tomato slices

In a bowl, combine the first eight ingredients. Crumble turkey over mixture and mix well. Shape into eight 1/2-in.-thick patties.

If using the grill, coat grill rack with nonstick cooking spray before starting the grill. Grill burgers, uncovered, over medium heat or broil 4-6 in. from the heat for 8-10 minutes on each side or until a meat thermometer reads 165°. Serve on rolls with lettuce and tomato. **Yield:** 8 servings.

Nutritional Analysis: One burger equals 355 calories, 13 g fat (4 g saturated fat), 77 mg cholesterol, 622 mg sodium, 35 g carbohydrate, 1 g fiber, 24 g protein. **Diabetic Exchanges:** 2 starch, 2 lean meat, 2 fat.

SLOW-COOKED TAMALE CASSEROLE

Diana Briggs, Veneta, Oregon

I've been making this recipe for years because my family really likes it. It's great for busy days.

      1 pound ground beef
      1 egg
1-1/2 cups milk
  3/4 cup cornmeal
      1 can (15-1/4 ounces) whole kernel corn,
          drained
      1 can (14-1/2 ounces) diced tomatoes,
          undrained
      1 can (2-1/4 ounces) sliced ripe olives,
          drained
      1 envelope chili seasoning
      1 teaspoon seasoned salt
      1 cup (4 ounces) shredded cheddar cheese

In a skillet, cook beef over medium heat until no longer pink; drain. In a bowl, combine the egg, milk and cornmeal until smooth. Add corn, tomatoes, olives, chili seasoning, seasoned salt and beef.

Transfer to a greased slow cooker. Cover and cook on high for 3 hours and 45 minutes. Sprinkle with cheese; cover and cook 15 minutes longer or until cheese is melted. **Yield:** 6 servings.

CHICKEN CARROT FRIED RICE
(Pictured below)

Peggy Spieckermann, Joplin, Missouri

A dear friend shared this colorful stir-fry when my four children were small.

  3/4 pound boneless skinless chicken
          breasts, cubed
      4 tablespoons soy sauce, *divided*
      2 garlic cloves, minced
1-1/2 cups chopped fresh broccoli
      3 green onions, sliced
      2 tablespoons vegetable oil, *divided*
      3 large carrots, shredded
      4 cups cold cooked rice
  1/4 teaspoon pepper

In a bowl, combine the chicken, 1 tablespoon soy sauce and garlic; set aside. In a large skillet or wok, stir-fry the broccoli and green onions in 1 tablespoon oil for 5 minutes. Add carrots; stir-fry 4 minutes longer or until crisp-tender. Remove and set aside.

In the same skillet, stir-fry chicken in remaining oil until no longer pink and juices run clear. Add the rice, pepper, vegetables and remaining soy sauce. Stir-fry until heated through. **Yield:** 4-6 servings.

STROGANOFF-STYLE PORK CHOPS

(Pictured below)

Kim Alpers, Traverse City, Michigan

Topped with a mustard and mushroom sauce, these tender, moist pork chops are Sunday-special. They're simply wonderful served with noodles…and are a welcome change from grilled or fried chops.

    4 boneless butterfly pork loin chops (1 inch thick)
    2 tablespoons vegetable oil
    1 large onion, chopped
    8 medium fresh mushrooms, sliced
1/4 cup water
    2 teaspoons prepared mustard
1/2 teaspoon salt
    1 tablespoon all-purpose flour
1/2 cup sour cream
Hot cooked noodles

In a large skillet over medium heat, brown pork chops in oil for 5-6 minutes on each side. Remove and keep warm. In the drippings, saute onion and mushrooms until tender.

Stir in the water, mustard and salt; bring to a boil. Return chops to pan. Reduce heat; cover and simmer for 15-20 minutes or until pork is tender. Remove chops and keep warm.

Combine flour and sour cream until smooth; add to the skillet. Bring to a boil; cook and stir for 1-2 minutes or until slightly thickened. Serve pork chops and mustard-mushroom sauce with noodles. **Yield:** 4 servings.

CHEESY ZUCCHINI BAKE

(Pictured above)

Sue Stanton, Linville, North Carolina

Ever since a friend shared this classic casserole with me, I actually look forward to our annual bounty of zucchini. This cheesy veggie bake makes a pretty entree or brunch item. I keep the recipe handy—I know I'll get requests!

4-1/2 cups sliced zucchini
    2 to 3 tablespoons olive *or* vegetable oil
Salt and pepper to taste
    1 large onion, chopped
    2 tablespoons minced garlic
    1 can (10-3/4 ounces) tomato puree
    1 can (6 ounces) tomato paste
    3 tablespoons sugar
    1 teaspoon Italian seasoning
    1 teaspoon dried basil
    2 cans (2-1/4 ounces *each*) sliced ripe olives, drained
    3 cups (12 ounces) shredded mozzarella cheese
    6 eggs, lightly beaten
1-1/2 cups grated Parmesan cheese

In a large skillet, saute zucchini in oil until tender. Sprinkle with salt and pepper; stir. Transfer to an ungreased 13-in. x 9-in. x 2-in. baking dish.

In the same skillet, saute onion until crisp-tender. Add garlic; saute 3 minutes longer. Stir in tomato puree, tomato paste, sugar, Italian seasoning and basil. Bring to a boil. Reduce heat; simmer, uncovered, for 10-15 minutes or until slightly thickened. Stir in olives. Pour over zucchini. Sprinkle with mozzarella.

Combine the eggs and Parmesan cheese; pour over zucchini. Bake, uncovered, at 375° for 25-30 minutes or until a knife inserted near the center comes out clean. Let the dish stand for 15 minutes before serving. **Yield:** 12-16 servings.

BARBECUED BEEF BRISKET
(Pictured at right)
Bettye Miller, Blanchard, Oklahoma

A guest at the RV park and marina my husband and I used to run gave me this flavorful brisket recipe. It's become the star of countless meal gatherings, from potlucks to holiday dinners. Husband Ed and our five grown children look forward to it as much as our Christmas turkey.

- 1/2 cup packed brown sugar
- 1/2 cup ketchup
- 1/4 cup water
- 1/4 cup cider vinegar
- 6 tablespoons vegetable oil, *divided*
- 3 tablespoons dark corn syrup
- 2 tablespoons prepared mustard
- 1 tablespoon prepared horseradish
- 1 garlic clove, minced
- 1 fresh beef brisket (2 to 2-1/2 pounds)*, trimmed

In a saucepan, combine the brown sugar, ketchup, water, vinegar, 4 tablespoons oil, corn syrup, mustard, horseradish and garlic. Cook and stir over medium heat until sugar is dissolved, about 3 minutes. Pour mixture into a disposable aluminum pan; set aside.

In a large skillet, brown brisket on both sides in remaining oil. Place brisket in pan; turn to coat with sauce. Cover pan tightly with foil.

Grill, covered, over indirect medium heat for 1 hour. Add 10 briquettes to coals. Cover and cook about 1-1/4 hours longer, adding more briquettes if needed, or until meat reaches desired doneness (for rare, a meat thermometer should read 140°; medium, 160°; well-done, 170°). Slice beef; serve with pan drippings. **Yield:** 6-8 servings.

*Editor's Note: This is a fresh brisket, not corned beef.

BEEF CABBAGE STROMBOLI
Pamela Courtney, Des Moines, Iowa

I served this hearty loaf to hungry workers who helped my husband and I move to our new house. It really satisfied their appetites.

> ✓ Uses less fat, sugar or salt. Includes Nutritional Analysis and Diabetic Exchanges.

- 2 loaves (1 pound *each*) frozen bread dough
- 1 pound lean ground beef
- 1/2 cup chopped onion
- 3 cups shredded cabbage
- 2 tablespoons Worcestershire sauce
- 2 tablespoons reduced-sodium soy sauce
- 2 teaspoons dried thyme
- 1-1/2 cups (6 ounces) shredded reduced-fat cheddar cheese
- 1-1/2 cups (6 ounces) shredded part-skim mozzarella cheese

Place each frozen loaf in a 9-in. x 5-in. x 3-in. loaf pan coated with nonstick cooking spray. Let rise until dough is 1 in. above top of pan. In a nonstick skillet, cook beef and onion over medium heat until meat is no longer pink; drain. Add cabbage, Worcestershire sauce, soy sauce and thyme. Cover and cook for 15 minutes or until cabbage is tender; drain.

Punch dough down. Place each loaf on an ungreased baking sheet; pat into a 16-in. x 10-in. rectangle. Spoon meat mixture lengthwise down one side of each rectangle to within 1 in. of edges. Sprinkle with cheeses. Fold dough over filling; turn edges under to seal. With a sharp knife, make four diagonal slashes on top of loaves. Bake at 375° for 20-22 minutes or until golden brown. Serve warm. **Yield:** 2 loaves (6 servings each).

Nutritional Analysis: One serving equals 367 calories, 13 g fat (5 g saturated fat), 31 mg cholesterol, 672 mg sodium, 42 g carbohydrate, 3 g fiber, 25 g protein. **Diabetic Exchanges:** 2-1/2 starch, 2 lean meat, 1 fat.

Fried Green Tomato Sandwiches

(Pictured below)

Mary Ann Bostic, Sinks Grove, West Virginia

This is one of my favorite quick-fix suppers. I'm sure a lot of people have never tried fried green tomatoes before, but they're yummy. They're especially satisfying in these sandwiches.

   1/4 cup all-purpose flour
   1/4 teaspoon *each* garlic powder, salt,
         pepper and paprika
     3 medium green tomatoes, sliced
    12 bacon strips
    12 slices sourdough bread, toasted
     6 slices provolone cheese
Lettuce, mayonnaise and Dijon mustard,
   optional

In a shallow dish, combine flour and seasonings; dip tomatoes in the mixture and set aside. In a skillet, cook bacon over medium heat until crisp. Remove to paper towels to drain. In the drippings, cook tomatoes for 2 minutes on each side; drain on paper towels.

Place six slices of toast on a baking sheet. Layer with three tomato slices, two bacon strips and a cheese slice. Broil 3-4 in. from the heat for 3-4 minutes or until cheese is melted. Top with lettuce if desired. Spread mayonnaise and mustard on remaining toast if desired; place over lettuce. **Yield:** 6 sandwiches.

 ## Spaghetti 'n' Meatballs

(Pictured above)

Marilou Krumm, Stanhope, Iowa

My mom's Italian friend taught her the secret to this saucy spaghetti dish. Our whole family is grateful! Mom gave me the recipe as a wedding present. It's the best-tasting spaghetti ever...and the meatballs are so tender.

     2 eggs
     1 cup dry bread crumbs
   1/2 cup grated Parmesan cheese
   1/2 cup tomato juice, milk *or* beef broth
   1/4 cup finely chopped green pepper
   1/4 cup finely chopped onion
     1 teaspoon Italian seasoning
   1/2 teaspoon *each* salt, poultry seasoning
         and garlic powder
     2 pounds bulk pork sausage
SAUCE:
     4 cups water
     2 cans (11-1/2 ounces *each*) tomato juice
     3 cans (6 ounces *each*) tomato paste
     1 jar (1/2 ounce) dried celery flakes
     1 bay leaf
     1 teaspoon Italian seasoning
     1 teaspoon salt
   1/2 teaspoon pepper
   1/2 cup finely chopped green pepper
   1/2 cup finely chopped onion
     2 garlic cloves, minced
Hot cooked spaghetti

In a large bowl, combine eggs, bread crumbs, Parmesan cheese, tomato juice, green pepper, onion and seasonings. Crumble sausage over mixture and mix well. Shape into 1-in. balls. In a skillet, brown meatballs over medium heat; drain.

In a large saucepan, combine the first eight sauce ingredients. Add green pepper, onion and garlic. Bring to a boil. Reduce heat; simmer, uncovered, for 30-45 minutes or until thickened, stirring occasionally. Discard bay leaf.

Add meatballs to sauce; simmer for 1 hour or until meat is no longer pink. Serve over spaghetti. **Yield:** 10 servings.

PORK CHOPS WITH ONIONS AND APPLES

(Pictured on front cover)

Lou Ann Marques-Bambera
Attleboro, Massachusetts

I've always liked pork chops made with apples or onions. I decided to combine both ingredients to create this delicious recipe. Many family members and friends have requested it.

  2 **teaspoons coarsely ground pepper**
1/2 **teaspoon salt**
1/2 **teaspoon garlic powder**
  4 **bone-in center-cut pork chops (1 inch thick)**
  2 **medium onions, thinly sliced**
  2 **medium tart apples, sliced**
  2 **tablespoons butter *or* margarine**
  2 **tablespoons brown sugar**

In a small bowl, combine the pepper, salt and garlic powder. Rub over pork chops. Grill chops, covered, over medium heat for 7-9 minutes on each side or until a meat thermometer reads 160° and juices run clear.

Meanwhile, in a skillet, saute onions and apples in butter until tender. Add brown sugar; cook until thickened and bubbly. Serve with the pork chops. **Yield:** 4 servings.

MEXICAN CHICKEN MANICOTTI

(Pictured at right)

Keely Jankunas, Corvallis, Montana

Our family of five enjoys trying different ethnic cuisines. This Italian specialty has a little Mexican zip. Be careful not to overcook the manicotti. If the filled shells happen to break, just place them in the pan seam-side down.

  1 **package (8 ounces) manicotti shells**
  2 **cups cubed cooked chicken**

  2 **cups (8 ounces) shredded Monterey Jack cheese, *divided***
1-1/2 **cups (6 ounces) shredded cheddar cheese**
  1 **cup (8 ounces) sour cream**
  1 **small onion, diced, *divided***
  1 **can (4 ounces) chopped green chilies, *divided***
  1 **can (10-3/4 ounces) condensed cream of chicken soup, undiluted**
  1 **cup salsa**
2/3 **cup milk**

Cook manicotti according to package directions. Meanwhile, in a large bowl, combine the chicken, 1-1/2 cups Monterey Jack cheese, cheddar cheese, sour cream, half of the onion and 6 tablespoons chilies.

In another bowl, combine the soup, salsa, milk, and remaining onion and chilies. Spread 1/2 cup in a greased 13-in. x 9-in. x 2-in. baking dish.

Drain manicotti; stuff each with about 1/4 cup chicken mixture. Arrange over sauce in baking dish. Pour remaining sauce over shells.

Cover and bake at 350° for 30 minutes. Uncover; sprinkle with remaining Monterey Jack cheese. Bake 10 minutes longer or until cheese is melted. **Yield:** 7 servings.

Roasts Are Fast to Fix

WHAT could be more fuss-free than popping a roast in the oven or slow cooker and letting it be while you tend to other tasks? The down-home meaty mainstays featured here take just minutes to assemble.

PORK WITH ORANGE SAUCE

(Pictured below)

Penny Niedhamer, Fresno, California

This flavorful orange sauce is a fast and easy way to dress up slices of leftover pork roast. It's very scrumptious.

> 1 tablespoon cornstarch
> 1 cup orange juice
> 1 tablespoon jellied cranberry sauce
> 1-1/2 teaspoons soy sauce
> Salt and pepper to taste
> 8 slices cooked pork (1/2 inch thick)

In a saucepan, combine cornstarch and orange juice until smooth. Stir in the cranberry sauce, soy sauce, salt and pepper. Bring to a boil; cook and stir for 2 minutes or until thickened. Add pork; heat through. **Yield:** 4 servings.

SLOW-COOKED COFFEE POT ROAST

Janet Dominick, Bagley, Minnesota

My family raves about my gravy when I prepare this recipe. Whenever I'm fishing for compliments, this pot roast is a sure hit!

> 2 medium onions, thinly sliced
> 2 garlic cloves, minced
> 1 boneless beef chuck roast (3-1/2 to 4 pounds), quartered
> 1 cup brewed coffee
> 1/4 cup soy sauce
> 1/4 cup cornstarch
> 6 tablespoons cold water

Place half of the onions in a 5-qt. slow cooker. Top with garlic and half of the beef. Top with remaining onion and beef. Combine coffee and soy sauce;

pour over beef. Cover and cook on low for 9-10 hours or until meat is tender.

Combine cornstarch and water until smooth; stir into cooking juices. Cover and cook on high for 30 minutes or until gravy is thickened. **Yield:** 10-12 servings.

🔳🔳🔳🔳🔳🔳🔳🔳

GLAZED PORK TENDERLOIN

Nancy Rollag, Kewaskum, Wisconsin

I like to serve this tenderloin for Christmas and other special occasions. It's impressive yet easy to make.

- 1/2 cup currant jelly
- 1 tablespoon prepared horseradish
- 2 pork tenderloins (3/4 pound *each*)
- 1/2 cup chicken broth
- 1/4 cup white grape juice
- 1/4 teaspoon salt
- 1/4 teaspoon pepper

In a microwave-safe bowl, combine the jelly and horseradish. Microwave on high for 1 minute or until jelly is melted; stir until smooth.

Place the tenderloins on a rack in a shallow roasting pan. Brush with half of the jelly mixture. Bake, uncovered, at 425° for 20 minutes. Turn the meat over; brush with the remaining jelly mixture. Bake 10 minutes longer or until a meat thermometer reads 160°. Remove the meat and keep warm.

Add broth and grape juice to roasting pan; stir to loosen browned bits. Transfer to a saucepan. Cook over medium-high heat until liquid is reduced to 1/2 cup, about 5 minutes. Strain sauce; add salt and pepper. Slice pork; serve with sauce. **Yield:** 6 servings.

🔳🔳🔳🔳🔳🔳🔳🔳

NO-FUSS PORK AND SAUERKRAUT

Joan Pereira, Avon, Massachusetts

I once tasted a similar dish at a restaurant and decided to try making it at home. This is the fabulous result.

- 1 boneless pork loin roast (4 to 5 pounds), quartered

- 1/3 cup Dijon mustard
- 1 teaspoon garlic powder
- 1 teaspoon rubbed sage
- 1 can (27 ounces) sauerkraut, drained
- 2 medium tart apples, sliced
- 1 cup apple juice

Rub roast with mustard; sprinkle with garlic powder and sage. Place sauerkraut and half of the apples in a slow cooker. Top with roast. Pour apple juice around roast; top with remaining apples.

Cover and cook on high for 4-5 hours or until a meat thermometer reads 160°. **Yield:** 12-16 servings.

🔳🔳🔳🔳🔳🔳🔳🔳

BEEFY TOMATO RIGATONI

Trudy Williams, Shannonville, Ontario

Sharing recipes with friends is a favorite pastime of mine, and I get many requests for this mouth-watering main dish.

- 1 large onion, chopped
- 1 tablespoon olive *or* vegetable oil
- 2 cans (14-1/2 ounces *each*) Italian diced tomatoes, undrained
- 1 can (8 ounces) tomato sauce
- 3 cups shredded fully cooked beef rump roast
- 1/4 teaspoon salt
- 1/4 teaspoon crushed red pepper flakes
- 4-1/2 cups rigatoni *or* other large tube pasta, cooked and drained
- 2 cups (8 ounces) shredded mozzarella cheese
- 1 cup (4 ounces) shredded provolone cheese

In a saucepan, saute onion in oil until tender. Stir in tomatoes and tomato sauce. Bring to a boil. Reduce heat; cover and simmer for 5 minutes. Stir in the beef, salt and pepper flakes. Cover and simmer for 5 minutes. Add pasta; toss to coat.

Transfer to a greased 13-in. x 9-in. x 2-in. baking dish. Sprinkle with cheeses. Bake, uncovered, at 400° for 20-25 minutes or until cheese is melted. **Yield:** 6-8 servings.

In a bowl, combine the flour and salt; make a well. Beat yolks, egg and water; pour into well and stir. Turn onto a floured surface; knead 8-10 times. Divide into thirds; roll out each as thin as possible. Let stand for 20 minutes or until partially dried. Cut into 1/4-in. strips, then into 2-in. pieces; set aside.

In a bowl, combine the egg, ketchup, oats, onion and salt. Add beef; mix well. Shape into 1-1/2-in. balls. Place in a greased 11-in. x 7-in. x 2-in. baking dish. Bake, uncovered, at 400° for 10-15 minutes or until no longer pink.

In a large saucepan, combine soup, sour cream, milk and paprika; heat through. Add meatballs; cover and cook until heated through, stirring frequently.

In another saucepan, bring water and salt to a boil; add noodles. Cook for 12-15 minutes or until tender; drain. Toss with butter and parsley. Serve with meatballs. **Yield:** 6 servings.

🔳🔳🔳🔳🔳🔳🔳🔳

BARBECUED TURKEY SLICES

(Pictured below)

Jerry Olsen, Ephraim, Utah

At banquets, church dinners and even wedding buffets, this tantalizing turkey is a "must" for the table. It was a hit with the 100-plus guests at our family reunion. I've served it with cheesy potatoes and assorted summer salads. It's a snap to fix ahead of time and keeps well in the freezer.

🔳🔳🔳🔳🔳🔳🔳🔳

MEATBALL STROGANOFF WITH NOODLES

(Pictured above)

Carol Schurvinske, Geneseo, Illinois

My great-nephews and great-niece ask me to whip up this Stroganoff as their special birthday treat. I've yet to have any left over.

>   2 cups all-purpose flour
>   1 teaspoon salt
>   3 egg yolks
>   1 egg
>   6 tablespoons water
> MEATBALLS:
>   1 egg, lightly beaten
>   2 tablespoons ketchup
>   1/4 cup quick-cooking oats
>   1 tablespoon finely chopped onion
>   1/2 teaspoon salt
>   1 pound ground beef
> SAUCE:
>   2 cans (10-3/4 ounces *each*) condensed
>   cream of mushroom soup, undiluted
>   1 cup (8 ounces) sour cream
>   1 cup milk
>   1 tablespoon paprika
>   2 quarts water
>   1 teaspoon salt
>   1 tablespoon butter *or* margarine
>   1 tablespoon minced parsley

Main Dishes

1/2 cup grapefruit *or* citrus soda
1/2 cup soy sauce
1/4 cup vegetable oil
2-1/2 teaspoons garlic powder
 1 teaspoon prepared horseradish
2-1/2 pounds boneless skinless turkey breast,
  cut into 3/4-inch slices

In a large resealable plastic bag, combine the soda, soy sauce, oil, garlic powder and horseradish. Add turkey slices. Seal bag and turn to coat; refrigerate for 6-8 hours or overnight.

Drain and discard marinade. Grill turkey, uncovered, over medium heat or broil 4 in. from the heat for 4-5 minutes on each side or until juices run clear. **Yield:** 8-10 servings.

PORK VEGGIE STIR-FRY

Jamilla Ivits, Cambridge, Ontario

This stir-fry is chockful of good-for-you veggies and pork.

☑ **Uses less fat, sugar or salt. Includes Nutritional Analysis and Diabetic Exchanges.**

 3 tablespoons reduced-sodium soy sauce
 1 tablespoon lemon juice
 1 teaspoon sugar
 1 teaspoon cornstarch
 1 teaspoon salt-free lemon-pepper
  seasoning
 1 teaspoon ground mustard
1/2 teaspoon Worcestershire sauce
 1 pound pork tenderloin, cut into
  1/4-inch strips
 1 cup thinly sliced carrots
 4 teaspoons canola oil, *divided*
 1 cup thinly sliced zucchini
1/2 cup thinly sliced celery
 2 cups sliced fresh mushrooms
 5 cups torn fresh spinach

In a bowl, combine the first seven ingredients; add pork and toss to coat. In a nonstick skillet or wok, stir-fry carrots in 2 teaspoons oil for 2 minutes. Add zucchini and celery; stir-fry for 2 minutes. Add mushrooms; stir-fry for 2-3 minutes or until vegetables are crisp-tender. Remove and keep warm.

Stir-fry pork with marinade in batches in remaining oil for 2-3 minutes or until meat is no longer pink. Return the vegetable mixture and all of the pork to the pan. Add spinach; stir-fry for 1-2 minutes or until spinach is tender. **Yield:** 4 servings.
Nutritional Analysis: One serving (1 cup) equals 251 calories, 11 g fat (3 g saturated fat), 75 mg cholesterol, 571 mg sodium, 10 g carbohydrate, 3 g fiber, 27 g protein. **Diabetic Exchanges:** 3 lean meat, 2 vegetable, 1 fat.

SAVORY VEGETABLE BEEF STEW

(Pictured above)

Lynn Franklin, Marietta, Georgia

I've been cooking since I was 10 years old. One day, I plan to own a bed-and-breakfast inn. I look forward to the challenge of cooking for my future guests.

 3 pounds beef stew meat, cut into 1-inch
  cubes
1/3 cup Italian salad dressing
 2 cups water
 2 teaspoons beef bouillon granules
 1 can (14-1/2 ounces) diced tomatoes,
  undrained
 1 can (10-1/2 ounces) condensed beef
  broth, undiluted
 1 can (8 ounces) tomato sauce
 1 garlic clove, minced
 1 bay leaf
 1 teaspoon salt
 1 teaspoon dried oregano
1/2 teaspoon pepper
 6 small potatoes, quartered
 6 medium carrots, cut into 1-inch pieces
 1 medium green pepper, cut into 1/2-inch
  pieces
 1 medium onion, chopped
 3 tablespoons all-purpose flour
 3 tablespoons cold water

In a Dutch oven, brown meat in salad dressing over medium heat. Add the next 10 ingredients; bring to a boil. Reduce heat; cover and simmer for 1-1/2 hours or until meat is tender.

Add the potatoes, carrots, green pepper and onion. Cover and simmer for 45 minutes or until vegetables are tender. Combine flour and cold water until smooth; stir into stew. Bring to a boil; cook and stir for 2 minutes or until thickened. Discard bay leaf before serving. **Yield:** 12 servings.

MEATY CHILI LASAGNA
(Pictured below)
Melba NeSmith, Corsicana, Texas

My mother-in-law has been gone for over 20 years now, but her recipe is still in great demand at family gatherings and potluck suppers. Serve this lasagna with salad, bread and a light dessert...and you'll satisfy the heartiest appetite.

  12 uncooked lasagna noodles
1-1/2 pounds ground beef
   1 medium onion, chopped
   1 medium green pepper, chopped
   2 to 3 jalapeno peppers, seeded and
     chopped*
   1 to 2 tablespoons chili powder
   1 garlic clove, minced
   1 can (10-3/4 ounces) condensed cream
     of mushroom soup, undiluted
   1 cup frozen corn
   1 can (8 ounces) tomato sauce
   3 tablespoons tomato paste
   1 can (2-1/4 ounces) sliced ripe olives,
     drained
   4 cups (16 ounces) shredded cheddar
     cheese

Cook noodles according to package directions. Meanwhile, in a large skillet, cook beef, onion, peppers, chili powder and garlic over medium heat until meat is no longer pink; drain. Add the soup, corn, tomato sauce, tomato paste and olives; simmer until heated through.

Drain noodles. Spread 1/2 cup meat sauce in a greased 13-in. x 9-in. x 2-in. baking dish. Layer with four noodles, half of the remaining sauce and a third of the cheese. Repeat layers once. Top with remaining noodles and cheese. Cover and bake at 350° for 30 minutes. Uncover; bake 15 minutes longer or until cheese is melted. Let stand for 15 minutes before cutting. **Yield:** 12 servings.

*Editor's Note: When cutting or seeding hot peppers, use rubber or plastic gloves to protect your hands. Avoid touching your face.

YANKEE POT ROAST
(Pictured above)
Vera Burke, West Pittston, Pennsylvania

Here's a traditional main dish that's tested and true. It's been a favorite with my family for many years.

   1 boneless beef chuck roast (4 to 5
     pounds)
   1 tablespoon vegetable oil
   2 large onions, coarsely chopped
   2 cups sliced carrots
   2 celery ribs, sliced
   2 cans (14-1/2 ounces *each*) Italian
     stewed tomatoes
1-3/4 cups water
   1 teaspoon salt
1/2 teaspoon dried thyme
1/4 teaspoon pepper
   4 medium potatoes, peeled and cut into
     eighths

In a large deep skillet over medium-high heat, brown roast on all sides in oil. Remove roast. Add onions, carrots, celery, tomatoes, water, salt, thyme and pepper to the skillet. Bring to a boil.

Return roast to skillet. Reduce heat; cover and simmer for 2 hours. Add potatoes; cover and cook 40 minutes longer or until meat and vegetables are tender. **Yield:** 12-14 servings.

SWEET BEEF STEW

Anne Graham, Los Osos, California

This is not your usual beef stew, which is why I get so many requests for the recipe. It's so easy to fix in the pressure cooker, which is one of the most underrated time-savers of all!

1-1/2 pounds beef stew meat, cut into 1-inch cubes
 2 medium onions, chopped
 3 garlic cloves, minced
 1 tablespoon vegetable oil
 1/2 teaspoon salt
 1/4 teaspoon ground ginger
 1/4 teaspoon pepper
 1/8 teaspoon ground nutmeg
 3/4 cup apricot nectar
 3 tablespoons soy sauce
 2 tablespoons molasses
 1 teaspoon brown sugar
 1 teaspoon cornstarch
 1 tablespoon water
Hot cooked rice *or* noodles

In a pressure cooker, brown beef, onions and garlic in oil over medium heat. Stir in salt, ginger, pepper and nutmeg. Combine the apricot nectar, soy sauce, molasses and brown sugar; pour over meat. Close cover securely; place pressure regulator on vent pipe.

Bring cooker to full pressure over high heat. Reduce heat to medium-high and cook for 20 minutes. (Pressure regulator should maintain a slow steady rocking motion; adjust heat if needed.) Remove from the heat; allow pressure to drop on its own.

Remove meat with a slotted spoon. Combine cornstarch and water until smooth; add to pan drippings. Bring to a boil; cook and stir for 2 minutes or until thickened. Stir in meat and serve over rice. **Yield:** 4 servings.

PEPPERONI PASTA BAKE
(Pictured at right)

Delores Marie Kolosovsky, Dodgeville, Wisconsin

Here's my homemade version of a family-favorite Italian restaurant entree. For a change of pace, I substitute hamburger for pepperoni, add Italian seasonings and use a mix of fun pasta shapes, including rotini and corkscrew.

 3 cups uncooked wagon wheel *or* spiral pasta
 1 can (4 ounces) mushroom stems and pieces, undrained
 1 package (3-1/2 ounces) sliced pepperoni, quartered
3/4 cup chopped green pepper
 1 medium onion, chopped
 1 jar (14 ounces) spaghetti sauce
 1 can (8 ounces) tomato sauce
 1 can (6 ounces) tomato paste
 1 cup (4 ounces) shredded cheddar cheese
 2 cups (8 ounces) shredded mozzarella cheese

Cook pasta according to package directions; drain and place in a large bowl. Add the mushrooms, pepperoni, green pepper and onion. Stir in the spaghetti sauce, tomato sauce, tomato paste and cheddar cheese; mix well.

Transfer to a greased 3-qt. baking dish. Cover and bake at 350° for 50 minutes. Uncover; sprinkle with mozzarella cheese. Bake 10 minutes longer or until cheese is melted. **Yield:** 6 servings.

▪▪▪▪▪▪▪▪▪▪▪▪
SPINACH CHEESE STRATA
(Pictured above)

Mary Laffey, Indianapolis, Indiana

Here's a delicious brunch dish for the holidays. I usually garnish it with red and green pepper rings overlapped in the center for a festive touch.

    1/2 cup chopped onion
    1/4 cup chopped sweet red pepper
    1/4 cup chopped green pepper
      2 tablespoons butter *or* margarine
      1 package (10 ounces) frozen chopped
        spinach, thawed and well drained
      2 cups Wheat Chex
    1/2 cup shredded cheddar cheese
    1/2 cup shredded Swiss cheese
      6 eggs
      2 cups milk
    1/3 cup crumbled cooked bacon
      1 teaspoon Dijon mustard
      1 teaspoon salt
    1/4 teaspoon white pepper

In a skillet, saute the onion and peppers in butter until crisp-tender. Remove from the heat. Add spinach and cereal; mix well. Spoon into a greased 11-in. x 7-in. x 2-in. baking dish. Sprinkle with cheeses.

In a bowl, combine the eggs, milk, bacon, mustard, salt and pepper. Pour over cheeses. Bake at 325° for 45-50 minutes or until knife inserted near the center comes out clean. Let stand for 10 minutes before cutting. **Yield:** 6-8 servings.

▪▪▪▪▪▪▪▪▪▪▪▪
LINGUINE WITH GARLIC
CLAM SAUCE

Perlene Hoekema, Lynden, Washington

I've tried other clam linguine recipes over the years, but this is our favorite. I usually keep the ingredients on hand.

      1 package (8 ounces) linguine
      2 to 3 garlic cloves, minced
      5 tablespoons butter *or* margarine
    1/4 cup olive *or* vegetable oil
      1 tablespoon all-purpose flour
      2 cans (6-1/2 ounces *each*) minced clams
      1 cup (4 ounces) shredded Monterey Jack
        cheese
    1/4 cup minced fresh parsley

Cook linguine according to package directions. Meanwhile, in a skillet, saute garlic in butter and oil until golden. Stir in flour until blended. Drain clams, reserving juice; set clams aside. Gradually add juice to the skillet. Bring to a boil; cook and stir for 2 minutes or until thickened. Reduce heat; stir in clams, cheese and parsley. Cook until cheese is melted and sauce has thickened. Drain linguine; top with clam sauce. **Yield:** 4 servings.

▪▪▪▪▪▪▪▪▪▪▪▪
 TROUT BAKED IN CREAM
(Pictured below)

Ann Nace, Perkasie, Pennsylvania

Here's a quick and delicious way to serve trout. It's definitely one of our family's favorites.

Reliable Roast Hints

- For added flavor, I make 1-in.-deep slits on the top of pork roasts and insert slivers of garlic into them before roasting.
—*Beth Henriquez*
Pittsburgh, Pennsylvania

- Cooking a pot roast in a slow cooker is great for two fuss-free meals. For one meal, we have pot roast with potatoes and carrots. The next day, I add a can of diced tomatoes and 2 cans of mixed vegetables to the leftover meat, vegetables and gravy for a satisfying dinner of vegetable beef soup.
—*Pam Naylor*
Elkton, Kentucky

- To spice up a pot roast, add a 12-ounce jar of pepperoncini peppers with the juice and cook as usual. We like this served over rice.
—*Carole Linton*
Evansville, Wyoming

- For a large get-together, I generally cook two roasts at the same time. I leave at least 1 inch of space between them to allow for even baking.
—*Ruth Snouffer*
Fairborn, Ohio

- When I make my mouth-watering pot roast, I add a few extra veggies. I puree and freeze the leftover vegetables, then add them to my homemade soups. They give the stock a wonderful flavor.
—*Joella Riddle*
Wichita, Kansas

- I add 1/2 cup of ketchup to my Italian Beef to give it a little sweetness.
—*Stacey Bradley-Handel*
Mt. Carroll, Illinois

- For an interesting flavor twist, I add a can of cola to my pot roast.
—*Gloria, Terveer*
Lincoln, Nebraska

- Sometimes I cut an uncooked beef roast into slices, then cook the slices like a cutlet. I find that if the roast is still partially frozen, it is easier to slice. —*Cathy Orsen*
Hanley, Saskatchewan

- I cut my leftover pot roast into slices and freeze with the gravy in individual serving portions. I reheat a portion and serve over buttered toast for a quick lunch or dinner.
—*Pamela Frazier*
Barhamsville, Virginia

- We enjoy pork roast and sauerkraut. I cook the sauerkraut right with the roast, adding a little water to prevent it from drying out.
—*Ronda Jay Holcomb*
Farmington, New Mexico

- I cut my leftover pork roast into bite-size pieces and add it to bottled barbecue sauce for a tasty planned-over. —*Diane Myers*
Elizabethtown, Pennsylvania

---

6 trout fillets (about 3-1/2 ounces *each*)
2 tablespoons lemon juice
1 teaspoon dill weed
1/2 teaspoon salt
1/8 teaspoon pepper
1 cup whipping cream
2 tablespoons seasoned bread crumbs

Place trout in a greased 13-in. x 9-in. x 2-in. baking dish. Sprinkle with lemon juice, dill, salt and pepper. Pour cream over all. Sprinkle with bread crumbs. Bake, uncovered, at 350° for 11-15 minutes or until fish flakes easily with a fork.
Yield: 4-6 servings.

HAM WITH VEGETABLES

Ernestine Beoughter, Lawrenceville, Illinois

There isn't a quicker complete meal than this one—it takes just minutes in the pressure cooker. The ham and vegetables turn out tender and delicious. This has been a favorite for years, especially with tiny new potatoes and fresh-from-the-garden green beans.

4 medium potatoes, cut into 1-inch cubes
4 cups cut fresh green beans (2-inch pieces)
4 medium carrots, halved widthwise
1 cup chicken broth
1 teaspoon dried minced onion
1/2 teaspoon salt
1 fully cooked ham steak (about 1 pound)

Place cooking rack in pressure cooker. Add the potatoes, beans, carrots, broth, onion and salt. Place ham over vegetables. Close cover securely; place pressure regulator on vent pipe.

Bring cooker to full pressure over high heat. Reduce heat to medium-high and cook for 4 minutes. (Pressure regulator should maintain a slow steady rocking motion; adjust heat if needed.) Immediately cool according to manufacturer's directions until pressure is completely reduced.
Yield: 4 servings.

PAIR *any of these heartwarming soups and savory sandwiches for a satisfying lunch or light supper.*

COMFORTING COMBOS. From top: Layered Ham and Spinach Salad, Hearty Vegetable Soup and Poppy Seed Dressing (all recipes on p. 47).

Soups & Salads

Soups & Salads

HEARTY VEGETABLE SOUP
(Pictured at left)

Janice Steinmetz, Somers, Connecticut

A friend gave me the idea to use V8 juice in soup recipes because it provides more flavor.

    8 medium carrots, sliced
    2 large onions, chopped
    4 celery ribs, chopped
    1 large green pepper, seeded and chopped
    1 garlic clove, minced
    1 tablespoon olive *or* vegetable oil
    4 cups water
    1 can (28 ounces) diced tomatoes,
        undrained
    2 cups V8 juice
    2 cups chopped cabbage
    2 cups frozen cut green beans
    2 cups frozen peas
    1 cup frozen corn
    1 can (15 ounces) garbanzo beans *or*
        chickpeas, rinsed and drained
    2 teaspoons chicken bouillon granules
1-1/2 teaspoons dried parsley flakes
    1 teaspoon salt
    1 teaspoon dried marjoram
    1 teaspoon dried thyme
    1 bay leaf
  1/2 teaspoon dried basil
  1/4 teaspoon pepper

In a Dutch oven or soup kettle, saute the carrots, onions, celery, green pepper and garlic in oil until crisp-tender. Stir in remaining ingredients. Bring to a boil. Reduce heat; cover and simmer for 1 to 1-1/2 hours or until vegetables are tender. Discard bay leaf before serving. **Yield:** 14-16 servings (4 quarts).

 LAYERED HAM AND SPINACH SALAD
(Pictured at left)

Beverly Sprague, Baltimore, Maryland

Here's a delicious salad that's sure to be a favorite with your family and friends. It's very easy to make yet looks so pretty layered in a glass bowl. I especially like to make it for luncheons and potlucks.

    16 cups torn fresh spinach
     1 teaspoon sugar
     1 teaspoon pepper
   1/4 teaspoon salt
     6 hard-cooked eggs, chopped
 1-1/2 cups cubed fully cooked ham
     1 medium red onion, sliced
     1 envelope ranch salad dressing mix
 1-1/2 cups mayonnaise
     1 cup (8 ounces) sour cream
     2 cups (8 ounces) shredded Swiss cheese
   1/2 pound sliced bacon, cooked and
         crumbled

Place two-thirds of the spinach in a 4-qt. salad bowl. Sprinkle with half of the sugar, pepper and salt. Top with eggs, ham and remaining spinach. Sprinkle with remaining sugar, pepper and salt. Arrange onion slices on top.

In a bowl, combine the dressing mix, mayonnaise and sour cream. Spread over onions. Sprinkle with cheese and bacon. Refrigerate until serving. **Yield:** 8-10 servings.

POPPY SEED DRESSING
(Pictured at left)

Deb Amrine, Grand Haven, Michigan

All of my favorite salads are topped off with homemade dressing. I use this sweet poppy seed concoction to drizzle over fruit salads with strawberries, grapes, oranges and bananas...or over spinach and toasted pecans.

    1/3 cup sugar
      5 tablespoons cider vinegar
  2-1/2 teaspoons poppy seeds
  1-1/2 teaspoons grated onion
      1 teaspoon ground mustard
    1/2 teaspoon salt
      1 cup vegetable oil
Assorted fresh fruit

In a small bowl, combine the first six ingredients. Slowly whisk in oil. Cover and refrigerate. Serve with fruit. **Yield:** 1-1/2 cups.

CHRISTMAS GELATIN RING
(Pictured above)

Dorothy Duzynski, Park Ridge, Illinois

This colorful salad with its red and green layers is fun to serve for a festive dinner or brunch. It's been my family's favorite for many years—everyone loves the Jell-O and cream cheese combination. It goes with all kinds of entrees.

    1 package (3 ounces) cherry gelatin
    3 cups boiling water, *divided*
    1 can (29 ounces) sliced pears, undrained
    1 package (3 ounces) lemon gelatin
    1 package (8 ounces) cream cheese,
      cubed and softened
    1 package (3 ounces) lime gelatin
    1 can (20 ounces) crushed pineapple

In a bowl, dissolve cherry gelatin in 1 cup boiling water. Drain pears, reserving 1 cup juice (discard remaining juice or save for another use). Stir pears and reserved juice into cherry gelatin. Pour into a 10-in. fluted tube pan or 3-qt. ring mold coated with nonstick cooking spray. Refrigerate until nearly set, about 1-1/4 hours.

In a bowl, dissolve the lemon gelatin in 1 cup boiling water; refrigerate until slightly thickened. Beat in the cream cheese until blended. Pour over the cherry layer.

In another bowl, dissolve lime gelatin in remaining boiling water. Drain pineapple well, reserving juice. Add enough water to juice to measure 3/4 cup. Stir pineapple and reserved juice into lime gelatin; spoon over lemon layer. Refrigerate until firm. Unmold onto a serving plate. **Yield:** 12 servings.

CHEESY CHICKEN CORN SOUP

Joyce Isenburger, Spring, Texas

This soup is always well-received at potlucks and other get-togethers. No one can believe how easy it is to make.

    2 cans (14-1/2 ounces *each*) chicken
      broth
    1 can (10 ounces) diced tomatoes and
      green chilies, undrained
    2 cups shredded cooked chicken
    2 cups frozen corn
1-1/2 cups water, *divided*
    1/4 cup finely chopped onion
Dash pepper
    1/2 cup all-purpose flour
    1 pound process American cheese, cubed

In a large saucepan, combine the broth, tomatoes, chicken, corn, 1 cup water, onion and pepper. Bring to a boil. Reduce heat; simmer, uncovered, for 5 minutes or until the corn is tender.

Combine the flour and remaining water until smooth; stir into the soup. Bring to a boil; cook and stir for 2 minutes or until thickened. Reduce heat to low; stir in the cheese until melted. **Yield:** 9 servings (about 2 quarts).

APPLE TOSSED SALAD
(Pictured below)

Jean Sickles, Columbus, Ohio

My husband doesn't normally like apples in his salad, but he really likes this. It has a nice mixture of ingredients and is very simple to toss together.

Soups & Salads

1/3 cup red wine vinegar *or* cider vinegar
1/4 cup olive *or* vegetable oil
3 tablespoons water
1 garlic clove, minced
1 teaspoon onion powder
1/2 teaspoon Italian seasoning
1/4 teaspoon dried parsley flakes
1/4 teaspoon salt
1/4 teaspoon pepper
8 cups torn romaine
1 medium red apple, thinly sliced
1 small sweet onion, sliced and separated into rings
1/4 cup sunflower kernels *or* walnuts

In a jar with a tight-fitting lid, combine the first nine ingredients; shake well. In a salad bowl, combine the romaine, apple, onion and sunflower kernels. Add the dressing and toss to coat. Let salad stand for 30 minutes before serving. **Yield:** 8-10 servings.

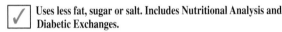

RASPBERRY CABBAGE SALAD

Janet Berge, Richfield, Minnesota

This salad goes great with any meaty main dish. Whenever I serve it for company, I'm asked to share the recipe. The flavorful combination of ingredients looks so pretty on salad plates.

✓ Uses less fat, sugar or salt. Includes Nutritional Analysis and Diabetic Exchanges.

1/3 cup seedless raspberry jam
2 tablespoons plus 1-1/2 teaspoons white wine vinegar *or* cider vinegar
2 tablespoons canola oil
1/2 teaspoon seasoned salt
1/2 teaspoon lemon-pepper seasoning
6 cups shredded napa (Chinese) cabbage
1-1/2 cups shredded red cabbage
2 medium tomatoes, cut into wedges
1 ripe avocado, peeled and cubed
1/2 medium cucumber, thinly sliced
1/2 cup unsweetened raspberries
2 tablespoons chopped green onion

In a bowl, combine the jam, vinegar, oil, seasoned salt and lemon-pepper; mix well. On plates, arrange cabbage, tomatoes, avocado and cucumber; sprinkle with raspberries and onion. Drizzle with dressing. **Yield:** 6 servings.
Nutritional Analysis: One serving (1-1/4 cups) equals 161 calories, 10 g fat (1 g saturated fat), 0 cholesterol, 183 mg sodium, 18 g carbohydrate, 6 g fiber, 3 g protein. **Diabetic Exchanges:** 1-1/2 vegetable, 1-1/2 fat, 1 fruit.

SPICY POTATO SALAD
(Pictured above)

Donna Lefurgey, Prescott, Arizona

This is a great potluck or picnic dish. It's always gobbled up quickly. One of the best things is that it's easy to prepare.

6 large red potatoes (about 3 pounds), cubed
1/3 cup vegetable oil
1/4 cup cider vinegar
1 tablespoon sugar
2-1/2 teaspoons chili powder
1-1/2 teaspoons hot pepper sauce
1 teaspoon salt
1/4 teaspoon onion powder
1/4 teaspoon ground cumin
1 can (15-1/4 ounces) whole kernel corn, drained
1 can (2-1/4 ounces) sliced ripe olives, drained
1/2 cup minced fresh cilantro *or* parsley
2 tablespoons chopped seeded jalapeno peppers*

Place potatoes in a large saucepan and cover with water; cover and bring to a boil. Reduce heat; cook for 20-30 minutes or until tender. Drain and place in a large bowl.
In a jar with a tight-fitting lid, combine the oil, vinegar, sugar, chili powder, hot pepper sauce, salt, onion powder and cumin; shake well. Pour over potatoes and toss to coat. Cover and refrigerate for at least 1 hour. Just before serving, stir in the corn, olives, cilantro and peppers. **Yield:** 8-10 servings.
*Editor's Note: When cutting or seeding hot peppers, use rubber or plastic gloves to protect your hands. Avoid touching your face.

CREAM CHEESE CHICKEN SOUP

(Pictured below)

Kathleen Rappleye, Mesa, Arizona

After tasting a similar soup in a restaurant, I went home and cooked up my own version. It's so soothing on a winter evening served with crusty French bread. For a change of pace, try substituting ham or turkey for the chicken.

      1 small onion, chopped
      1 tablespoon butter *or* margarine
      3 cups chicken broth
      3 medium carrots, cut into 1/4-inch slices
      2 medium potatoes, peeled and cubed
      2 cups cubed cooked chicken
      2 tablespoons minced fresh parsley
Salt and pepper to taste
      1/4 cup all-purpose flour
      1 cup milk
      1 package (8 ounces) cream cheese, cubed

In a large saucepan, saute the onion in butter. Add broth, carrots and potatoes. Bring to a boil. Reduce heat; cover and simmer for 15 minutes or until vegetables are tender. Add the chicken, parsley, salt and pepper; heat through.

Combine flour and milk until smooth; add to the vegetable mixture. Bring to a boil; cook and stir for 2 minutes or until thickened. Reduce heat. Add the cream cheese; cook and stir until melted. **Yield:** 8 servings.

SUN KERNEL DELIGHT

Kelly Culp, Clinton, Ohio

This delightfully different cold pasta salad features apples, pineapple and sunflower kernels, which add a nice crunch. My family loves it.

   1-1/4 cups sugar
      4 eggs, lightly beaten
      1/2 cup lemon juice
      1 package (7 ounces) ring macaroni, cooked and drained
      6 medium apples, chopped
      1 can (8 ounces) crushed pineapple, drained
      1 carton (8 ounces) frozen whipped topping, thawed
      1/2 to 1 cup salted sunflower kernels

In a saucepan, combine the sugar, eggs and lemon juice; cook and stir over low heat until temperature reaches 160° and mixture is thickened, about 5 minutes. Cool completely. Fold in the macaroni, apples, pineapple and whipped topping. Refrigerate until ready to serve; stir in sunflower kernels. **Yield:** 12 servings.

PICKLED CARROTS

Cecilia Grondin
Grand Falls, New Brunswick

The trick to pickled carrots is cooking them just long enough to retain a harvest-fresh "snap". These tangy treats are terrific for perking up a buffet table or relish tray or serving alongside a hearty sandwich.

      1 pound carrots, cut into 3-inch julienne strips
      3/4 cup water
      2/3 cup white vinegar
      3/4 cup sugar
      1 cinnamon stick (3 inches), broken
      3 whole cloves
      1 tablespoon mustard seed

Place 1 in. of water in a saucepan; add carrots. Bring to a boil. Reduce heat; cover and simmer for 3-4 minutes or until carrots are crisp-tender. Drain and rinse in cold water. Place in a bowl and set aside.

In a saucepan, combine water, vinegar, sugar,

cinnamon, whole cloves and mustard seed. Bring to a boil. Reduce heat; simmer, uncovered, for 10 minutes. Cool; pour over the carrots.

Cover and refrigerate for 8 hours or overnight. Discard cloves and cinnamon. Serve carrots with a slotted spoon. **Yield:** 6-8 servings.

CHILLED MARINATED ASPARAGUS
(Pictured above)

Nicole LeCroy, Nashville, Tennessee

My mother had surgery a few years back in spring, so my two sisters and I were challenged to prepare dishes like this that would keep well and still taste great as leftovers. Mom got her appetite back when she tried this cool and crunchy asparagus.

    2/3 cup packed brown sugar
    2/3 cup cider vinegar
    2/3 cup soy sauce
    2/3 cup vegetable oil
      4 teaspoons lemon juice
      1 teaspoon garlic powder
      2 pounds fresh asparagus, trimmed
      1 cup chopped pecans, toasted

In a saucepan, combine the brown sugar, vinegar, soy sauce, oil, lemon juice and garlic powder. Bring to a boil. Reduce heat; simmer, uncovered, for 5 minutes. Refrigerate until cool. Meanwhile, in a large skillet, bring 1/2 in. of water to a boil. Add asparagus. Reduce heat; cover and simmer for 3-5 minutes or until crisp-tender. Drain and rinse in cold water.

Place asparagus in a large resealable plastic bag; add marinade. Seal bag and turn to coat; refrigerate for 2 hours or overnight, turning occasionally. Drain and discard marinade. Place asparagus on a serving plate; sprinkle with pecans. **Yield:** 8 servings.

FESTIVE TOSSED SALAD
(Pictured below)

Isabell Burrows, Livermore, California

This is a delightful salad that has a wonderful blend of flavors. It has a crunchy texture and looks good, too, with its variety of colors.

      1 cup coarsely chopped walnuts
      3 tablespoons butter *or* margarine
    1/4 cup sugar
      1 teaspoon coarsely ground pepper
    1/4 teaspoon salt
     12 cups torn mixed salad greens
    3/4 cup dried cranberries
      4 ounces crumbled feta *or* blue cheese
DRESSING:
    1/4 cup red wine vinegar *or* cider vinegar
    1/4 cup vegetable oil
    1/2 cup loosely packed fresh parsley sprigs
    1/4 cup chopped red onion
      2 garlic cloves, peeled
      1 tablespoon sugar
    1/2 teaspoon dried oregano
    1/8 teaspoon salt
    1/8 teaspoon pepper

In a skillet, cook and stir walnuts in butter until toasted, about 5 minutes. Remove from the heat; stir in the sugar, pepper and salt. In a salad bowl, toss the greens, cranberries, cheese and walnuts.

Place the dressing ingredients in a blender or food processor; cover and process until smooth. Drizzle desired amount over salad; toss to coat. Serve immediately. Refrigerate leftover dressing. **Yield:** 12 servings.

1 package (6 ounces) strawberry *or* lemon gelatin
3 cups boiling water
1 can (16 ounces) whole-berry cranberry sauce
1 can (8 ounces) crushed pineapple, undrained
1 cup chopped pecans
Sour cream, optional

In a large bowl, dissolve gelatin in water. Stir in cranberry sauce and pineapple. Cover and refrigerate for 1 hour or until slightly thickened. Stir in nuts. Pour into a 1-1/2-qt. gelatin mold coated with nonstick cooking spray. Refrigerate until set. Unmold onto a serving platter. Serve with sour cream if desired. **Yield:** 8-10 servings.

CRAB PASTA SALAD

(Pictured below)

Kathryn Anderson, Wallkill, New York

This salad has a very good blend of flavors. It's easy to make and especially delicious on a hot day.

2 cups uncooked medium shell pasta
1-1/2 cups imitation crabmeat, chopped
1 cup broccoli florets
1/2 cup diced green pepper
1/2 cup quartered cherry tomatoes
1/4 cup chopped green onions
DRESSING:
1/2 cup mayonnaise
1/4 cup creamy Italian salad dressing
1/4 cup grated Parmesan cheese

CREAMY CAULIFLOWER SALAD

(Pictured above)

Pat Payne, Harrison, Tennessee

Friends always ask for this recipe whenever I make this dish for a special occasion. It tastes so good and goes a long way.

1 medium head cauliflower, broken into florets
1 cup thinly sliced radishes
3/4 cup thinly sliced green pepper
1 cup (8 ounces) sour cream
2 tablespoons grated onion
4 to 5 teaspoons lemon juice
1 tablespoon Caesar salad dressing mix
1 teaspoon vegetable oil
1/4 teaspoon seasoned salt
1/4 teaspoon pepper

In a large bowl, combine the cauliflower, radishes and green pepper. In a small bowl, combine the remaining ingredients; mix well. Pour over cauliflower mixture and toss to coat. Cover and refrigerate for at least 2 hours before serving. **Yield:** 8-10 servings.

CRANBERRY GELATIN MOLD

Jane Walker, Dewey, Arizona

With a heavy meal, this cool refreshing salad with tart cranberry flavor is a welcome side dish. Plus, it has an eye-catching rosy color that brightens any festive meal.

Soups & Salads

Cook pasta according to package directions; drain and rinse in cold water. Place in a large bowl. Stir in the crab, broccoli, green pepper, tomatoes and onions. Combing dressing ingredients; pour over salad and toss gently to coat. Cover and refrigerate for 2-4 hours before serving. **Yield:** 4-6 servings.

NUTTY CARROT SALAD

Esther Bane, Glidden, Iowa

Peanut butter is a scrumptious addition to this simple salad. With just a few basic ingredients, you can have it ready in no time.

1/3 cup mayonnaise *or* salad dressing
2 tablespoons peanut butter
2 cups shredded carrots
1/3 cup raisins

In a bowl, combine the mayonnaise and peanut butter. Stir in carrots and raisins. Cover and refrigerate until serving. **Yield:** 3-4 servings.

ANGEL HAIR PASTA SALAD

Kimberly Garner, Batesville, Arkansas

This is a refreshing salad that keeps a summer kitchen cool. It's a tasty way to get my family to eat their vegetables.

 Uses less fat, sugar or salt. Includes Nutritional Analysis and Diabetic Exchanges.

1 package (7 ounces) angel hair pasta
4 plum tomatoes, seeded and chopped
1 cup thinly sliced carrots
1 medium cucumber, chopped
6 green onions, thinly sliced
2 tablespoons olive *or* canola oil
2 tablespoons cider vinegar
1/2 teaspoon salt
1/4 teaspoon pepper

Cook pasta according to package directions; drain and rinse in cold water. Place in a large bowl; add the tomatoes, carrots, cucumber and onions. In a small bowl, whisk together the oil, vinegar, salt and pepper. Pour over pasta mixture and toss to coat. Cover and refrigerate for 4 hours. **Yield:** 8 servings.

Nutritional Analysis: One serving (3/4 cup) equals 121 calories, 4 g fat (trace saturated fat), 0 cholesterol, 241 mg sodium, 18 g carbohydrate, 2 g fiber, 4 g protein. **Diabetic Exchanges:** 1-1/2 vegetable, 1 starch.

CREAMY CARROT PARSNIP SOUP

(Pictured above)

Phyllis Clinehens, Maplewood, Ohio

Our farm family would eat soup every day as long as it didn't come from a can! This smooth creamy concoction tastes like it's fresh from the garden. A subtle hint of horseradish and ginger sparks every steaming spoonful.

8 cups chopped carrots
6 cups chopped peeled parsnips
4 cups chicken broth
3 cups water
2 teaspoons sugar
1 teaspoon salt
1 medium onion, chopped
4 garlic cloves, minced
1 teaspoon grated fresh horseradish
1/4 teaspoon ground ginger *or* 1 teaspoon grated fresh gingerroot
3 tablespoons butter *or* margarine
2 cups buttermilk
2 tablespoons sour cream
Fresh dill sprigs, optional

In a Dutch oven or soup kettle, combine the carrots, parsnips, broth, water, sugar and salt; bring to a boil. Reduce heat; cover and cook for 25-30 minutes or until vegetables are tender.

In a skillet, saute onion, garlic, horseradish and ginger in butter until tender. Add to the carrot mixture.

Transfer soup to a blender in batches; cover and process until smooth. Return to the pan. Stir in buttermilk; heat through (do not boil).

Garnish servings with sour cream and dill if desired. **Yield:** 12 servings (3 quarts).

3 cups broccoli florets

3 cups broccoli florets
2 cups diced peeled potatoes
2 cups water
1/3 cup sliced green onions
1 teaspoon salt
1/2 teaspoon pepper
3 tablespoons butter *or* margarine
3 tablespoons all-purpose flour
1/8 teaspoon ground nutmeg
2 cups milk
1/2 cup shredded cheddar cheese

In a large saucepan, combine the first six ingredients. Bring to a boil. Reduce heat; cover and simmer for 12-14 minutes or until vegetables are tender.

Meanwhile, in another saucepan, melt butter. Stir in flour and nutmeg until smooth. Gradually add milk. Bring to a boil; cook and stir for 2 minutes or until thickened. Stir into vegetable mixture; heat through. Sprinkle with cheese. **Yield:** 6 servings.

ORANGE-AVOCADO TOSSED SALAD

(Pictured above)

Janis Engle, San Jose, California

This salad grabs the mealtime spotlight whenever I serve it. The grapes, mandarin oranges and almonds add sweetness and crunch to the greens and avocado…and the dressing has a mild curry flavor.

1/2 cup vegetable oil
1/3 cup white wine vinegar *or* cider vinegar
1 garlic clove, minced
2 tablespoons brown sugar
1 teaspoon curry powder
1 teaspoon soy sauce
10 cups torn red leaf lettuce
1 cup torn fresh spinach
1 can (11 ounces) mandarin oranges, drained
1 cup halved green grapes
1/2 cup slivered almonds, toasted
1 ripe avocado, peeled and sliced

In a jar with a tight-fitting lid, combine the first six ingredients; shake well. In a large salad bowl, toss the lettuce, spinach, oranges, grapes and almonds. Add dressing and toss to coat. Garnish with avocado. **Yield:** 12 servings.

BROCCOLI CHOWDER

(Pictured on page 56)

Sue Call, Beech Grove, Indiana

I serve this comforting soup on chilly stay-at-home evenings. Nutmeg seasons the light creamy broth that's chock-full of tender broccoli florets and diced potatoes.

CHEESY VEGETABLE SOUP

(Pictured on page 57)

Dana Worley, Lebanon, Tennessee

Shredded cheddar cheese adds flavor to this smooth-as-silk soup that's loaded with good-for-you cabbage, carrots, lima beans and potatoes. This filling dish is always a crowd pleaser on cold winter days.

1 large onion, chopped
5 tablespoons butter *or* margarine, *divided*
2 cups water
2 cups shredded cabbage
1 package (10 ounces) frozen lima beans, thawed
1 cup sliced carrots
1 cup diced peeled potatoes
1 tablespoon chicken bouillon granules
3 tablespoons all-purpose flour
1/4 teaspoon paprika
1/4 teaspoon pepper
2 cups milk
1 cup half-and-half cream
1-1/2 cups (6 ounces) shredded cheddar cheese
Minced fresh parsley

In a large saucepan, saute onion in 2 tablespoons butter until tender. Add water, vegetables and bouillon. Bring to a boil. Reduce heat; cover and simmer for 20 minutes or until vegetables are tender.

Meanwhile, in a small saucepan, melt remaining butter. Stir in the flour, paprika and pepper until smooth. Gradually add milk and cream.

Bring to a boil; cook and stir for 2 minutes or until thickened. Reduce heat; stir in cheese until melted. Add to soup; heat through. Sprinkle with parsley. **Yield:** 8 servings (2 quarts).

SOUTHWESTERN CHICKEN BARLEY SOUP

(Pictured on page 57)

Kell Ferrell, Alamo, North Dakota

I drive 80 miles round-trip every day for my job, so I need quick, healthy dishes to fix for my family. This is a huge favorite. If I don't have leftover chicken, I simply boil or poach some chicken breasts. I use the cooking liquid to replace part of the water in the recipe to add even more flavor.

    1 medium onion, chopped
    1 garlic clove, minced
    1 tablespoon olive *or* vegetable oil
    3 cups water
    1 can (15-1/4 ounces) whole kernel corn,
      drained
    1 can (15 ounces) black beans, rinsed and
      drained
    1 can (15 ounces) tomato sauce
    1 can (14-1/2 ounces) diced tomatoes,
      undrained
    1 can (14-1/2 ounces) chicken broth
    1/2 cup medium pearl barley
    1 can (4 ounces) chopped green chilies,
      drained
    1 tablespoon chili powder
    1/2 to 1 teaspoon ground cumin
    3 cups cubed cooked chicken

In a Dutch oven or soup kettle, saute onion and garlic in oil until tender. Add the next 10 ingredients. Bring to a boil. Reduce heat; cover and simmer for 45 minutes.

Stir in the chicken; cook 15 minutes longer or until chicken is heated through and barley is tender. **Yield:** 12 servings (3 quarts).

CHICKEN FAJITA SALAD

(Pictured at right)

Audrey Thibodeau, Mesa, Arizona

Living in the Southwest, I've learned to create all sorts of Mexican dishes. This nicely spiced salad is one of my favorites. It's a winner with my luncheon guests. They appreciate the change of pace from typical cold chicken salad.

    6 tablespoons vegetable oil, *divided*
    1/2 cup lime juice
    2 tablespoons minced fresh parsley
    2 garlic cloves, minced
    1 teaspoon ground cumin
    1 teaspoon dried oregano
1-1/4 pounds boneless skinless chicken
      breasts, cut into 1-inch pieces
    1 cup sliced green onions
    1 medium sweet red pepper, julienned
    1 can (4 ounces) chopped green chilies,
      drained
    1 cup chopped pecans, toasted
Shredded lettuce
    2 medium tomatoes, cut into wedges
    1 medium ripe avocado, peeled and sliced
Tortillas, warmed, optional

In a bowl, combine 4 tablespoons oil, lime juice, parsley, garlic, cumin and oregano. Pour half into a large resealable plastic bag; add the chicken. Seal bag and turn to coat; refrigerate for 1 hour or overnight. Cover and refrigerate remaining marinade.

Drain and discard marinade from chicken. In a large skillet, saute onions in remaining oil for 2 minutes. Add chicken; stir-fry for 2-3 minutes or until chicken just begins to brown. Add the red pepper, chilies and reserved marinade; stir-fry for 2 minutes. Stir in pecans.

Place lettuce on individual plates; top with chicken mixture, tomatoes and avocado. Serve with tortillas if desired. **Yield:** 4 servings.

SPOONFUL after steaming spoonful, these savory soups heat things up when temperatures cool down.

SUPER SOUPS. Clockwise from top left: Vegetable Beef Soup (p. 58), Southwestern Chicken Barley Soup (p. 55), Cheesy Vegetable Soup (p. 54), Split Pea Soup (p. 59) and Broccoli Chowder (p. 54).

ROASTED VEGGIE CHILI

C.J. Counts, Murphy, North Carolina

You're sure to get a kick out of this spicy entree, which placed third at a chili contest. I wanted to make a good-for-you chili that also used veggies from my garden. My husband and I are chefs, but we also like to have fun and use our imaginations when we cook.

        2 cups fresh *or* frozen corn
        2 cups *each* cubed zucchini, yellow
          summer squash and eggplant
        2 *each* medium green peppers and sweet
          red peppers, cut into 1-inch pieces
        2 large onions, chopped
      1/2 cup garlic cloves, peeled
      1/4 cup olive *or* vegetable oil
        4 quarts chicken broth
        2 cans (14-1/2 ounces *each*) stewed
          tomatoes
        2 cans (14-1/2 ounces *each*) tomato puree
      1/4 cup lime juice
        4 teaspoons chili powder
    1-1/4 teaspoons cayenne pepper
        1 teaspoon ground cumin
      1/2 cup butter *or* margarine
      1/2 cup all-purpose flour
        3 cans (15 ounces *each*) white kidney *or*
          cannellini beans, rinsed and drained
      1/2 cup minced fresh cilantro *or* parsley
Sour cream and chopped green onions, optional

Place the vegetables and garlic in a roasting pan. Drizzle with oil; toss to coat. Cover and bake at 400° for 20-30 minutes or until vegetables are tender; cool slightly. Remove and chop garlic cloves.

In a Dutch oven or soup kettle, combine the broth, tomatoes, tomato puree, lime juice, chili powder, cayenne and cumin. Bring to a boil. Reduce heat; simmer, uncovered, for 25-35 minutes or until mixture is reduced by a quarter.

In a saucepan, melt butter; stir in flour until smooth. Cook and stir until bubbly and starting to brown. Slowly whisk into tomato mixture. Add roasted vegetables, garlic, beans and cilantro; mix well. Cook until thickened. Garnish with sour cream and green onions if desired. **Yield:** 24 servings (6 quarts).

HEARTY CHICKEN VEGETABLE SOUP

(Pictured above)

Bertha Vogt, Tribune, Kansas

I experimented with various combinations, and this is the recipe I came up with. It's especially good to take to potlucks or share with friends. I often take a bowl to work to heat up for a fast lunch.

        1 roasting chicken (about 5 pounds), cut
          up and skin removed
        2 celery ribs, sliced
        1 large onion, chopped
    2-1/2 quarts water
        1 can (14-1/2 ounces) stewed tomatoes
        4 medium carrots, sliced
        2 medium potatoes, peeled and cubed
        1 medium turnip, peeled and cubed
        2 tablespoons chicken bouillon granules
      1/2 teaspoon minced fresh parsley
      3/4 teaspoon *each* dried basil, oregano and
          tarragon
      3/4 teaspoon salt
      3/4 teaspoon pepper
      1/2 teaspoon garlic powder
        2 cups broccoli florets
        2 cups frozen peas, optional

Place the chicken, celery, onion and water in a Dutch oven or soup kettle; bring to a boil. Skim fat. Reduce heat; cover and simmer for 1-1/2 to 2 hours or until chicken is tender. Remove chicken; cool. Remove meat from bones and cut into bite-size pieces; return to pan.

Add tomatoes, carrots, potatoes, turnip, bouillon and seasonings; bring to a boil. Reduce heat; cover and simmer for 20 minutes. Add broccoli and peas if desired; simmer 15-20 minutes longer or until vegetables are tender. **Yield:** 16 servings (about 4 quarts).

VEGETABLE BEEF SOUP

(Pictured on page 56)

Ruby Williams, Bogalusa, Louisiana

Brimming with chunks of beef, potatoes, carrots, green beans and mushrooms, this satisfying soup is a meal in itself. When unexpected guests come to visit, this is one of my favorite recipes to prepare because it's ready in no time. I like to serve it with warm corn bread and a fruit salad.

- 2 cans (14-1/2 ounces *each*) beef broth
- 1 tablespoon Worcestershire sauce
- 1 teaspoon ground mustard
- 1/2 teaspoon salt
- 1/4 teaspoon pepper
- 3 medium potatoes, peeled and cubed
- 6 medium carrots, cut into 1/2-inch slices
- 3 cups cubed cooked beef
- 2 cups frozen cut green beans, thawed
- 2 cups sliced fresh mushrooms
- 1 cup frozen peas, thawed
- 1 can (15 ounces) tomato sauce
- 2 tablespoons minced fresh parsley

In a Dutch oven or soup kettle, combine the broth, Worcestershire sauce, mustard, salt and pepper. Stir in potatoes and carrots. Bring to a boil. Reduce heat; cover and simmer for 12 minutes or until carrots are crisp-tender.

Stir in the remaining ingredients. Return to a boil. Reduce heat; simmer, uncovered, for 5 minutes or until the vegetables are tender. **Yield:** 12 servings (3 quarts).

☗☗☗☗☗☗☗☗☗☗☗☗

SPLIT PEA SOUP

(Pictured on page 57)

Laurie Todd, Columbus, Mississippi

This old-fashioned favorite is not only a snap to make but it's economical, too. Carrots, celery and onion accent the subtle flavor of the split peas, while a ham bone adds a meaty touch to this hearty soup. It's sure to chase away autumn's chill!

- 1 package (16 ounces) dry green split peas
- 1 ham bone
- 1 large onion, chopped
- 1 teaspoon salt
- 1/2 teaspoon pepper
- 1/2 teaspoon dried thyme
- 1 bay leaf
- 1 cup diced carrots
- 1 cup diced celery

Place peas in a Dutch oven or soup kettle; add water to cover by 2 in. Bring to a boil; boil for 2 minutes. Remove from the heat; cover and let stand for 1 hour. Drain and rinse peas, discarding liquid.

Return peas to Dutch oven. Add 2-1/2 qts. water, ham bone, onion, salt, pepper, thyme and bay leaf. Bring to a boil. Reduce heat; cover and

simmer for 1-1/2 hours, stirring occasionally.

Remove the ham bone; when cool enough to handle, remove meat from bone. Discard bone; dice meat and return to soup. Add carrots and celery. Simmer, uncovered, for 45-60 minutes or until soup reaches desired thickness and vegetables are tender. Discard bay leaf. **Yield:** 10 servings (about 2-1/2 quarts).

☗☗☗☗☗☗☗☗☗☗☗☗

COOL CUCUMBER SALAD

(Pictured below)

Joy Sauers, Sioux Falls, South Dakota

Whenever I pack a picnic, this salad comes along. It's great with grilled entrees or sandwiches. In summer and fall, it's among my most requested side dishes. It keeps well in the refrigerator, so you can make it ahead of time.

- 1 medium cucumber, quartered and sliced
- 1 medium tomato, chopped
- 1/2 cup chopped green pepper
- 1/3 cup chopped sweet onion
- 2 tablespoons lime juice
- 2 tablespoons red wine vinegar *or* cider vinegar
- 3/4 teaspoon dill weed
- 1/2 teaspoon salt
- 1/4 teaspoon pepper

In a large bowl, combine the cucumber, tomato, green pepper and onion. In a small bowl, combine lime juice, vinegar, dill, salt and pepper. Pour over cucumber mixture; toss to coat. Cover and refrigerate for 15 minutes. Serve with a slotted spoon. **Yield:** 4 servings.

WHITE BEAN AND PASTA SOUP

(Pictured below)

Michelle Harbour, Lebanon, Tennessee

My husband and I savor every spoonful of this hearty soup. It makes a real stick-to-your-ribs meal when served with crusty oven-fresh bread.

> 1-1/2 cups dry great northern beans
> 3/4 pound Italian sausage links, casings removed
> 1 large onion, chopped
> 1 large carrot, chopped
> 3 garlic cloves, minced
> 6 cups chicken broth
> 3 cups water
> 2 tablespoons dried currants
> 1 teaspoon dried basil
> 1 can (14-1/2 ounces) diced tomatoes, undrained
> 1 cup uncooked small shell pasta

Grated Parmesan cheese

Place beans in a Dutch oven or soup kettle; add water to cover by 2 in. Bring to a boil; boil for 2 minutes. Remove from the heat; cover and let stand for 1 hour. Drain and rinse beans, discarding liquid.

In the same pan, cook the sausage, onion, carrot and garlic over medium heat until the meat is no longer pink; drain. Add the broth, water, currants, basil and beans. Bring to a boil. Reduce heat; cover and simmer for 1-1/2 to 2 hours or until the beans are tender, stirring occasionally.

Add the tomatoes and pasta; bring to a boil. Reduce heat; cover and simmer for 15 minutes or until pasta is tender. Serve with Parmesan cheese. **Yield:** 12 servings (3 quarts).

CITRUSY AVOCADO CRAB SALAD

(Pictured above)

Jackie Allen, Belfair, Washington

My husband and I love to treat family and friends to favorite dishes like this refreshing salad.

> 1 cup (8 ounces) sour cream
> 1/4 cup orange juice concentrate
> 2 to 4 tablespoons milk
> 8 cups torn salad greens
> 1 pound frozen crabmeat, thawed, flaked and cartilage removed *or* 2-1/2 cups flaked imitation crabmeat
> 2 ripe avocados, peeled and sliced
> 1 medium grapefruit, peeled and sectioned
> 1 medium navel orange, peeled and sectioned
> 1 can (8 ounces) sliced pineapple, drained and halved
> 3 hard-cooked eggs, sliced
> 1/4 cup sliced almonds, toasted

In a bowl, combine sour cream and orange juice concentrate until smooth. Add enough milk to reach desired consistency. Cover and refrigerate until serving.

On a serving platter, arrange greens, crab, avocados, fruit and eggs. Drizzle with dressing. Sprinkle with almonds. **Yield:** 8 servings.

ITALIAN POTATO SALAD

Jeannette Macera, Utica, New York

You'll want to take this simple-to-assemble potato salad to all your picnics and outings.

> 5 to 6 medium red potatoes, cooked and cut into 1-inch pieces
> 2 garlic cloves, minced

1/2 cup chopped red onion
3 to 4 plum tomatoes, quartered
1/3 cup olive *or* vegetable oil
3 to 4 fresh basil leaves, chopped
1 jar (5-3/4 ounces) stuffed olives,
  drained and halved
1 teaspoon dried oregano
1-1/2 teaspoons salt
1/4 teaspoon pepper
Lettuce leaves, optional

In a large bowl, combine the first 10 ingredients; toss to coat. Cover and refrigerate until serving. Serve salad in a lettuce-lined bowl if desired. **Yield:** 12 servings.

TOMATO SOUP SALAD DRESSING

Betty Jean Coachman, Tipton, Indiana

This is a nice refreshing dressing for simple lettuce salads. The onion adds a lot of flavor.

1 can (10-3/4 ounces) condensed tomato
  soup, undiluted
1 cup vegetable oil
1/2 cup cider vinegar
1 cup sugar
1 small onion, quartered
1/2 teaspoon salt
Salad greens and vegetables of your choice

In a blender, combine the first six ingredients. Cover and process until smooth. Refrigerate for at least 4 hours. Serve with salad. **Yield:** about 3 cups.

 CRANBERRY ORANGE
    VINAIGRETTE

Toni Serpe, Dania, Florida

I eat a lot of salad and this is one of my favorite dressings. Living in Florida, I like using orange products produced in our state.

1/4 cup cranberry juice concentrate
1/4 cup orange juice concentrate
1/4 cup red wine vinegar *or* cider vinegar
1/4 cup olive *or* vegetable oil
1 teaspoon Dijon mustard
1/2 teaspoon salt
1/2 teaspoon pepper
Torn salad greens
Sliced radishes and sweet yellow and
  orange peppers *or* vegetables of your choice

In a jar with a tight-fitting lid, combine the first seven ingredients; shake well. Serve over greens and vegetables. Store in the refrigerator. **Yield:** 1 cup.

FIESTA VEGETABLE SALAD

(Pictured below)

Betty Claycomb, Alverton, Pennsylvania

A friend shared this recipe with me. Not only does it look pretty, it can be made ahead and kept in the refrigerator for several days.

1 package (16 ounces) frozen cut green
  beans, thawed and drained
1 package (16 ounces) frozen peas,
  thawed and drained
1 package (16 ounces) frozen corn,
  thawed and drained
1 *each* medium green, sweet yellow and
  red pepper, diced
1 cup chopped celery
1 cup chopped onion
1 cup sugar
3/4 cup cider vinegar
1/2 cup vegetable oil
1 tablespoon water
1 teaspoon salt
1/2 teaspoon pepper

In a large bowl, combine the vegetables; set aside. In a saucepan, heat the sugar, vinegar, oil, water, salt and pepper over medium heat until sugar is dissolved. Pour warm dressing over vegetables; toss to coat. Cover and refrigerate for 2 hours or overnight. Serve with a slotted spoon. **Yield:** 12-14 servings.

SUNSHINE FRUIT SALAD

(Pictured above)

Delores Jones, Spokane, Washington

This is an excellent salad any time of the year. Other fruits can be substituted when they're in season.

- 2 medium oranges, peeled, sectioned and chopped
- 1 tablespoon sugar
- 2 green *or* red tart apples, chopped
- 3 kiwifruit, peeled and chopped
- 1 cup green seedless grapes
- 1/2 cup red seedless grapes
- 1 can (8 ounces) pineapple chunks, drained
- 1/2 cup vanilla yogurt
- 1 large firm banana, sliced

In a salad bowl, combine oranges and sugar. Let stand for 10 minutes. Add apples, kiwi, grapes, pineapple and yogurt; toss gently. Cover and refrigerate for 30 minutes. Add the banana just before serving. **Yield:** 6-8 servings.

BLUE CHEESE APPLE SALAD

Nancy Stolp, Wisconsin Rapids, Wisconsin

We have a lot of apple orchards in our state, so this definitely represents our area. This is one of my favorite apple recipes. It has a nice combination of flavors.

- 3 medium unpeeled red apples, cubed
- 2 teaspoons lemon juice
- 3 cups cantaloupe cubes *or* balls
- 2 cups sliced celery
- 1/2 cup sour cream
- 1/2 cup crumbled blue cheese
- 1/3 cup mayonnaise *or* salad dressing

Lettuce leaves

In a large bowl, toss apples with lemon juice. Add cantaloupe and celery; mix well. In a small bowl, combine the sour cream, blue cheese and mayonnaise. Pour over apple mixture and toss to coat. Cover and refrigerate for 1 hour. Serve in a lettuce-lined bowl. **Yield:** 10-12 servings.

GOLDEN APPLE POTATO SALAD

Mary Pipkin, Melba, Idaho

This is a wonderful variation on an American summertime standby. Since Idaho is the potato state and a lot of apples are also grown here, I thought this would be an excellent blend of ingredients.

- 6 medium russet potatoes
- 2/3 cup mayonnaise
- 1/2 cup plain yogurt
- 2 tablespoons cider vinegar
- 2 teaspoons prepared mustard
- 1 garlic clove, minced
- 1 teaspoon salt
- 5 bacon strips, cooked and crumbled
- 1 medium onion, grated
- 2 medium Golden Delicious apples, cubed

Place potatoes in a large saucepan and cover with water; bring to a boil over medium-high heat. Cover and cook for 20-30 minutes or until tender.

In a small bowl, combine the mayonnaise, yogurt, vinegar, mustard, garlic and salt. Peel warm potatoes and slice into a large bowl; add the bacon and onion. Pour dressing over potato mixture and gently toss to coat. Fold in apples. Cover and refrigerate for several hours before serving. **Yield:** 10 servings.

VEGETABLE PASTA SALAD

Helen Phillips, Horseheads, New York

It's always fun to incorporate the vegetables we grow in our garden into different dishes. This salad not only gives me the opportunity to use our vegetables, it looks and tastes great.

- 2 cups broccoli florets
- 4 cups cooked spiral pasta
- 2 medium carrots, julienned

1/2 cup frozen peas, thawed
1/2 cup cubed fully cooked ham
1/2 cup cubed cheddar cheese
1/3 cup sliced green onions
DRESSING:
3/4 cup mayonnaise
2 tablespoons cider vinegar
1 tablespoon Dijon mustard
1 garlic clove, minced
1 teaspoon dill weed
1/4 teaspoon pepper

In a saucepan, cook broccoli in a small amount of water for 2-3 minutes; rinse in cold water and drain. In a large bowl, combine the broccoli, pasta, carrots, peas, ham, cheese and onions.

In another bowl, combine the dressing ingredients; mix well. Pour over salad and toss to coat. Cover and refrig-erate for 1 hour or until serving. **Yield:** 10-12 servings.

CORN AND SAUSAGE SOUP

(Pictured above)

Rebecca Clark, Hammond, Louisiana

I created this recipe about 15 years ago when I received an abundance of fresh sweet corn from friends. The soup is easy to make and has always been a big hit with family and friends. I usually serve it with bread and a tossed salad.

2-1/2 cups chopped onions
1/2 cup *each* chopped green pepper, sweet red pepper and celery
6 tablespoons butter *or* margarine
1-1/2 pounds fully cooked smoked sausage, cut into 1/4-inch pieces
3 garlic cloves, minced
4 cans (15 ounces *each*) Italian-style tomato sauce
3 packages (16 ounces *each*) frozen corn
2 cans (14-1/2 ounces *each*) Italian diced tomatoes, undrained
2 cups water
3 bay leaves
1-1/2 teaspoons *each* dried basil, oregano and thyme
1/2 teaspoon pepper
1/4 teaspoon dried marjoram
1/4 teaspoon hot pepper sauce, optional

In a Dutch oven or soup kettle, saute onions, peppers and celery in butter until tender. Add sausage and garlic; cook for 8-10 minutes or until heated.

Stir in the remaining ingredients. Bring to a boil. Reduce heat; simmer, uncovered, for 1 hour, stirring occasionally. Discard bay leaves before serving. **Yield:** 16-18 servings (about 5 quarts).

BROCCOLI SLAW

(Pictured below)

Konny Thomas, Citrus Heights, California

Here's a new twist on traditional coleslaw. It's easy to make and so delicious.

4 cups broccoli florets
1 medium carrot, shredded
2 cups shredded red cabbage
1/2 cup raisins
1 small sweet onion, chopped
1 bottle (16 ounces) coleslaw dressing

In a serving bowl, combine all ingredients. Cover and refrigerate for at least 2 hours. Stir before serving. **Yield:** 6 servings.

SPINACH SALAD WITH SPICY HONEY DRESSING

(Pictured below)

Barbara Martinefau, Hudson, Wisconsin

Here's a salad with some zip to it. I've also served the spicy dressing with mixed vegetables, fruit and tossed salads.

    4 cups torn fresh spinach
    1 cup minced fresh parsley
    1 cup sliced fresh mushrooms
    2 medium tomatoes, cut into wedges
    2 celery ribs, chopped
    1 cup canned bean sprouts, rinsed and drained
1-1/2 cups (6 ounces) shredded cheddar cheese
    1 cup salted sunflower kernels
    1/4 teaspoon *each* salt, pepper and garlic salt
DRESSING:
    1/2 cup vegetable oil
    1/4 cup honey
    1/4 cup cider vinegar
    1/4 cup chopped onion
    3 tablespoons chili sauce
1-1/2 teaspoons Worcestershire sauce
    1/4 teaspoon salt

In a large salad bowl, combine the spinach, parsley, mushrooms, tomatoes, celery, bean sprouts, cheese, sunflower kernels and seasonings.

In a jar with a tight-fitting lid, combine the dressing ingredients; shake well. Drizzle desired amount over salad and toss to coat. Serve immediately. Refrigerate any leftover dressing. **Yield:** 12 servings.

FLOWER GARDEN SOUP

(Pictured above)

Fresh vegetables flavor traditional chicken soup in this bountiful blend from our Test Kitchen. For fun, cut notches in the carrots and zucchini to make "petals", slice the veggies, then simmer up bowls of blooms!

    6 medium carrots
    1 medium zucchini
    4 celery ribs, chopped
    1 medium onion, chopped
    8 cans (14-1/2 ounces *each*) chicken broth
    1 teaspoon dried basil
    1 teaspoon dried oregano
    4 cups cubed cooked chicken

Using a zest stripper or paring knife, cut a lengthwise strip on each carrot, forming a notch. Repeat at equal intervals around carrot. Repeat with zucchini. Cut carrots and zucchini into 1/4-in. slices; set zucchini aside.

In a Dutch oven or soup kettle, combine the carrots, celery, onion, broth, basil and oregano. Bring to a boil. Reduce heat; cover and simmer for 20-30 minutes or until vegetables are crisp-tender. Add chicken and reserved zucchini; simmer, uncovered, for 10 minutes or until zucchini is tender. **Yield:** 8 servings (2 quarts).

VEGETABLE SALAD MEDLEY

Darala Taylor, Covina, California

I like to take this salad to potlucks because it feeds a lot of people, and it's so easy to make.

    1 cup sugar
    3/4 cup red wine vinegar *or* cider vinegar
    1/2 cup vegetable oil
    1 teaspoon salt
    1/2 teaspoon pepper

2 cups frozen French-style green beans,
    thawed and drained
1 can (15 ounces) garbanzo beans *or*
    chickpeas, rinsed and drained
1-1/2 cups frozen peas, thawed and drained
1-1/2 cups frozen corn, thawed and drained
1 cup *each* chopped celery, red onion and
    sweet red pepper
1 cup cauliflowerets
2 cans (2-1/4 ounces *each*) sliced ripe
    olives, drained
1 jar (4 ounces) diced pimientos, drained

In a saucepan, bring the sugar, vinegar, oil, salt
and pepper to a boil. In a large bowl, combine
the remaining ingredients. Add sugar mixture and
toss to coat. Cover and refrigerate for several
hours or overnight, stirring occasionally. Serve
with a slotted spoon. **Yield:** 12-14 servings.

MAPLE-DIJON SALAD DRESSING

Kristin Curtis, Sterling, Pennsylvania

*I believe maple syrup is one of Mother Nature's
finest ingredients. I use it in everything from cheese-
cakes to this salad dressing.*

3/4 cup olive *or* vegetable oil
1/4 cup balsamic vinegar *or* cider vinegar
1/4 cup maple syrup
1/4 cup Dijon mustard
2 garlic cloves, minced
1/4 teaspoon pepper

In a jar with a tight-fitting lid, combine all ingredients; shake well. Store in the refrigerator.
Shake before serving. **Yield:** 1-2/3 cups.

GRAPE AND CABBAGE SALAD

Dorothy Raymond, Mira Loma, California

*This is a recipe I created using the grapes grown in our
state. The flavor and texture brings many compliments, and its combination of color adds to its appeal.*

2 cups finely shredded cabbage
1 cup halved red grapes
1/2 cup chopped green pepper
2 tablespoons minced fresh parsley
1/4 cup Italian salad dressing
2 tablespoons water
1 tablespoon cider vinegar

In a bowl, combine the cabbage, grapes, green
pepper and parsley. In another bowl, whisk together salad dressing, water and vinegar. Pour over
cabbage mixture and toss to coat. Cover and refrigerate overnight. **Yield:** 4-6 servings.

WILD RICE WALDORF

(Pictured below)

Dorothy Banken, Norman, Oklahoma

*I used to live in Minnesota, where a lot of wild rice is
grown. The addition of wild rice to this salad gives it
a robust flavor.*

1 can (8 ounces) pineapple chunks *or*
    tidbits
1/2 cup sour cream
1/2 cup mayonnaise
2 tablespoons sugar
1 tablespoon lemon juice
2 cups cooked wild rice
2 medium green apples, diced
2 medium red apples, diced
1 celery rib, thinly sliced
1/2 cup chopped walnuts
Lettuce leaves, optional

Drain pineapple, reserving 1 tablespoon juice (discard remaining juice or save for another use); set
pineapple aside. In a small bowl, combine sour
cream, mayonnaise, sugar, lemon juice and reserved pineapple juice.

In a large bowl, combine the rice, apples, celery and pineapple. Add the dressing and toss to
coat. Cover and refrigerate for 2 hours. Just before
serving, stir in walnuts. Serve in a lettuce-lined
bowl if desired. **Yield:** 10-12 servings.

SCALLOPED CARROTS
(Pictured below)

Joyce Tornholm, New Market, Iowa

A cookbook my husband gave me as a wedding gift included this recipe—he remembers having the dish as a child at church dinners. Now I make it whenever I need a special vegetable side. It's rich and cheesy even after reheating.

  6 cups water
 12 medium carrots, sliced 1/4 inch thick
    (about 4 cups)
  1 medium onion, finely chopped
 1/2 cup butter *or* margarine, *divided*
 1/4 cup all-purpose flour
  1 teaspoon salt
 1/4 teaspoon ground mustard
 1/4 teaspoon celery salt
Dash pepper
  2 cups milk
  2 cups (8 ounces) shredded cheddar
    cheese
  3 slices whole wheat bread, cut into small
    cubes

In a saucepan, bring water to a boil; add carrots. Return to a boil; cover and cook for 4 minutes. Drain and immediately place the carrots in ice water; drain and pat dry.

In a saucepan, saute onion in 1/4 cup butter. Stir in the flour, salt, mustard, celery salt and pepper until blended. Gradually add milk. Bring to a boil; cook and stir for 2 minutes or until thickened.

In a greased 11-in. x 7-in. x 2-in. baking dish, layer half of the carrots, cheese and white sauce. Repeat layers. Melt remaining butter; toss with bread cubes. Sprinkle over the top. Bake, uncovered, at 350° for 35-40 minutes or until hot and bubbly. **Yield:** 4-6 servings.

CREAMY PARMESAN SAUCE

Maria Bacher, Westminster, South Carolina

Try this sauce over a variety of vegetables. It has a wonderful cheesy flavor.

  1 package (8 ounces) cream cheese,
    cubed
 3/4 cup milk
 1/2 cup shredded Parmesan cheese
Ground nutmeg and pepper to taste

In a 1-qt. microwave-safe dish, combine the cream cheese, milk and Parmesan cheese. Cover and microwave at 50% power for 3 minutes; stir. Cook 3-5 minutes longer or until cheeses are melted. Add nutmeg and pepper. Serve over vegetables. **Yield:** 2 cups.

Editor's Note: Shredded Parmesan cheese will give the sauce a creamier texture than grated Parmesan. This recipe was tested in an 850-watt microwave.

CORN AND PEPPERS

Carol Gaus, Itasca, Illinois

Add a little pep to plain corn with this flavorful recipe. It's as colorful as it is fresh tasting.

✓ **Uses less fat, sugar or salt. Includes Nutritional Analysis and Diabetic Exchanges.**

  3 cups fresh *or* frozen corn
  1 cup chopped green pepper
  1 cup chopped sweet red pepper
  1 tablespoon chopped seeded jalapeno
    pepper*
  2 teaspoons chili powder
 3/4 teaspoon salt
 1/2 teaspoon ground cumin
  1 cup chopped fresh tomato
  2 tablespoons minced fresh parsley *or*
    cilantro

In a saucepan, bring 1 in. of water to a boil; place the corn and peppers in a steamer basket over water. Sprinkle with the chili powder, salt and cumin. Cover and steam for 8-10 minutes or until

vegetables are crisp-tender. Transfer vegetable mixture to a serving bowl. Add tomato and parsley; toss gently. **Yield:** 6 servings.

Nutritional Analysis: One serving (about 3/4 cup) equals 84 calories, 1 g fat (trace saturated fat), 0 cholesterol, 212 mg sodium, 20 g carbohydrate, 3 g fiber, 3 g protein. **Diabetic Exchange:** 1 starch.

*Editor's Note: When cutting or seeding hot peppers, use rubber or plastic gloves to protect your hands. Avoid touching your face.

CHEDDAR CAULIFLOWER

Karen Jean Johann, Kewaskum, Wisconsin

This cheesy cauliflower side dish has long been a family favorite. It always makes a pretty presentation on our holiday table.

- 1 medium head cauliflower, broken into florets
- 1/4 cup water
- 1 cup (8 ounces) sour cream
- 2 teaspoons minced chives
- 1/4 teaspoon salt
- 1/8 teaspoon pepper
- 1-1/2 cups (6 ounces) shredded cheddar cheese

Place the cauliflower and water in a 2-qt. microwave-safe dish. Cover and microwave on high for 6 minutes; stir. Cook 6-8 minutes longer or until tender. Drain.

In a bowl, combine the sour cream, chives, salt and pepper; spoon over the cauliflower. Sprinkle with cheese. Microwave, uncovered, on high for 2 minutes or until cheese is melted. **Yield:** 6 servings.

Editor's Note: This recipe was tested in an 850-watt microwave.

HOMEMADE CAJUN SEASONING

Onietta Loewer, Branch, Louisiana

We in Louisiana love seasoned foods. I use this in gravy, over meats and with salads. It makes an excellent gift for teachers. Many have asked for the recipe.

- 1 carton (26 ounces) salt
- 2 containers (1 ounce *each*) cayenne pepper
- 1/3 cup pepper
- 1/3 cup chili powder
- 3 tablespoons garlic powder

In a bowl, combine all of the ingredients. Store in an airtight container. Use to season pork, chicken, seafood, steaks or vegetables. **Yield:** about 3-1/2 cups.

RICH 'N' CHEESY MACARONI

(Pictured above)

Gwen Miller, Rolling Hills, Alberta

This delicious dish puts a new twist on traditional macaroni and cheese. The three different cheese flavors blend wonderfully. Plus, it's easy to prepare—I plan to make it often when my husband and I start traveling.

- 2-1/2 cups uncooked elbow macaroni
- 6 tablespoons butter *or* margarine, *divided*
- 1/4 cup all-purpose flour
- 1 teaspoon salt
- 1 teaspoon sugar
- 2 cups milk
- 8 ounces process American cheese, cubed
- 1-1/3 cups small-curd cottage cheese
- 2/3 cup sour cream
- 2 cups (8 ounces) shredded sharp cheddar cheese
- 1-1/2 cups soft bread crumbs

Cook macaroni according to package directions; drain. Place in a greased 2-1/2-qt. baking dish. In a saucepan, melt 4 tablespoons butter. Stir in the flour, salt and sugar until smooth. Gradually stir in milk. Bring to a boil; cook and stir for 2 minutes or until thickened.

Reduce heat; stir in American cheese until melted. Stir in cottage cheese and sour cream. Pour over macaroni. Sprinkle with cheddar cheese. Melt remaining butter and toss with bread crumbs; sprinkle over top. Bake, uncovered, at 350° for 30 minutes or until golden brown. **Yield:** 6-8 servings.

SOUTH LIBERTY HALL RELISH

Melinda Winchell, Las Vegas, Nevada

My grandparents originated this recipe that's been treasured in our family for four generations. It's named after a dance hall they ran in rural Iowa. Whenever I bite into a hot dog or hamburger dressed up with this taste bud-tingling relish, I think of them and their delicious country cooking.

　　1 pint dill pickles, drained
1/4 cup chopped onion
　　2 to 3 tablespoons sugar
1/2 cup yellow mustard

Place the pickles and onion in a food processor; cover and process until finely chopped. Transfer to a bowl; stir in sugar and mustard. Cover and store in the refrigerator for up to 1 week. **Yield:** 2 cups.

SWEET POTATO BAKE

(Pictured below)

Pam Holloway, Marion, Louisiana

This is an easy dish to prepare and is a perfect addition to a special holiday meal. The topping is flavorful and gives a nice contrast of textures.

　　7 large sweet potatoes (about 6 pounds), peeled and cubed
1/4 cup butter *or* margarine
1/2 cup orange marmalade
1/4 cup orange juice
1/4 cup packed brown sugar
　　2 teaspoons salt
　　1 teaspoon ground ginger
TOPPING:
　12 oatmeal cookies, crumbled
　　6 tablespoons butter *or* margarine, softened

Place sweet potatoes in a Dutch oven and cover with water; bring to a boil. Reduce heat; cover and cook just until tender, about 15 minutes. Drain well. Mash potatoes with butter. Add marmalade, orange juice, brown sugar, salt and ginger.

Transfer to a greased 13-in. x 9-in. x 2-in. baking dish. Toss cookie crumbs with butter; sprinkle over the top. Bake, uncovered, at 400° for 20 minutes or until browned. Let stand for 15 minutes before serving. **Yield:** 10-12 servings.

CONFETTI CARROT FRITTERS

Peggy Camp, Twain, California

Crispy, sweet and savory, these delicate fritters are a fun twist on the traditional fruit-filled variety. They're yummy served with a mustard dipping sauce, but our kids enjoy them with a drizzle of warm maple syrup, too.

　　6 cups water
2-1/2 cups finely chopped carrots
1/4 cup all-purpose flour
1/4 teaspoon salt
1/4 teaspoon pepper
　　2 eggs, *separated*
　　3 tablespoons milk
　　2 tablespoons finely chopped onion
　　2 tablespoons minced fresh parsley
Vegetable oil for deep-fat frying
MUSTARD SAUCE:
　　1 tablespoon minced fresh parsley
　　1 tablespoon red wine vinegar *or* cider vinegar
　　1 tablespoon Dijon mustard
　　1 teaspoon finely chopped green onion
1/4 cup olive *or* vegetable oil

In a saucepan, bring water to a boil; add carrots. Return to a boil; cover and cook for 2 minutes. Drain and immediately place the carrots in ice water; drain and pat dry.

In a bowl, combine the flour, salt and pepper. Combine egg yolks and milk; stir into the flour mixture until smooth. Stir in the onion, parsley and carrots.

In a mixing bowl, beat egg whites until stiff peaks form; fold into batter.

In an electric skillet, heat 1/4 in. of oil to 375°. Drop batter by 1/3 cupfuls into oil. Fry until golden brown, about 2 minutes on each side.

For mustard sauce, combine the parsley, vinegar, mustard and green onion in a bowl. Slowly whisk in oil until blended. Serve with the fritters. **Yield:** 9 servings.

A Bushel of Carrot Tips

• When preparing my favorite Italian or Mexican recipes, I often substitute shredded carrots for part of the ground beef or sausage. It reduces the fat and makes the recipe more economical, too.   —Trudy Overlin
Rigby, Idaho

• When I roast carrots, I pat them dry with a paper towel first so they'll brown better.   —Marlene Schott
Devine, Texas

• I've found that a sprinkle of nutmeg enhances the flavor of steamed buttered carrots.   —Esther Bane
Glidden, Iowa

• Before we freeze our carrots, we cook them in a pressure cooker for 2 minutes, then quickly cool them. They are great in soups and other cooked dishes.   —Callie Dalton
Brookfield, Connecticut

• Scalloped carrots are a great make-ahead dish. I do all the prep work the day before and refrigerate. The next day, I just pop the carrots in the oven and increase the baking time a little. This dish also freezes well.
—Patricia Fitchett
Clifton Park, New York

• My family thinks carrot pie is tastier and more colorful than pumpkin pie. At harvesttime, I cook all the small carrots and make carrot puree for pies. I freeze the puree in 2-cup packages. When my family is clamoring for carrot pie, I can quickly whip it up using the premeasured puree.
—Gail Dinwoodie
Minton, Saskatchewan

• Around the second week in April, I plant my carrots at 25 seeds per foot, 1/4 inch deep with rows 12 inches apart. Later, I thin the seedlings to 3 inches apart.   —Ruth Brant
Dallastown, Pennsylvania

• We enjoy carrot cake so much that I generally bake two cakes at one time. The second cake keeps moist and delicious in the freezer for up to 3 months. It's best to frost the cake after it's thawed.   —Irene O'Dell
Pembroke, Virginia

• I always keep carrots and low-fat dip on hand for a quick, nutritious snack.   —Anne Powers
Munford, Alabama

• My carrot muffins are so chock-full of apples, coconut, carrots, etc., that they tend to stick to paper liners. So I grease the muffin cups with nonstick cooking spray instead.
—Loraine Meyer
Bend, Oregon

• When I'm pinched for time, I used jarred strained carrots baby food in my carrot cookies.   —Patricia Morrow
Mapleton, Minnesota

• For a delicious addition to sauteed carrots, sprinkle with toasted nuts. To quickly toast nuts, spread them in a single layer in a dry skillet and heat over medium heat. Stir or shake the pan constantly until nuts are lightly browned. Remove from pan and let cool. If you leave the nuts in the hot pan, they'll continue to brown and may burn.   —Carol Gaus
Itasca, Illinois

SWISS CHEESE POTATO PANCAKES
(Pictured above)

Ferne Moe, Northbrook, Illinois

Years ago, when I was searching for just the right thing to perk up a meal, my neighbor suggested these pancakes. They did the trick! Golden brown, crisp and cheesy, they make a deliciously different dish any time of day.

 1 package (3 ounces) cream cheese, softened
 2 eggs
 2 tablespoons all-purpose flour
 4 cups shredded peeled potatoes (about 1 pound)
 1/4 cup shredded Swiss cheese
 2 tablespoons grated onion
 1/4 teaspoon salt
 1/8 teaspoon pepper
Dash cayenne pepper
 3 tablespoons butter *or* margarine
 3 tablespoons vegetable oil

In a mixing bowl, beat cream cheese until smooth. Add eggs, one at a time, beating well after each addition. Add flour; mix well. Stir in potatoes, Swiss cheese, onion, salt, pepper and cayenne pepper.

In a large skillet, heat butter and oil over medium heat. Drop batter by 1/4 cupfuls; press lightly to flatten. Fry until golden and crisp, about 5 minutes on each side. Drain on paper towels. **Yield: 16 pancakes.**

CANDIED SWEET POTATOES
Essie Nealey, Tabor City, North Carolina

My town is known as the Yam Capital of the United States. This is a simple recipe that goes well with baked ham or roasted turkey.

 3 pounds sweet potatoes *or* yams
 1/2 cup packed brown sugar
 1 teaspoon ground cinnamon
 1/4 cup butter *or* margarine, cubed
 1/4 cup corn syrup

Place sweet potatoes in a large kettle and cover with water; cover and boil gently for 30-45 minutes or until potatoes can be easily pierced with the tip of a sharp knife. When cool enough to handle, peel the potatoes and cut into wedges.

Place in an ungreased 11-in. x 7-in. x 2-in. baking dish. Sprinkle with brown sugar and cinnamon. Dot with butter; drizzle with corn syrup. Bake, uncovered, at 375° for 15-20 minutes or until bubbly, basting with sauce occasionally. **Yield: 8-10 servings.**

BROCCOLI SUPREME
(Pictured below)

Maretta Ballinger, Visalia, California

Here's a creamy side dish that goes well with many entrees. It's easy to make and can be prepared ahead.

1 package (16 ounces) frozen chopped
  broccoli, thawed and drained
1 can (10-3/4 ounces) condensed cream
  of mushroom soup, undiluted
1/2 cup sour cream
1/2 cup chopped celery
1 jar (2 ounces) diced pimientos, drained
1/2 teaspoon salt
1/2 teaspoon pepper
1/2 cup shredded cheddar cheese

In a bowl, combine the first seven ingredients; stir
to coat. Transfer to a greased 1-1/2-qt. baking dish.
Sprinkle with cheese. Bake, uncovered, at 350°
for 20 minutes or until heated through. **Yield:** 4-
6 servings.

OVEN-ROASTED CARROTS

(Pictured on front cover)

Marlene Schott, Devine, Texas

*My seven children and 15 grandchildren really look
forward to carrots when they're prepared this flavorful way. As a cook at our local school, I served two
generations of my brood, plus relatives and friends
from all over our area.*

2 pounds baby carrots
4 small onions, quartered
6 garlic cloves, peeled
2 tablespoons olive *or* vegetable oil
2 teaspoons white wine vinegar *or* cider
  vinegar
1 to 2 teaspoons dried thyme
1/2 teaspoon salt
1/8 teaspoon pepper

Place carrots, onions and garlic in two greased 15-
in. x 10-in. x 1-in. baking pans. Drizzle with oil
and vinegar. Sprinkle with thyme, salt and pepper; gently toss to coat.

Cover and bake at 450° for 20 minutes; stir.
Bake, uncovered, for 10 minutes; stir again. Bake
10 minutes longer or until carrots are crisp-tender.
Yield: 8 servings.

CHEESY EGGPLANT BAKE

(Pictured above right)

Frances Sayre, Cinnaminson, New Jersey

*Since New Jersey is the Garden State, I think this
recipe represents our region. This dish uses a lot of vegetables out of the garden.*

1 medium eggplant, peeled
2 teaspoons salt
3/4 cup dry bread crumbs
3 teaspoons garlic salt
1/2 teaspoon pepper
3 eggs
3 tablespoons olive *or* vegetable oil,
  divided
1 large green pepper, chopped
1 medium onion, chopped
1/2 pound fresh mushrooms, sliced
2 cans (14-1/2 ounces *each*) stewed
  tomatoes
1 package (6 ounces) sliced mozzarella
  cheese

Cut eggplant into 1/4-in.-thick slices. Place in a
colander over a plate; sprinkle with salt. Let
stand 30 minutes. In a shallow bowl, combine the
bread crumbs, garlic salt and pepper. In another
shallow bowl, beat eggs. Pat eggplant slices with
paper towels; dip into eggs, then coat with crumb
mixture.

In a skillet, cook eggplant in 2 tablespoons oil
for 2 minutes on each side or until lightly
browned. Transfer to an ungreased 13-in. x 9-in.
x 2-in. baking dish. In the same skillet, saute the
green pepper, onion and mushrooms in remaining
oil for 5 minutes or until crisp-tender. Sprinkle
over eggplant. Top with tomatoes. Bake, uncovered, at 350° for 25 minutes. Place cheese slices
over the top. Bake 25-30 minutes longer or until
cheese is lightly browned. **Yield:** 6-8 servings.

Carrots Cook Up in Minutes

FOR quick and colorful cuisine, nothing beats garden-fresh carrots. They're a staple in every home and available in all seasons. You can create any of these sensational sides to round out a meal in 30 minutes or less...so start peeling!

In a saucepan, combine cornstarch and cinnamon. Add the brown sugar, butter and reserved juice. Bring to a boil; cook and stir for 2 minutes or until thickened. Stir in the carrots and pineapple; heat through. **Yield:** 4 servings.

CARROTS AND PINEAPPLE

(Pictured below)

Cora Christian, Church Hill, Tennessee

This simple side dish has been a favorite with family and friends for years.

    2 cups baby carrots
    1 can (20 ounces) pineapple chunks
    4 teaspoons cornstarch
    1/2 teaspoon ground cinnamon
    1/2 cup packed brown sugar
    1 tablespoon butter *or* margarine

In a saucepan, bring 1 in. of water to a boil; place carrots in a steamer basket over water. Cover and steam for 8-10 minutes or until crisp-tender. Drain pineapple, reserving juice; set pineapple aside.

MICROWAVE CARROT CASSEROLE

Ruth Barry, Sacramento, California

I received this speedy recipe from a cooking class when I bought my first microwave years ago. It always gets rave reviews.

1-1/2 pounds carrots, shredded
    1/4 cup water
      1 can (10-3/4 ounces) condensed cream of celery soup, undiluted
      1 cup (4 ounces) shredded cheddar cheese
      1 medium onion, chopped
    1/4 cup milk
    1/2 teaspoon ground mustard
      2 tablespoons dry bread crumbs
      1 tablespoon butter *or* margarine, melted

In a 1-1/2-qt. microwave-safe dish, combine carrots and water. Cover and microwave on high for 6-8 minutes or until crisp-tender, stirring once; drain and return to dish.

In a bowl, combine the soup, cheese, onion, milk and mustard. Pour over carrots; stir to coat. Cover and microwave on high for 2 minutes. Toss the bread crumbs and butter; sprinkle over the top. Cover and microwave on high 2 minutes longer. Let stand for 2 minutes. **Yield: 4 servings.**

Editor's Note: This recipe was tested in an 850-watt microwave.

HONEY-MUSTARD CARROTS

Kim Jorgensen, Coulee City, Washington

This recipe comes from my husband's grandmother. It is "the" veggie side dish to be served at Thanksgiving.

3-1/2 cups sliced *or* baby carrots
   2 tablespoons olive *or* vegetable oil
   1 tablespoon honey
   1 tablespoon maple syrup
   1 tablespoon Dijon mustard
   2 teaspoons dried parsley flakes

In a saucepan, bring 1 in. of water to a boil; place carrots in a steamer basket over water. Cover and steam for 8-10 minutes or until crisp-tender. In a saucepan, combine the oil, honey, syrup and mustard; bring to a boil. Stir in carrots and parsley. **Yield: 4-5 servings.**

FLAVORFUL CARROTS

Kathryn Gleason, Unadilla, New York

When my mom passed away, I went through her cookbooks to find the favorite recipes she prepared for our family gatherings. These tasty carrots were one of them.

   5 cups sliced carrots
   3 tablespoons finely chopped green pepper
   2 tablespoons finely chopped green onion
   1 package (3 ounces) cream cheese, softened
   1 cup (8 ounces) sour cream

   1/2 teaspoon salt
   1/2 teaspoon grated lemon peel
   1/8 teaspoon pepper

Place 1 in. of water in a saucepan; add carrots. Bring to a boil. Reduce heat; cover and simmer for 7-9 minutes or until crisp-tender. Drain and place carrots in a bowl; add green pepper and onion.

In a mixing bowl, beat cream cheese, sour cream, salt, lemon peel and pepper until smooth. Pour over vegetables; gently stir to coat. **Yield: 6 servings.**

SAUTEED CARROTS

Mildred Sherrer, Bay City, Texas

My aunt passed this recipe down to me. It's requested often by family.

1-1/2 pounds carrots, cut into 1-inch julienne strips
   4 teaspoons olive *or* vegetable oil
   1/3 cup chicken broth
   1/2 teaspoon pepper
   2 tablespoons brown sugar
   2 tablespoons butter *or* margarine, melted
   1 tablespoon lemon juice
   1 tablespoon grated lemon peel
   1 tablespoon minced fresh parsley

In a large skillet, saute carrots in oil for 3 minutes. Add the broth and pepper. Cover and cook for 5-6 minutes or until carrots are crisp-tender.

Combine the brown sugar, butter, lemon juice and peel; pour over carrots. Cook until sugar is dissolved and liquid is thickened. Sprinkle with parsley. **Yield: 4-5 servings.**

A SWEET IDEA

ADDING 1/2 to 1 teaspoon sugar to cooked vegetables such as carrots, corn and peas reduces starchy flavors and highlights natural sweetness.

Save any liquid in which you've cooked vegetables and use for soups, stews or sauces. If you don't want to use it right away, freeze the liquid for up to 6 months.

4 medium potatoes, peeled and thinly sliced
1/4 cup chopped onion

In a saucepan, melt the butter. Stir in flour, salt and pepper until smooth. Gradually stir in milk. Bring to a boil; cook and stir for 2 minutes or until thickened. Reduce heat. Stir in cheese until melted. In a 2-1/2-qt. microwave-safe dish coated with nonstick cooking spray, layer a third of the potatoes, onion and cheese sauce. Repeat the layers twice. Cover and microwave on high for 35-40 minutes, stirring every 5 minutes until the potatoes are tender. **Yield:** 8 servings.

Editor's Note: This recipe was tested in an 850-watt microwave.

MAPLE APPLE RINGS
(Pictured below)

Alma Jacklin, New Durham, New Hampshire

I live in maple syrup country and got this recipe from a sugarhouse. These apple rings are wonderful served with baked beans.

- 3/4 cup all-purpose flour
- 1 egg, beaten
- 1/4 cup maple syrup
- 1/4 cup buttermilk
- 3 large apples, peeled, cored and cut into 1/4-inch rings
Oil for deep-fat frying
Confectioners' sugar

In a shallow bowl, combine the flour, egg, syrup and buttermilk. Dip apple rings on both sides into

BROCCOLI NOODLE SUPREME
(Pictured above)

Lila McNamara, Dickinson, North Dakota

I found this recipe in a cookbook my daughter gave me years ago. I like it because it's quick to prepare and it tastes so good.

- 3 cups uncooked egg noodles
- 2 cups broccoli florets
- 1 can (10-3/4 ounces) condensed cream of chicken and broccoli soup, undiluted
- 1/2 cup sour cream
- 1/3 cup grated Parmesan cheese
- 1/8 teaspoon pepper

In a saucepan, cook noodles according to package directions. Add broccoli during the last 5 minutes of cooking; drain. Set aside and keep warm. In the same pan, combine the soup, sour cream, Parmesan cheese and pepper; cook and stir until heated through. Return noodles and broccoli to the pan; toss to coat. **Yield:** 6 servings.

MICROWAVE SCALLOPED POTATOES

Mary Hufford-Baker, Sweet Home, Oregon

I adapted this recipe from one that came with our microwave oven. The results were delicious.

- 3 tablespoons butter *or* margarine
- 3 tablespoons all-purpose flour
- 1 to 1-1/2 teaspoons salt
- 1/4 teaspoon pepper
- 3 cups milk
- 1-1/4 cups shredded cheddar cheese

batter. In an electric skillet or deep-fat fryer, heat 2 in. of oil to 375°. Fry apple rings, a few at a time, for 2 minutes or until golden brown. Drain on paper towels. Dust with confectioners' sugar. **Yield:** 4 servings.

SWEET-SOUR BEETS

Irene Heller, Hellertown, Pennsylvania

I've been making these beets for special occasions ever since I found this recipe. They're so tasty and liked by just about everyone who's tried them. I grow beets in my garden, so I make them often.

  1/4 cup packed brown sugar
    2 tablespoons all-purpose flour
  1/4 teaspoon salt
  3/4 cup water
  1/3 cup vinegar
    2 tablespoons butter *or* margarine
    2 cans (13-1/4 ounces *each*) sliced beets, drained
    1 can (8 ounces) crushed pineapple, undrained
  1/2 cup raisins

In a large saucepan, combine the brown sugar, flour and salt. Add the water, vinegar and butter. Bring to a boil; cook and stir for 2 minutes or until thickened and bubbly. Gently stir in beets, pineapple and raisins; heat through. **Yield:** 8 servings.

EARLY-BIRD ASPARAGUS SUPREME

Joyce Speckman, Stockton, California

My husband and I pick, pack and ship 1,500 tons of asparagus each year. This recipe using that springtime veggie is a favorite.

    3 pounds fresh asparagus, cut into 1-inch pieces
    3 tablespoons butter *or* margarine, melted
    1 envelope onion soup mix
    1 cup (4 ounces) shredded mozzarella *or* Monterey Jack cheese

In a saucepan or microwave, cook asparagus in a small amount of water until crisp-tender; drain. Place in a 13-in. x 9-in. x 2-in. baking dish coated with nonstick cooking spray. Combine butter and soup mix; drizzle over asparagus. Sprinkle with cheese. Bake, uncovered, at 450° for 10-12 minutes or until asparagus is tender and cheese is melted. **Yield:** 6-8 servings.

PATCHWORK RICE PILAF

(Pictured above)

Brenda Scarbeary, Oelwein, Iowa

Colorful and versatile, this side dish is always popular at a picnic, potluck or special dinner. The apples bring a subtle sweetness to the rice. This pilaf goes well with a variety of main dish meats and always disappears quickly.

    4 celery ribs, chopped
    2 large onions, chopped
    4 medium carrots, chopped
    1 large green pepper, chopped
  1/4 cup butter *or* margarine
    2 medium tart red apples, chopped
    2 cups sliced fresh mushrooms
    2 packages (6.2 ounces *each*) fast-cooking long grain and wild rice mix
    2 cans (10-1/2 ounces *each*) condensed chicken broth, undiluted
1-1/2 cups water
  1/2 cup slivered almonds

In a large skillet or saucepan, saute the celery, onions, carrots and green pepper in butter until crisp-tender. Add the apples and mushrooms; saute for 2 minutes. Stir in rice, contents of seasoning packets, broth and water; bring to a boil.

Reduce heat; cover and simmer according to rice package directions or until rice is tender and liquid is absorbed. Sprinkle with almonds. **Yield:** 12 servings.

SAUCY GREEN BEAN BAKE

June Formanek, Belle Plaine, Iowa

Here's a different way to serve green beans. It's a nice change of pace from plain vegetables.

- 1 can (8 ounces) tomato sauce
- 2 tablespoons diced pimientos
- 1 tablespoon prepared mustard
- 1/4 teaspoon salt
- 1/8 teaspoon pepper
- 1 pound fresh *or* frozen cut green beans, cooked
- 1/2 cup chopped onion
- 1/3 cup chopped green pepper
- 1 garlic clove, minced
- 2 tablespoons butter *or* margarine
- 3/4 cup shredded process cheese (Velveeta)

In a bowl, combine the first five ingredients. Add the green beans; toss to coat. Transfer to an ungreased 1-qt. baking dish. Cover and bake at 350° for 20 minutes.

Meanwhile, in a skillet, saute onion, green pepper and garlic in butter until tender. Sprinkle over beans. Top with cheese. Bake, uncovered, for 3 minutes or until the cheese is melted. **Yield:** 4-6 servings.

ARTICHOKES AU GRATIN

(Pictured below)

Marjorie Bowen, Colorado Springs, Colorado

This makes a great side dish for Thanksgiving, Christmas or any dinner. My niece served this at a family gathering and was kind enough to share the recipe.

- 2 cans (14 ounces *each*) water-packed artichoke hearts, drained and quartered
- 1 garlic clove, minced

- 1/4 cup butter *or* margarine, *divided*
- 2 tablespoons all-purpose flour
- 1/2 teaspoon salt
- 1/4 teaspoon pepper
- 1-1/2 cups milk
- 1 egg, lightly beaten
- 1/2 cup shredded Swiss cheese, *divided*
- 1 tablespoon dry bread crumbs
- 1/8 teaspoon paprika

In a skillet, saute the artichokes and garlic in 2 tablespoons butter until tender. Transfer to a greased 1-qt. baking dish.

In a saucepan, melt the remaining butter. Stir in flour, salt and pepper until smooth. Gradually add milk. Bring to a boil; cook and stir for 2 minutes or until thickened. Remove from the heat. Stir a small amount of hot mixture into egg; return all to pan, stirring constantly. Stir in 1/4 cup cheese until melted.

Pour over artichokes; sprinkle with remaining cheese. Combine crumbs and paprika; sprinkle over top. Bake, uncovered, at 400° for 20-25 minutes or until heated through. **Yield:** 4-6 servings.

ORANGE SWEET POTATOES

Bonnie Baumgardner, Sylva, North Carolina

Seconds are common once folks try these wonderfully satisfying sweet potatoes—they're smothered with a cinnamon-orange sauce and dotted with walnuts.

- 8 medium sweet potatoes (about 4 pounds)
- 2/3 cup packed brown sugar
- 4 teaspoons cornstarch
- 1/2 teaspoon salt
- 1/2 teaspoon ground cinnamon
- 1 cup orange juice
- 1/4 cup honey
- 3 tablespoons butter *or* margarine
- 2 tablespoons water
- 2 tablespoons grated orange peel
- 1/2 cup chopped walnuts

Place sweet potatoes in a Dutch oven or soup kettle and cover with water. Bring to a boil. Reduce heat; cover and simmer for 25-30 minutes or until tender. Drain. When potatoes are cool, peel and cut into 1/2-in. slices. Arrange in a greased shallow 3-qt. baking dish; set aside.

In a saucepan, combine the brown sugar, cornstarch, salt and cinnamon. Stir in the orange juice, honey, butter, water and orange peel. Bring to a boil; cook and stir for 2 minutes or until thickened. Stir in the walnuts. Pour the mixture over the potatoes. Bake, uncovered, at 350° for 25 minutes or until heated through. **Yield:** 12 servings.

CHEESE-STUFFED POTATOES

Patricia Richardson, Bend, Oregon

These cheesy potatoes are so hearty, my husband and I often eat them as a main dish.

✓ **Uses less fat, sugar or salt. Includes Nutritional Analysis and Diabetic Exchanges.**

  4 medium baking potatoes (2 pounds)
  1 cup chopped leeks (white portion only)
  1 cup chopped onion
  2 garlic cloves, minced
  2 teaspoons olive *or* canola oil
3/4 cup fresh *or* frozen corn
1/2 cup 2% cottage cheese
1/2 cup reduced-fat plain yogurt
1/2 teaspoon salt
1/4 teaspoon pepper

Wrap each potato in foil. Bake at 375° for 1 hour or until tender. Cool. Remove foil; cut potatoes in half lengthwise. Scoop out pulp, leaving a 1/4-in. shell; set shells aside. In a bowl, mash pulp until smooth.

In a skillet, saute the leeks, onion and garlic in oil. Add to mashed potatoes. Stir in the corn, cottage cheese, yogurt, salt and pepper. Spoon into potato shells. Place on a baking sheet. Broil 6 in. from the heat for 3-5 minutes or until tops are golden. **Yield:** 8 servings.

Nutritional Analysis: One serving (half of a potato) equals 183 calories, 2 g fat (1 g saturated fat), 2 mg cholesterol, 224 mg sodium, 36 g carbohy-drate, 4 g fiber, 6 g protein. **Diabetic Exchanges:** 2 starch, 1 vegetable, 1/2 fat.

CHEDDAR CABBAGE CASSEROLE

Alice Jones, Demorest, Georgia

The flavors really blend well in this casserole. The crunch of the cornflakes adds to the texture contrast.

2-1/2 cups coarsely crushed cornflakes
  1/2 cup butter *or* margarine, melted
4-1/2 cups shredded cabbage
  1/4 cup chopped onion
  1/4 to 1/2 teaspoon salt
  1/4 to 1/2 teaspoon pepper
    1 can (10-3/4 ounces) condensed cream of celery soup, undiluted
    1 cup milk
  1/2 cup mayonnaise*
    2 cups (8 ounces) shredded cheddar cheese

Toss the cornflakes and butter; sprinkle half into a greased 13-in. x 9-in. x 2-in. baking dish. Layer with the cabbage, onion, salt and pepper. In a

bowl, combine the soup, milk and mayonnaise until smooth. Spoon over top; sprinkle with cheese and remaining cornflake mixture. Bake, uncovered, at 350° for 45-50 minutes or until golden brown. **Yield:** 8-10 servings.

*Editor's Note: Reduced-fat or fat-free mayonnaise may not be substituted for regular mayonnaise.

ACORN SQUASH WITH SPINACH STUFFING

(Pictured above)

Mary Bruff, Westminster, Maryland

Here's a recipe that combines two of my favorite vegetables—squash and spinach.

  3 small acorn squash
  1 cup chopped celery
  3 green onions, chopped
  1 tablespoon vegetable oil
  1 package (10 ounces) fresh spinach, chopped
1/2 teaspoon salt, *divided*
  6 tablespoons dry bread crumbs
  2 tablespoons chopped pecans
  1 tablespoon butter *or* margarine

Cut squash in half; discard seeds. Place squash, cut side down, in an ungreased 15-in. x 10-in. x 1-in. baking pan. Fill pan with hot water to a depth of 1/2 in. Bake, uncovered, at 350° for 40 minutes.

Meanwhile, in a skillet, saute celery and onions in oil until tender. Add the spinach and 1/4 teaspoon salt; cook and stir until spinach is wilted. In a bowl, combine the bread crumbs, pecans and remaining salt.

Drain water from baking pan. Turn squash cut side up. Stuff with spinach mixture; sprinkle crumb mixture over top. Dot with butter. Bake 15 minutes longer or until the squash is tender. **Yield:** 6 servings.

THIS BOUNTY *of from-scratch breads and rolls will rise to the occasion, at breakfast, lunch or dinner...or any time between.*

UNBEATABLE BREADS. From top: Oatmeal Yeast Bread (p. 82), Light Candied Fruitcake (p. 81) and Strawberry Rhubarb Coffee Cake (p. 81).

Breads & Rolls

Strawberry Rhubarb Coffee Cake

(Pictured at left)

Benita Thomas, Falcon, Colorado

We have a rhubarb patch, so I'm always looking for recipes featuring this "fruit". I've served this coffee cake to people who say they don't like rhubarb, and they've always told me how much they enjoyed it.

- 2/3 cup sugar
- 1/3 cup cornstarch
- 2 cups chopped rhubarb
- 1 package (10 ounces) frozen sweetened sliced strawberries, thawed
- 2 tablespoons lemon juice

CAKE:
- 3 cups all-purpose flour
- 1 cup sugar
- 1 teaspoon baking powder
- 1 teaspoon baking soda
- 1 cup cold butter *or* margarine
- 2 eggs
- 1 cup buttermilk
- 1 teaspoon vanilla extract

TOPPING:
- 3/4 cup sugar
- 1/2 cup all-purpose flour
- 1/4 cup cold butter *or* margarine

In a saucepan, combine sugar and cornstarch; stir in rhubarb and strawberries. Bring to a boil over medium heat; cook for 2 minutes or until thickened. Remove from the heat; stir in lemon juice. Cool.

For cake, combine flour, sugar, baking powder and baking soda in a large bowl. Cut in butter until mixture resembles coarse crumbs. Beat the eggs, buttermilk and vanilla; stir into crumb mixture just until moistened. Spoon two-thirds of the batter into a greased 13-in. x 9-in. x 2-in. baking pan. Spoon cooled filling over batter. Top with remaining batter.

For topping, combine sugar and flour. Cut in butter until mixture resembles coarse crumbs; sprinkle over batter. Bake at 350° for 45-50 minutes or until golden brown. Cool on a wire rack. **Yield:** 12-16 servings.

Light Candied Fruitcake

(Pictured at left)

Nancy Adams, Las Vegas, Nevada

Light as a feather and full of flavor, this fruitcake makes a delectable treat to take to a potluck or to give to a friend. Folks who taste a slice always request the recipe.

- 2 packages (1/4 ounce *each*) active dry yeast
- 1/2 cup warm water (110° to 115°)
- 1/3 cup warm milk (110° to 115°)
- 1/2 cup butter *or* margarine, softened
- 1/4 cup sugar
- 2 eggs, beaten
- 1 teaspoon salt
- 1 teaspoon ground cinnamon
- 1 teaspoon ground ginger
- 1/2 teaspoon ground nutmeg
- 3-1/4 to 3-1/2 cups all-purpose flour
- 1 cup chopped mixed candied fruit
- 1 cup raisins
- 1 cup chopped walnuts
- 1-1/2 teaspoons grated orange peel

ORANGE GLAZE:
- 2 cups confectioners' sugar
- 1 teaspoon grated orange peel
- 4 to 6 tablespoons orange juice

Red candied cherries

In a large mixing bowl, dissolve yeast in warm water. Add the milk, butter, sugar, eggs, salt, spices and 2 cups flour. Beat on medium speed for 2 minutes. Stir in enough remaining flour to form a firm dough (do not knead). Cover and let rise in a warm place for 20 minutes.

Stir dough down. Stir in fruit, raisins, nuts and orange peel. Transfer to a greased 10-in. fluted tube pan. Cover and let rise until doubled, about 1-1/2 hours.

Bake at 375° for 35-40 minutes or until golden brown. Cool for 5 minutes before removing from pan to a wire rack to cool completely.

For glaze, in a bowl, combine sugar, orange peel and enough orange juice to achieve a drizzling consistency; spoon over cake. Decorate with cherries. **Yield:** 14-16 servings.

until smooth and elastic, about 6-8 minutes. Place in a greased bowl, turning once to grease top. Cover and let rise in a warm place until doubled, about 1 hour.

Meanwhile, for filling, in a small mixing bowl, combine the butter, sugar, extract and orange peel; set aside. Toss the fruit and almonds with flour; set aside.

Punch dough down. Turn onto a lightly floured surface. Roll into a 30-in. x 9-in. rectangle. Spread filling to within 1/2 in. of edges; sprinkle with fruit mixture. Roll up jelly-roll style, starting with a long side; pinch seam to seal. With a sharp knife, cut roll in half lengthwise. Place on a greased baking sheet; gently twist the ropes together cut side up. Coil into a circle; tuck ends under. Cover and let rise until doubled, about 1 hour.

Bake at 325° for 30-35 minutes or until golden. Remove from pan to a wire rack to cool. In a mixing bowl, combine orange butter ingredients. Refrigerate until serving. Serve with coffee cake. **Yield:** 1 coffee cake (1/2 cup orange butter).

HOLIDAY BREAKFAST BRAID
(Pictured above)

Sarah Miller, Wauconda, Washington

This fruity braid rounds out my Christmas morning menu. Slathered with orange butter, the bread is just delicious.

 1 package (1/4 ounce) active dry yeast
1/4 cup warm water (110° to 115°)
1/2 cup warm milk (110° to 115°)
1/3 cup sugar
1/3 cup butter *or* margarine, softened
 2 eggs, beaten
 1 teaspoon salt
 1 teaspoon grated orange peel
1/2 teaspoon ground cardamom
1/8 teaspoon ground mace
3-1/2 cups all purpose flour
FILLING:
1/4 cup butter *or* margarine, softened
 2 tablespoons sugar
3/4 teaspoon almond extract
1/2 teaspoon grated orange peel
1/2 cup chopped mixed candied fruit
1/2 cup chopped almonds
 2 teaspoons all-purpose flour
ORANGE BUTTER:
1/2 cup butter (no substitutes), softened
 2 tablespoons confectioners' sugar
 1 teaspoon grated orange peel

In a large mixing bowl, dissolve yeast in warm water. Add the milk, sugar, butter, eggs, salt, orange peel, cardamom, mace and 2 cups flour. Beat until smooth. Stir in enough remaining flour to form a soft dough. Turn onto a floured surface; knead

POTATO ROLLS
(Pictured below)

Loraine Meyer, Bend, Oregon

This is my favorite recipe for dinner rolls since they rise nice and high and bake up fluffy and golden brown. I won a ribbon at the county fair with these rolls two years in a row.

 7 to 8 cups all-purpose flour
1/2 cup sugar
 1 package (1/4 ounce) active dry yeast
 1 teaspoon salt
 2 cups milk

2/3 cup shortening
1/2 cup water
1 cup mashed potatoes (prepared without milk *or* butter)
2 eggs

In a large mixing bowl, combine 2 cups flour, sugar, yeast and salt. In a saucepan, heat milk, shortening and water to 120°-130°. Add to dry ingredients; beat until moistened. Add mashed potatoes and eggs; beat until smooth. Stir in enough remaining flour to form a stiff dough. Do not knead. Place in a greased bowl, turning once to grease top. Cover and refrigerate for several hours or overnight.

Turn dough onto a lightly floured surface and punch down. Divide in half. With greased hands, shape each portion into 12 balls. Roll each ball into an 8-in. rope; tie into a knot. Place 2 in. apart on greased baking sheets; tuck ends under. Cover and let rise until doubled, about 2 hours. Bake at 375° for 25-30 minutes or until golden brown. Remove from pans to wire racks. **Yield:** 2 dozen.

BUTTERMILK PAN ROLLS

Patricia Young, Bella Vista, Arkansas

These wonderful rolls can be made very quickly. Hot, fresh rolls go well with just about any meal.

2 packages (1/4 ounce *each*) active dry yeast
1/4 cup warm water (110° to 115°)
1-1/2 cups warm buttermilk* (110° to 115°)
1/2 cup vegetable oil
3 tablespoons sugar
4-1/2 cups all-purpose flour
1 teaspoon baking soda
1/2 teaspoon salt

In a large mixing bowl, dissolve yeast in warm water. Add buttermilk, oil and sugar. Combine flour, baking soda and salt; add to yeast mixture and beat until smooth. Do not knead. Let stand for 10 minutes.

Turn dough onto a lightly floured surface; punch down. Shape into 24 balls and place in two greased 9-in. square baking pans. Cover and let rise in a warm place until doubled, about 30 minutes. Bake at 400° for 20 minutes or until golden brown. Remove to wire racks. **Yield:** 2 dozen.

*Editor's Note: Warmed buttermilk will appear curdled.

HOLIDAY FRUITCAKE
(Pictured above)

Allene Spence, Delbarton, West Virginia

I came up with this fruitcake recipe all by myself, and it's a family favorite. The mixture of fruits and nuts helps make it a tasty treat.

3 cups whole red and green candied cherries
3 cups diced candied pineapple
1 package (1 pound) shelled walnuts
1 package (10 ounces) golden raisins
1 cup shortening
1 cup sugar
5 eggs
4 tablespoons vanilla extract
3 cups all-purpose flour
3 teaspoons baking powder
1 teaspoon salt

In a bowl, combine the cherries, pineapple, walnuts and raisins; set aside. In a mixing bowl, cream shortening and sugar. Beat in eggs and vanilla. Combine the flour, baking powder and salt; add to the creamed mixture and mix well. Pour over fruit mixture and stir to coat.

Pour into a greased and floured 10-in. tube pan. Bake at 300° for 2 hours or until a toothpick inserted near the center comes out clean. Cool for 10 minutes before removing from pan to a wire rack to cool completely.

Wrap tightly and store in a cool place. Slice with a serrated knife; bring to room temperature before serving. **Yield:** 12-16 servings.

LOOKING *for something sweet to snack on?*
Look no further than these from-scratch
cookies, bars and candies.

COOKIE CLASSICS. Clockwise from top left: Cinnamon Snaps, Sour Cream Chocolate Cookies and Swedish Butter Cookies (all recipes on p. 91).

Cookies, Bars & Candies

SWEDISH BUTTER COOKIES
(Pictured at left)

Sue Soderland, Elgin, Illinois

My husband Ernie's great-grandmother came from Sweden and brought this tasty tradition with her. When I joined the family, my mother-in-law shared the recipe with me, along with one of the key ingredients—a bottle of pure maple syrup. My family always requests these butter cookies for holidays and other special occasions.

    1 cup butter (no substitutes), softened
    1 cup sugar
    2 teaspoons maple syrup
    2 cups all-purpose flour
    1 teaspoon baking soda
Confectioners' sugar

In a mixing bowl, cream butter and sugar. Add syrup; mix well. Combine flour and baking soda; gradually add to creamed mixture. Divide dough into eight portions. Roll each portion into a 9-in. log.

Place 3 in. apart on ungreased baking sheets. Bake at 300° for 25 minutes or until lightly browned. Cut into 1-in. slices. Remove to wire racks to cool. Dust with confectioners' sugar. **Yield:** about 6 dozen.

CINNAMON SNAPS
(Pictured at left)

Cathy Cain, Carmel, California

Since I'm a longtime cinnamon fan, I decided to give traditional gingersnaps a different twist. My husband and son agree I spiced them up just right. We live on a ranch overlooking the ocean and also own a machine shop business.

    3/4 cup shortening
    1 cup packed brown sugar
    1 egg
    1/4 cup molasses
2-1/4 cups all-purpose flour
    2 teaspoons baking soda
    2 teaspoons ground cinnamon
    1/2 teaspoon salt
Additional sugar

In a mixing bowl, cream shortening and brown sugar. Add egg and molasses. Combine the flour, baking soda, cinnamon and salt; gradually add to creamed mixture. Roll into 1-in. balls, then roll in additional sugar.

Place 2 in. apart on ungreased baking sheets. Bake at 350° for 10-12 minutes or until cookies are set and tops are cracked. Remove to wire racks to cool. **Yield:** 4-1/2 dozen.

SOUR CREAM CHOCOLATE COOKIES
(Pictured at left)

Tina Sawchuk, Ardmore, Alberta

These soft chocolaty cookies can be easily altered to make several different varieties—I've added everything from mints to macadamia nuts to them. My husband and I live on a mixed farm with our young daughter and son. Among my favorite hobbies are gardening and baking.

    1/2 cup butter *or* margarine, softened
    3/4 cup sugar
    1/2 cup packed brown sugar
    1 egg
    1/2 cup sour cream
    1 teaspoon vanilla extract
1-3/4 cups all-purpose flour
    1/2 cup baking cocoa
    1 teaspoon baking powder
    1/2 teaspoon baking soda
    1/4 teaspoon salt
    1 cup (6 ounces) semisweet chocolate chips
    1/2 cup vanilla *or* white chips

In a mixing bowl, cream butter and sugars. Beat in egg, sour cream and vanilla. Combine dry ingredients; gradually add to the creamed mixture. Stir in chips.

Drop by rounded tablespoonfuls 2 in. apart onto greased baking sheets. Bake at 350° for 12-15 minutes or until set. Cool for 2 minutes before removing to wire racks to cool completely. **Yield:** about 3 dozen.

Helpful Cookie Hints

• I roll the dough from my family's favorite chocolate chip cookies into balls, place them on baking sheets, then put in the freezer. When the dough balls are frozen, I place them in plastic freezer bags.

Then, whenever we want fresh-baked chocolate chip cookies, I just take a bag out of the freezer, pop the cookies in the oven and add 3 to 5 minutes to the baking time. —*Carolyn Filippo* *Wake Forest, North Carolina*

• To make my sugar cookies more festive, I dip the bottom of a glass in colored sugar, rather than plain sugar, before flattening the cookies.
—*Donna Harvey* *Tunkhannock, Pennsylvania*

• For an elegant dessert, I top saucer-sized sugar cookies with fruit and cream. —*Wynn Simmons* *Vance, Alabama*

• As a special treat for my family, I'll wrap some of my chocolate chip cookie dough around miniature Snickers bars before baking. My family searches the cookie jar for these hidden treasures! —*Hazel Staley* *Gaithersburg, Maryland*

• To tint your sugar cookie dough, mix food coloring with a little milk before adding it to the dough.
—*Deb Coffey, Cincinnati, Ohio*

• To give my sugar cookies a little different look and taste, I roll them in powdered strawberry-flavored gelatin before baking. —*Mary Anne Daniels* *Genesco, Illinois*

• Try crumbling old-fashioned sugar cookies on top of ice cream for a yummy topping. —*Judy Swartz* *Lancaster, California*

• I bake my cookies on parchment-lined baking sheets to make cleanup a breeze.

To keep cookies fresh when the weather turns humid, I store them in a tin in the refrigerator.
—*Mrs. Edna Wieland* *Grandville, Michigan*

• Before I roll my peanut butter cookie dough into balls, I spray my hands with nonstick cooking spray to make handling the dough easier.
—*Edna Havens* *Bartlesville, Oklahoma*

• A clean, empty potato chip tube makes an ideal container for shipping cookies. —*Kimberly Wyatt* *Keokuk, Iowa*

• Since I prefer a daintier cookie, I roll my soft molasses cookie dough into smaller balls than the recipe calls for, then adjust the baking time.
—*Linda Weber, Bartlett, Texas*

• To dress up my sugar cookies, I flatten them with a glass that has a textured bottom. —*Mrs. Roger Seekins* *Prescott, Wisconsin*

• I roll my sugar cookie dough into balls, then dip one side in nonpareils. I place them, nonpareils side up, on a baking sheet and flatten with a glass for a pretty presentation. —*Pamela Davis* *Graham, Washington*

POPCORN COOKIES

Leigh Ann Preston, Palmyra, Indiana

My sister-in-law shared this recipe with me. It is just one of the ways I put the popcorn we grow on our farm to good use.

 1/2 cup butter *or* margarine, softened
   1 cup sugar
   1 egg
   1 teaspoon vanilla extract
 1-1/4 cups all-purpose flour
 1/2 teaspoon baking soda
Pinch salt
   2 cups popped popcorn, slightly crushed
   1 cup (6 ounces) semisweet chocolate chips
 1/2 cup chopped pecans

In a mixing bowl, cream the butter and sugar. Beat in egg and vanilla. Combine flour, baking soda and salt; add to the creamed mixture. Stir in the popcorn, chocolate chips and pecans. Drop by tablespoonfuls 2 in. apart onto greased baking sheets. Bake at 350° for 13-14 minutes or until golden brown. Cool on wire racks. **Yield:** 2-1/2 dozen.

SUNFLOWER FUDGE

Pam Clemens, Wimbledon, North Dakota

My family grows sunflowers on our farm, so I'm always on the lookout for new recipes to use the tasty kernels. This fudge is a favorite.

 1-1/2 teaspoons plus 1 tablespoon butter (no substitutes), *divided*
   3 cups (18 ounces) semisweet chocolate chips
  10 milk chocolate candy bars (1.55 ounces *each*), chopped
   2 jars (7 ounces *each*) marshmallow creme
 3/4 cup salted sunflower kernels
 4-1/2 cups sugar
 1-2/3 cups evaporated milk
   1 teaspoon vanilla extract

Line a 13-in. x 9-in. x 2-in. pan with foil and grease the foil with 1-1/2 teaspoons butter; set aside. In a large bowl, combine the chocolate chips, candy bars, marshmallow creme and sunflower kernels; set aside.

In a saucepan, combine the sugar, milk and remaining butter. Cook and stir over medium heat until sugar is dissolved. Bring to a rapid boil; boil for 5 minutes, stirring constantly.

Remove from the heat; stir in vanilla. Pour

over chocolate mixture and stir until chocolate is melted. Pour into prepared pan. Refrigerate until firm. Using foil, lift fudge out of pan; cut into 1-in. squares. Store in the refrigerator. **Yield:** about 6 pounds.

PEPPERMINT CANDY COOKIES

(Pictured above)

Gloria McKenzie, Panama City, Florida

These buttery mint treats practically melt in your mouth. Food coloring gives them a lively look.

 1-1/4 cups butter (no substitutes), softened
 3/4 cup confectioners' sugar
 2-1/2 cups all-purpose flour
 1/2 teaspoon salt
 1/2 teaspoon peppermint extract
Green and red paste *or* gel food coloring

In a mixing bowl, cream butter and sugar. Add the flour, salt and extract; mix well. Divide dough into fourths. Tint one portion green and one red; leave the remaining portions plain.

Divide each portion into thirds; shape each into a 6-in. log. Flatten into triangular logs, bending the top of one point slightly (to give finished cookies a pinwheel effect). Assemble one large roll by alternating three green and three plain logs. Wrap in plastic wrap. Repeat with red and remaining plain dough. Refrigerate for 4 hours or until firm.

Unwrap and cut into 1/4-in. slices. Place 2 in. apart on ungreased baking sheets. Bake at 375° for 8-10 minutes or until edges are golden brown. Cool for 1 minute before removing to wire racks.

Cut 6-in.-square pieces of cellophane or plastic wrap to wrap each cookie; twist ends securely or tie with a ribbon. **Yield:** about 4 dozen.

■■■■■■■■■■■■■

DOUBLE CHOCOLATE FUDGE

(Pictured above)

Marilyn Jordan, Hoosick Falls, New York

If you love chocolate, here's a recipe that's sure to please. This rich treat is a favorite of our family.

1-1/2 teaspoons plus 2 tablespoons butter (no
    substitutes), *divided*
4-1/2 cups sugar
    1 can (12 ounces) evaporated milk
Pinch salt
    1 jar (7 ounces) marshmallow creme
    2 cups (12 ounces) semisweet chocolate
    chips
    3 packages (4 ounces *each*) German
    sweet chocolate, broken into pieces
    2 cups chopped walnuts, optional

Line a 15-in. x 10-in. x 1-in. baking pan with foil. Grease the foil with 1-1/2 teaspoons butter; set aside. In a large saucepan, combine the sugar, milk, salt and remaining butter. Cook and stir over medium heat until sugar is dissolved. Bring to a rapid boil; boil for 5 minutes, stirring constantly.

Remove from heat; stir in marshmallow creme until melted. Stir in chips and German sweet chocolate until melted. Add walnuts if desired; mix well. Pour into prepared pan. Refrigerate overnight or until firm. Using foil, remove fudge from pan; peel off foil. Cut into 1-in. squares. Store in the refrigerator. **Yield:** 5 pounds.

■■■■■■■■■■■■■

CHOCO-CLOUD BROWNIES

(Pictured at right)

Linda Roecker, Hazelton, North Dakota

True to its name, this mild chocolate brownie is covered by a cloud of light fluffy frosting. The recipe has earned raves at our table. My husband, a pastor,
and I have three young daughters who like to cook as much as I do.

    1 cup butter (no substitutes), softened
    2 cups sugar
    4 eggs
    1 milk chocolate candy bar (7 ounces),
    melted
    3 teaspoons vanilla extract
    2 cups all-purpose flour
1/2 teaspoon salt
    2 cups chopped pecans
FROSTING:
    5 tablespoons all-purpose flour
    1 cup milk
    1 cup butter (no substitutes), softened
    1 cup confectioners' sugar
    2 teaspoons vanilla extract
Baking cocoa

In a mixing bowl, cream butter and sugar. Add eggs, one at a time, beating well after each. Add chocolate and vanilla; mix well. Gradually add flour and salt. Stir in pecans. Spread into a greased 13-in. x 9-in. x 2-in. baking pan. Bake at 350° for 35-40 minutes or until center is set and edges pull away from pan. Cool on a wire rack.

For frosting, combine flour and milk in a small saucepan until smooth. Bring to a boil; cook and stir for 2 minutes or until thickened. Remove from the heat; cool completely. In a mixing bowl, cream butter and confectioners' sugar. Add vanilla; mix well. Gradually add milk mixture; beat for 5 minutes or until fluffy. Frost brownies; dust with cocoa. Cut into bars. Store in the refrigerator. **Yield:** about 2-1/2 dozen.

Cookies, Bars & Candies

BUCKEYES

Merry Kay Opitz, Elkhorn, Wisconsin

These candies are always popular at my church's annual Christmas fund-raiser.

5-1/2 cups confectioners' sugar
1-2/3 cups peanut butter
1 cup butter *or* margarine, melted
4 cups (24 ounces) semisweet chocolate chips
1 teaspoon shortening

In a bowl, combine the sugar, peanut butter and butter; mix well. Shape into 1-in. balls; set aside. In a heavy saucepan or microwave, melt chocolate chips and shortening; stir until smooth. Dip balls in chocolate; place on a wire rack over waxed paper. Refrigerate for 15 minutes or until firm. Cover and store in the refrigerator. **Yield:** about 5-1/2 dozen.

HONEY SPICE COOKIES

Joan Gerber, Bluffton, Indiana

With four children, I bake a lot of cookies. These nicely-seasoned sweets are a family favorite.

✓ Uses less fat, sugar or salt. Includes Nutritional Analysis and Diabetic Exchanges.

2 cups honey
2 cups sugar
3 eggs
7-1/2 cups all-purpose flour
3 teaspoons baking soda
3 teaspoons ground cinnamon
1 teaspoon salt
1 teaspoon ground allspice
1 teaspoon ground cloves
2 cups confectioners' sugar
3 tablespoons fat-free milk

In a mixing bowl, beat honey and sugar. Add eggs, one at a time, beating well after each addition. Combine the flour, baking soda, cinnamon, salt, allspice and cloves; gradually add to honey mixture. Shape dough into five 10-in. rolls; wrap in plastic wrap. Refrigerate for 2 hours or until firm.

Unwrap dough and cut into 1/4-in. slices. Place 2 in. apart on baking sheets coated with non-stick coating spray. Combine confectioners' sugar and milk; lightly brush over cookies. Bake at 350° for 8-10 minutes or until lightly browned. Remove to wire racks to cool. **Yield:** 12-1/2 dozen.

Nutritional Analysis: One cookie equals 54 calories, trace fat (trace saturated fat), 4 mg cholesterol, 43 mg sodium, 13 g carbohydrate, trace fiber, 1 g protein. **Diabetic Exchange:** 1/2 starch.

CHOCOLATE CHIP CHEESECAKE BARS

(Pictured above)

Jane Nolt, Narvon, Pennsylvania

These bars combine two favorite flavors—chocolate chip cookies and cheesecake—in one bite.

3/4 cup shortening
3/4 cup sugar
1/3 cup packed brown sugar
1 egg
1-1/2 teaspoons vanilla extract
1-1/2 cups all-purpose flour
1 teaspoon salt
3/4 teaspoon baking soda
1-1/2 cups miniature chocolate chips
3/4 cup chopped pecans
FILLING:
2 packages (8 ounces *each*) cream cheese, softened
3/4 cup sugar
2 eggs
1 teaspoon vanilla extract

In a mixing bowl, cream shortening and sugars. Beat in egg and vanilla. Combine the flour, salt and baking soda; add to the creamed mixture and mix well. Fold in the chocolate chips and pecans. Set aside a third of the dough for topping. Press remaining dough into a greased 13-in. x 9-in. x 2-in. baking pan. Bake at 350° for 8 minutes.

Meanwhile, in a small mixing bowl, beat cream cheese and sugar until smooth. Add eggs and vanilla; mix well. Spoon over crust. Drop teaspoonfuls of reserved dough over filling. Bake at 350° for 35-40 minutes or until golden brown. Cool on a wire rack. Cover and store in the refrigerator. **Yield:** 3 dozen.

CHEESECAKE DIAMONDS

(Pictured below)

Gloria Williams, Chesapeake, Virginia

Here's a simple recipe that's good to have on hand when guests are coming over. I found it in an old cookbook.

    5 tablespoons butter *or* margarine,
      softened
  1/3 cup packed brown sugar
    1 cup all-purpose flour
  1/4 cup chopped pecans
FILLING:
    1 package (8 ounces) cream cheese,
      softened
  1/2 cup sugar
    1 egg
    2 tablespoons whipping cream
    1 tablespoon lemon juice
    2 teaspoons lemon peel
  1/2 teaspoon vanilla extract

In a small mixing bowl, cream butter and brown sugar. Add flour and pecans; mix well. Set aside 1 cup for topping. Press the remaining mixture into a greased 8-in. square baking pan. Bake at 350° for 10-12 minutes or until set. Cool on a wire rack. In another mixing bowl, beat cream cheese and sugar until smooth. Add egg, beating just until combined. Beat in the cream, lemon juice, peel and vanilla. Spread over crust. Sprinkle with reserved topping.

Bake at 350° for 20-22 minutes or until center is almost set. Cool on a wire rack for 1 hour. Refrigerate overnight. Cut into diamonds. Refrigerate leftovers. **Yield:** 16 servings.

BROWNIES FROM HEAVEN

Linda Eldridge, Lake Alfred, Florida

There's always a flurry of activity around the snack bar in my kitchen, especially when I set out a plate of these brownies. Topped with a fluffy chocolaty frosting, they really live up to their name.

    1 cup butter *or* margarine, softened
    2 cups sugar
    2 eggs
    1 teaspoon vanilla extract
    2 cups all-purpose flour
  1/2 cup baking cocoa
    1 cup chopped walnuts
FROSTING:
  1/2 cup butter *or* margarine, softened
3-1/2 cups confectioners' sugar
  1/3 cup baking cocoa
  1/4 cup milk
    1 teaspoon vanilla extract

In a mixing bowl, cream butter and sugar. Add eggs, one at a time, beating well after each addition. Beat in vanilla. Combine flour and cocoa; add to creamed mixture just until combined. Stir in walnuts.

Spread into an ungreased 13-in. x 9-in. x 2-in. baking pan. Bake at 350° for 23-28 minutes or until a toothpick inserted near the center comes out clean. Cool on a wire rack.

For frosting, in a mixing bowl, beat butter until fluffy. Beat in the confectioners' sugar, cocoa, milk and vanilla until smooth. Spread over brownies. Cut into bars. **Yield:** 2 dozen.

 ## CHOCOLATE SURPRISE COOKIES

(Pictured on page 98)

Grace Crary, West Linn, Oregon

Chocolate and peanut butter are popular with our clan, so I roll them together in this recipe. It's fun watching folks' faces when they bite into the middle.

  3/4 cup peanut butter*
  3/4 cup confectioners' sugar
CHOCOLATE DOUGH:
  1/2 cup butter *or* margarine, softened
  1/4 cup peanut butter
  1/2 cup sugar
  1/2 cup packed brown sugar
    1 egg white
    1 teaspoon vanilla extract
1-1/2 cups all-purpose flour
  1/2 cup baking cocoa

1/2 teaspoon baking soda
ICING:
   2 tablespoons shortening
   1 cup confectioners' sugar
   1/4 teaspoon vanilla extract
   1 to 2 tablespoons milk

In a mixing bowl, cream peanut butter and confectioners' sugar until smooth. Roll into thirty 3/4-in. balls. Cover and refrigerate for 30 minutes. Meanwhile, in a mixing bowl, cream butter, peanut butter and sugars. Beat in egg white and vanilla. Combine flour, cocoa and baking soda; gradually add to creamed mixture. Roll into thirty 1-1/2-in. balls.

Using floured hands, flatten chocolate balls and shape one around each peanut butter ball, sealing edges. Place 2 in. apart on greased baking sheets. Flatten with a glass dipped in sugar. Bake at 375° for 7-9 minutes or until cookies are set and tops are cracked. Cool for 1 minute before removing to wire racks.

For icing, in a small mixing bowl, cream shortening and confectioners' sugar. Beat in vanilla and enough milk to reach spreading consistency. Spoon into a resealable plastic bag or pastry bag; cut a small hole in corner of bag. Pipe icing over cookies in a zigzag pattern. **Yield:** 2-1/2 dozen.

*Editor's Note: Reduced-fat or generic brands of peanut butter are not recommended for this recipe.

WHITE CHOCOLATE OATMEAL COOKIES

(Pictured on page 99)

Edith Pluhar, Cohagen, Montana

My sons and grandsons manage our ranch...and they always seem to have one hand in the cookie jar—especially when I bake these crunchy morsels!

   1 cup butter (no substitutes), softened
   1/2 cup sugar
   1/2 cup packed brown sugar
   1 egg
   3 teaspoons vanilla extract
   1 teaspoon coconut extract
1-1/2 cups quick-cooking oats
1-1/4 cups all-purpose flour
   1 teaspoon salt
   1 teaspoon baking soda
   1 cup flaked coconut, toasted
   6 squares (1 ounce *each*) white baking chocolate, cut into 1/2-inch chunks
Additional sugar

In a mixing bowl, cream the butter and sugars. Add the egg and extracts; mix well. Combine the oats, flour, salt and baking soda; gradually add to creamed mixture. Stir in the coconut and chocolate.

Drop by tablespoonfuls 3 in. apart onto ungreased baking sheets. Flatten with a glass dipped in sugar. Bake at 350° for 8-9 minutes or until golden brown. Cool for 1 minute before removing to wire racks. **Yield:** about 5 dozen.

RASPBERRY CITRUS BARS

(Pictured above)

Ruby Nelson, Mountain Home, Arkansas

This dessert was an instant hit with my family when I first made it. The combination of raspberries, lemon juice and orange peel gives it a unique taste.

   1 cup butter *or* margarine, softened
   3/4 cup confectioners' sugar
2-1/4 cups all-purpose flour, *divided*
   4 eggs
1-1/2 cups sugar
   1/3 cup lemon juice
   2 tablespoons grated orange peel
   1 teaspoon baking powder
1-1/2 cups unsweetened raspberries

In a mixing bowl, cream butter and confectioners' sugar. Add 2 cups flour; beat until combined. Press mixture into a greased 13-in. x 9-in. x 2-in. baking pan. Bake at 350° for 20 minutes or until lightly browned.

Meanwhile, in a mixing bowl, beat the eggs, sugar, lemon juice and orange peel. Add the baking powder and remaining flour; mix well. Sprinkle raspberries over the crust. Pour filling over the berries.

Bake for 30-35 minutes or until lightly browned and filling is set. Cool on a wire rack. Store in the refrigerator. **Yield:** 12-15 servings.

WHATEVER *flavor you favor, you'll find the cookie you're craving here.*

BAKER'S BEST. Clockwise from top left: Chocolate Surprise Cookies (p. 96), White Chocolate Oatmeal Cookies (p. 97), Toffee Malted Cookies (p. 101), Fruit-Filled Spritz Cookies (p. 100) and Chocolate Meringues (p. 100).

they make a perfect holiday pastry. I'm the grand-mother of six and stay active with a German folk dance group.

1-1/2 cups chopped dates
    1 cup water
  1/2 cup sugar
    2 teaspoons orange juice
    2 teaspoons grated orange peel
    1 cup maraschino cherries, chopped
  1/2 cup flaked coconut
  1/2 cup ground nuts
DOUGH:
    1 cup butter (no substitutes), softened
    1 cup sugar
  1/2 cup packed brown sugar
    3 eggs
  1/2 teaspoon almond extract
  1/2 teaspoon vanilla extract
    4 cups all-purpose flour
  1/2 teaspoon baking soda
  1/2 teaspoon salt
Confectioners' sugar

In a saucepan, combine the first five ingredients; bring to a boil, stirring constantly. Reduce heat; cook and stir for 8 minutes or until thickened. Cool completely. Stir in cherries, coconut and nuts; set aside.

In a mixing bowl, cream butter and sugars. Beat in eggs and extracts. Combine the flour, baking soda and salt; gradually add to creamed mixture.

Using a cookie press fitted with a bar disk, press a 12-in.-long strip of dough onto an ungreased baking sheet. Spread fruit filling over dough. Press another strip over filling. Cut into 1-in. pieces (there is no need to separate the pieces). Repeat with remaining dough and filling.

Bake at 375° for 12-15 minutes or until edges are golden. Recut into pieces if necessary. Remove to wire racks to cool. Dust with confectioners' sugar. **Yield:** about 7-1/2 dozen.

STRAWBERRY-NUT PINWHEEL COOKIES

(Pictured above)

Ruth Gillmore, Alden, New York

All the "cookie monsters" I know love these treats. I enjoy the cookies because they're easy to roll up, cut and bake. Plus, the filling is very tasty!

  1/2 cup butter (no substitutes), softened
    1 cup sugar
    1 egg
    1 teaspoon vanilla extract
    2 cups all-purpose flour
    1 teaspoon baking powder
  1/2 cup strawberry jam
    1 cup chopped walnuts

In a mixing bowl, cream butter and sugar. Add egg and vanilla; mix well. Combine flour and baking powder; gradually add to creamed mixture. On a lightly floured surface, roll dough into a 14-in. x 10-in. rectangle. Spread jam to within 1/2 in. of edges. Sprinkle nuts over jam. Roll up jelly-roll style, starting with a long side. Wrap in plastic wrap; refrigerate for at least 3 hours or overnight.

Unwrap and cut into 1/4-in. slices. Place 1 in. apart on greased baking sheets. Bake at 375° for 10-12 minutes or until lightly browned. Remove to wire racks to cool. **Yield:** 4 dozen.

FRUIT-FILLED SPRITZ COOKIES

(Pictured on page 98)

Ingeborg Keith, Newark, Delaware

From the first time I baked these cookies, they've been a lip-smacking success. Old-fashioned and attractive,

---

CHOCOLATE MERINGUES

(Pictured on page 98)

Nancy Grace, San Diego, California

These cookies are great for fancy occasions, but easy enough to make as a snack. My grandma was an avid baker, known in her neighborhood as the "cookie lady". With 18 nieces and nephews, I'm carrying on her tradition.

    1 cup (6 ounces) semisweet chocolate chips
    2 egg whites

1/4 teaspoon cream of tartar
1/8 teaspoon salt
1/2 cup sugar
1/2 teaspoon white vinegar
1/2 teaspoon vanilla *or* almond extract
1/2 cup flaked coconut
1/4 cup chopped almonds

In a microwave or heavy saucepan, melt chocolate chips and stir until smooth; set aside. In a mixing bowl, beat egg whites, cream of tartar and salt until soft peaks form. Add sugar, 1 tablespoon at a time, beating until stiff peaks form, about 5 minutes. Beat in vinegar and vanilla. Fold in melted chocolate until combined; fold in coconut and almonds.

Drop by tablespoonfuls 2 in. apart onto lightly greased baking sheets. Bake at 350° for 10-11 minutes or until firm. Remove to wire racks to cool. Store in an airtight container. **Yield:** about 2-1/2 dozen.

🏵 ## TOFFEE MALTED COOKIES

(Pictured on page 99)

Sharon Timpe, Mequon, Wisconsin

As much as I delight in sharing these goodies, my family considers them "keepers". It's a wonder I ever get them out the door to take to meetings! With their buttery melt-in-your-mouth texture, they're always popular.

1 cup butter *or* margarine, softened
1/2 cup sugar
1/2 cup packed brown sugar
2 eggs
1 package (3.4 ounces) instant vanilla pudding mix
1 teaspoon vanilla extract
2-1/4 cups all-purpose flour
1 cup quick-cooking oats
1 teaspoon baking soda
1/2 teaspoon salt
1 cup malted milk balls, chopped
3/4 cup English toffee bits *or* almond brickle chips

In a mixing bowl, cream the butter and sugars. Add eggs, one at a time, beating well after each addition. Add pudding mix and vanilla. Combine the flour, oats, baking soda and salt; add to creamed mixture. Fold in the malted milk balls and the toffee bits (dough will be stiff).

Drop by rounded teaspoonfuls 2 in. apart onto ungreased baking sheets. Bake at 350° for 12-15 minutes or until golden brown. Cool for 2 minutes before removing to wire racks. **Yield:** about 6 dozen.

ORANGE TRUFFLES

(Pictured below)

Delicious citrus is the tasty surprise when folks try these chocolate candies developed by our Test Kitchen. For an elegant effect, our cooks drizzle them with melted white chips.

3 cups plus 2 tablespoons semisweet chocolate chips, *divided*
2/3 cup whipping cream
2 tablespoons butter (no substitutes)
1 teaspoon orange extract
2 tablespoons shortening
1/3 cup vanilla *or* white chips

Place 1 cup plus 2 tablespoons chocolate chips in a blender or food processor; cover and process until crushed, about 30 seconds. In a microwave-safe bowl, heat cream and butter on high for 1-2 minutes or until almost boiling.

While blender or processor is running, gradually pour cream mixture and extract over chips in a steady stream until smooth. Cover and refrigerate for 20-30 minutes or until firm. Roll into 1-in. balls.

In a microwave-safe bowl, heat shortening and remaining chocolate chips on high for 1 minute; stir. Microwave in 10- to 20-second intervals until melted; stir until smooth. Dip truffles; place on waxed paper to harden.

In another microwave-safe bowl, heat vanilla chips at 70% power for 15 seconds; stir. Microwave in 5-second intervals until melted; stir until smooth. Transfer to a pastry or plastic bag; cut a hole in the corner of bag. Drizzle over truffles. **Yield:** about 4 dozen.

Editor's Note: This recipe was tested in an 850-watt microwave.

SANTA SUGAR COOKIES

(Pictured below)

Jill Boruff, Soap Lake, Washington

Ho ho ho! St. Nick can drop in any time at all when you bake these cute-as-can-be treats. It's easy to form these scrumptious Santas with heart-shaped cookie cutters.

  1-1/2 cups butter *or* margarine, softened
  1-1/2 cups shortening
  1-1/2 cups sugar
  1-1/2 cups confectioners' sugar
     3 eggs
  4-1/2 teaspoons vanilla extract
  6-3/4 cups all-purpose flour
  1-1/2 teaspoons baking soda
  1-1/2 teaspoons cream of tartar
  1-1/2 teaspoons salt
FROSTING:
    1/4 cup semisweet chocolate chips
Brown and red miniature M&M's
    1 carton (12 ounces) soft whipped frosting
    1 tablespoon butter *or* margarine, softened
    1 cup confectioners' sugar
Red colored sugar
Red jimmies

In a mixing bowl, cream the butter, shortening and sugars. Add eggs, one at a time, beating well after each addition. Beat in vanilla. Combine the flour, baking soda, cream of tartar and salt; gradually add to creamed mixture. Refrigerate for 1-2 hours or until easy to handle.

On a lightly floured surface, roll out dough to 1/4-in. thickness. Cut with a 3-1/2-in. heart-shaped cookie cutter. Place 1 in. apart on ungreased baking sheets. Bake at 375° for 8-10 minutes or until firm (do not overbake). Remove to wire racks to cool.

In a microwave or heavy saucepan, melt chocolate chips. Cut a small hole in the corner of a pastry or plastic bag; insert #2 round pastry tip. Add melted chocolate. For eyes, pipe two dots in the center of each cookie; attach brown M&M's. Pipe a small dot of chocolate below eyes; attach a red M&M for nose. Pipe eyelashes.

In a bowl, combine the frosting, butter and sugar; mix well. For hat, frost the top 1 in. of the pointed end of cookie. Sprinkle with red sugar. Frost the sides and rounded ends for beard. Place two jimmies for the mouth. Cut a hole in the corner of a small plastic or pastry bag; insert #16 star tip. Fill with remaining frosting. Pipe a zigzag border under hat for fur hatband. Pipe a pom-pom on top of hat. **Yield:** about 8 dozen.

PUMPKIN SPICE BARS

Sheila Compton, Summerside, Prince Edward Island

Most of the year, my family runs a pretty garden-variety vegetable stand. Come October, however, it becomes a popular Halloween haunt, where I showcase our pick-of-the-patch pumpkins. This recipe calls for canned pumpkin, but I like to use my home-grown produce instead.

    4 eggs
    2 cups sugar
    1 can (15 ounces) solid-pack pumpkin
    1 cup vegetable oil
    2 cups all-purpose flour
    2 teaspoons baking powder
    2 teaspoons ground cinnamon
    1 teaspoon baking soda
  1/2 teaspoon salt
  1/2 teaspoon ground ginger
  1/4 teaspoon ground cloves
  1/2 cup dried cranberries
    1 can (16 ounces) *or* 2 cups cream cheese frosting

In a mixing bowl, beat eggs, sugar, pumpkin and oil until blended. Combine the flour, baking powder, cinnamon, baking soda, salt, ginger and cloves; add to pumpkin mixture just until combined. Stir in cranberries.

Pour into a greased 15-in. x 10-in. x 1-in. baking pan. Bake at 350° for 25-30 minutes or until a toothpick inserted near the center comes out clean. Cool completely on a wire rack. Frost with cream cheese frosting. **Yield:** 2-1/2 dozen.

Line an 8-in. square pan with foil; butter the foil with 1-1/2 teaspoons butter. In a heavy saucepan, melt chips over very low heat, stirring frequently. Or microwave at 70% power for 1 minute; stir. Microwave in 10- to 20-second intervals or until melted. Remove from the heat; stir in the frosting and extract until blended. Pour into prepared pan.

Randomly place drops of food coloring over fudge; cut through fudge with a knife to swirl. Cover and refrigerate for 4 hours or until firm before cutting into squares. **Yield:** 5 dozen.

Editor's Note: This recipe was tested in an 850-watt microwave.

CRANBERRY WALNUT BARS

(Pictured above)

Sylvia Gidwani, Milford, New Jersey

This recipe was given to me by a friend. My family enjoys these bars as is or topped with ice cream.

    1/4 cup butter *or* margarine, softened
    1/2 cup sugar
    1/2 cup packed brown sugar
      1 egg
      1 teaspoon vanilla extract
1-1/4 cups all-purpose flour
      1 teaspoon baking powder
    1/4 teaspoon salt
    1/4 teaspoon ground cinnamon
      1 cup chopped fresh *or* frozen cranberries
    1/2 cup chopped walnuts

In a mixing bowl, cream butter and sugars. Beat in egg and vanilla. Combine the flour, baking powder, salt and cinnamon; gradually add to creamed mixture. Fold in cranberries and walnuts.

Spread into a greased 9-in. square baking pan. Bake at 350° for 30-35 minutes or until a toothpick inserted near the center comes out clean. Cool on a wire rack. Cut into bars. **Yield:** 1-1/2 dozen.

CHERRY SWIRL FUDGE

For Christmas fudge with a new "twist", give this confection a whirl! Our kitchen staff used vanilla chips instead of chocolate ones and added fruit flavoring.

1-1/2 teaspoons butter (no substitutes)
      1 package (10 to 12 ounces) vanilla *or* white chips
      1 can (16 ounces) *or* 2 cups vanilla frosting
      1 teaspoon cherry *or* almond extract
      4 drops red liquid food coloring

REINDEER TREATS

(Pictured below)

You'll hardly be able to rein folks in once they see these crispy critters! Our Test Kitchen cooks hurried the herd together using a sweetened mix of chocolate rice cereal and peanut butter, then designed deer with pretzels and candies.

      6 cups crisp chocolate rice cereal
      1 cup packed brown sugar
      1 cup light corn syrup
      1 cup peanut butter
     40 miniature pretzel twists, halved
     80 miniature peanut butter candies
     40 red-hot candies

Place cereal in a large bowl; set aside. In a saucepan, combine brown sugar and corn syrup. Bring to a boil; cook and stir for 2 minutes. Remove from heat; stir in peanut butter until well blended. Pour over cereal; stir until coated.

Shape into 1-1/2-in. balls; place on waxed paper-lined baking sheets. Let stand until set. Place two pretzel halves in each ball for antlers. Position two peanut butter candies on each for eyes and one red-hot for nose. **Yield:** 3-1/2 dozen.

Batches of Cookies–Fast!

IN A HURRY to satisfy your sweet tooth? You can whip up a batch of these yummy cookies in just minutes. They're short on ingredients but long on flavor.

▰▰▰▰▰▰▰▰▰▰▰
NO-FUSS PEANUT BUTTER COOKIES
(Pictured below)

Mary Browning, North Ogden, Utah

These quick-and-easy peanut butter cookies go great with a cold glass of milk.

    1 cup peanut butter*
    1/4 cup butter-flavored shortening
    1/2 cup sugar
    1/2 cup packed brown sugar
    1/3 cup boiling water
    2 cups biscuit/baking mix
Additional sugar

In a mixing bowl, cream peanut butter, shortening and sugars. Beat in water. Gradually add biscuit mix. Roll dough into 1-in. balls. Place 2 in. apart on greased baking sheets. Flatten with a fork dipped in sugar, forming a crisscross pattern. Bake at 400° for 9-11 minutes or until edges are golden brown. **Yield:** 4-1/2 dozen.

*Editor's Note: This recipe does not use eggs. Reduced-fat or generic brands of peanut butter are not recommended for this recipe.

▰▰▰▰▰▰▰▰▰▰▰
EASY MACAROONS

Judy Farlow, Boise, Idaho

These crispy cookies are great for family get-togethers since they yield a large amount. They're always well received.

    1 pint lemon *or* orange sherbet
    2 tablespoons almond extract
    1 package (18-1/4 ounces) white cake mix
    6 cups flaked coconut

In a mixing bowl, beat sherbet and almond extract until sherbet is slightly softened. Gradually add cake mix. Stir in coconut. Drop by rounded teaspoonfuls 2 in. apart onto greased baking sheets.

Bake at 350° for 12-15 minutes or until edges are lightly browned. Remove to wire racks. **Yield:** about 10-1/2 dozen.

ORANGE DROP COOKIES

Lou Borcherding, Dodgeville, Wisconsin

It's easy to whip up a batch of these cookies in no time. A friend shared the recipe with me years ago.

  1 package (18-1/4 ounces) white cake mix*
  2 eggs
  1/2 cup vegetable oil
  1 teaspoon grated orange peel
  1 teaspoon orange extract
  1 cup flaked coconut
ICING:
  2 cups confectioners' sugar
  1/4 cup orange juice
  2 tablespoons butter (no substitutes), melted

In a mixing bowl, combine the cake mix, eggs, oil, orange peel and extract; mix well. Fold in coconut. Drop by rounded teaspoonfuls 2 in. apart onto ungreased baking sheets.

Bake at 350° for 8-10 minutes or until bottoms are golden brown. Remove to wire racks to cool. In a small bowl, combine icing ingredients until smooth. Drizzle over the cooled cookies. **Yield:** about 5 dozen.

*Editor's Note: Orange cake mix may be substituted for the white cake mix. Omit the orange extract.

CHOCOLATE CHUNK SHORTBREAD

Brenda Mumma, Airdrie, Alberta

Chocolate is a nice addition to shortbread, as this scrumptious recipe proves.

  3/4 cup butter (no substitutes), softened
  1/2 cup confectioners' sugar
  1 cup all-purpose flour
  1/2 cup cornstarch
  3 squares (1 ounce *each*) semisweet chocolate, coarsely chopped
Additional confectioners' sugar

In a mixing bowl, cream butter and sugar. Gradually add flour and cornstarch. Stir in chocolate. Shape into 1-in. balls. Place 1 in. apart on

ungreased baking sheets. Flatten with a glass dipped in confectioners' sugar.

Bake at 300° for 30-33 minutes or until edges are lightly brown. Remove to wire racks to cool. **Yield:** about 3-1/2 dozen.

PEANUT BUTTER 'N' JELLY COOKIES

Ruth Ramsdell, Spring Lake Heights, New Jersey

Kids especially love these tasty cookies. They're a cinch to make since no baking is involved.

  3 tablespoons peanut butter*
  38 butter-flavored crackers
  3 tablespoons jam *or* jelly
  6 ounces chocolate candy coating

Spread peanut butter on the bottoms of half of the crackers. Spread jam on the bottoms of remaining crackers; place, jam side down, over peanut butter crackers, forming a sandwich. In a saucepan over low heat, melt candy coating; dip cookies. Place on a waxed paper-lined baking sheet; let stand until set. **Yield:** 19 cookies.

*Editor's Note: Reduced-fat or generic brands of peanut butter are not recommended for this recipe.

MOLASSES BUTTERBALLS

Zelda Halloran, Dallas, Texas

Better hide these if you want any left—it's hard to eat just one! Good thing they're quick to make.

  1 cup butter (no substitutes), softened
  1/4 cup light molasses
  2 cups all-purpose flour
  1/2 teaspoon salt
  2 cups chopped walnuts
Confectioners' sugar

In a mixing bowl, cream butter and molasses. Combine flour and salt; gradually add to creamed mixture. Stir in walnuts. Roll into 1-in. balls. Place 1 in. apart on greased baking sheets. Bake at 350° for 15 minutes or until set. Remove to wire racks to cool. Roll cooled cookies in confectioners' sugar. **Yield:** 4-1/2 dozen.

CRISPY BUTTER COOKIES

(Pictured above)

Betty Ferrell, Jasper, Georgia

These cookies are easy to make and taste so good. They're very crisp and light, perfect with milk or coffee.

    1 cup butter (no substitutes), softened
1-1/2 cups confectioners' sugar
    2 egg whites
    1 teaspoon vanilla extract
2-1/2 cups all-purpose flour
    1/2 teaspoon baking powder
    1/2 teaspoon baking soda
Sugar

In a mixing bowl, cream butter and confectioners' sugar. Beat in egg whites and vanilla. Combine flour, baking powder and baking soda; gradually add to the creamed mixture.

Roll into 1-1/2-in. balls, then roll in sugar. Place 2 in. apart on greased baking sheets. Flatten with a fork. Bake at 350° for 12-14 minutes or until edges are lightly browned. Remove to wire racks to cool. **Yield:** about 4 dozen.

STAR SANDWICH COOKIES

Patti Schmidt, Canton, Ohio

I baked these treats for a church tea. The night before, I gave a sample to the folks setting up. They liked the cookies so much, they saved the rest to ensure they'd get some the next day!

    1 cup butter (no substitutes), softened
    2 cups all-purpose flour
    1/3 cup whipping cream
Sugar
FILLING:
    1/2 cup butter, softened
 1-1/2 cups confectioners' sugar
    2 teaspoons vanilla extract
    4 to 8 teaspoons whipping cream
Liquid *or* paste food coloring, optional

In a mixing bowl, beat the butter, flour and cream. Cover and refrigerate for 1 hour or until easy to handle.

On a lightly floured surface, roll out dough to 1/8-in. thickness. Cut with a floured 2-in. star cookie cutter. Sprinkle tops of cookies with sugar; place on ungreased baking sheets. Prick each cookie 3-4 times with a fork. Bake at 375° for 7-9 minutes or until set. Remove to wire racks to cool.

For filling, combine the butter, confectioners' sugar, vanilla and enough cream to achieve desired spreading consistency. Tint with food coloring if desired. Carefully spread filling on the bottom of half of the cookies; top with remaining cookies. **Yield:** about 5 dozen.

TERRIFIC TOFFEE

(Pictured below)

Carol Gillespie, Chambersburg, Pennsylvania

This candy is one of those must-make treats my family requests at Christmas. The buttery toffee, rich chocolate and crunchy nuts are a triple treat. Everyone who tries a piece asks for more.

1-1/2 teaspoons plus 1 cup butter (no substitutes), *divided*
    1 cup semisweet chocolate chips

1 cup milk chocolate chips
1 cup sugar
3 tablespoons water
2 cups coarsely chopped almonds, toasted, *divided*

Butter a large baking sheet with 1-1/2 teaspoons butter; set aside.

In a bowl, combine semisweet and milk chocolate chips; set aside. In a heavy saucepan, combine the sugar, water and remaining butter. Cook and stir over medium heat until a candy thermometer reaches 290° (soft-crack stage). Remove from the heat; stir in 1 cup almonds. Immediately pour onto prepared baking sheet.

Sprinkle with chocolate chips; spread with a knife when melted. Top with remaining almonds; cool. Break into 2-in. pieces. **Yield:** about 2 pounds.

Editor's Note: We recommend that you test your candy thermometer before each use by bringing water to a boil; the thermometer should read 212°. Adjust your recipe temperature up or down based on your test.

ALMOND ROCK CANDY

Nancy Bohlen, Brookings, South Dakota

This isn't your ordinary rock candy! The difference lies in the almond extract added to the mix. I regularly give batches to our daughter's Sunday school teachers for Christmas.

1-1/2 teaspoons butter (no substitutes)
2 cups sugar
1 cup water
3/4 cup light corn syrup
1 to 1-1/2 teaspoons almond extract
6 drops green *or* red food coloring

Butter a baking sheet with 1-1/2 teaspoons butter; set aside. In a heavy saucepan, combine the sugar, water and corn syrup. Bring to a boil over medium heat, stirring occasionally. Cover and cook for 3 minutes. Uncover; cook, without stirring, over medium-high heat until a candy thermometer reads 310° (hard-crack stage).

Remove from the heat; stir in almond extract and food coloring. Immediately pour onto prepared baking sheet. Quickly spread into a 13-in. x 9-in. rectangle. Using a sharp knife and working quickly, score into 1-in. squares. Recut rectangle along score lines until candy is cut into squares. Let stand at room temperature until dry. Separate into squares, using a knife if necessary, or break into bite-size pieces. **Yield:** 1 pound.

Editor's Note: We recommend that you test your candy thermometer before each use by

bringing water to a boil; the thermometer should read 212°. Adjust your recipe temperature up or down based on your test.

CHOCOLATE CAPPUCCINO COOKIES

(Pictured above)

Eleanor Senske, Rock Island, Illinois

These chocolaty cookies have a mild coffee flavor that makes them a hit with whoever tries them.

✓ **Uses less fat, sugar or salt. Includes Nutritional Analysis and Diabetic Exchanges.**

1 tablespoon instant coffee granules
1 tablespoon hot water
1 egg white
3/4 cup plus 1 tablespoon sugar, *divided*
1/4 cup canola oil
2 tablespoons corn syrup
2 teaspoons vanilla extract
1-1/4 cups all-purpose flour
1/2 cup baking cocoa
1/4 teaspoon salt

In a small bowl, dissolve coffee granules in hot water. In a mixing bowl, combine the egg white, 3/4 cup sugar, oil, corn syrup, vanilla and coffee; beat until well blended. Combine the flour, cocoa and salt; gradually add to coffee mixture.

Roll into 1-in. balls. Place 2 in. apart on ungreased baking sheets. Flatten to 1/4-in. thickness with a glass dipped in the remaining sugar. Bake at 350° for 5-7 minutes or until center is set. Remove to wire racks to cool. Store in an airtight container. **Yield:** 3-1/2 dozen.

Nutritional Analysis: One cookie equals 43 calories, 1 g fat (trace saturated fat), 0 cholesterol, 15 mg sodium, 8 g carbohydrate, trace fiber, 1 g protein. **Diabetic Exchange:** 1/2 starch.

ANY WAY *you slice it, this chapter's appealing assortment of cakes, pies and desserts is simply scrumptious!*

PICTURE-PERFECT PIES. From top: Raspberry Meringue Pie (p. 109), Peaches 'n' Cream Pie (p. 109) and Apple Blackberry Pie (p. 110).

Cakes, Pies & Desserts

Cakes, Pies & Desserts

RASPBERRY MERINGUE PIE
(Pictured at left)

Karen Rempel Arthur, Wainfleet, Ontario

Whether my husband and I are hosting a backyard barbecue or a formal dinner, we love treating guests to this raspberry pie. I transport it to potlucks or family gatherings in my extra-deep cake carrier so the meringue stays intact.

    1/3 cup plus 1/4 cup sugar, *divided*
      3 tablespoons cornstarch
1-1/2 cups milk
      4 eggs, *separated*
      1 teaspoon butter *or* margarine
    1/4 teaspoon almond extract
      1 graham cracker crust (10 inches)
1-1/8 teaspoons unflavored gelatin
      2 tablespoons plus 1/4 teaspoon cold
        water, *divided*
      1 can (21 ounces) raspberry pie
        filling
    3/4 teaspoon cream of tartar

In a saucepan, combine 1/3 cup sugar and cornstarch. Stir in the milk until smooth. Cook and stir over medium heat until thickened and bubbly. Reduce heat; cook and stir 2 minutes longer. Remove from the heat. Stir a small amount of mixture into the egg yolks. Return all to the pan, stirring constantly. Bring to a gentle boil; cook and stir 2 minutes longer. Remove from the heat; stir in the butter and extract. Pour hot filling into the crust.

Sprinkle gelatin over 2 tablespoons cold water; let stand for 2 minutes. In a saucepan, bring raspberry filling and gelatin mixture to a boil. Reduce heat; simmer, uncovered, for 5 minutes.

Meanwhile, in a mixing bowl, beat egg whites and cream of tartar on medium speed until soft peaks form. Beat in remaining water. Gradually beat in remaining sugar on high until stiff glossy peaks form and sugar is dissolved.

Pour hot raspberry filling over custard. Spread meringue evenly over hot filling, sealing edges to crust. Bake at 325° for 15-18 minutes or until meringue is golden. Cool on a wire rack for 1 hour.

Refrigerate for at least 3 hours before serving. Refrigerate leftovers. **Yield:** 8-10 servings.

PEACHES 'N' CREAM PIE
(Pictured at left)

Tamrah Tso, Flagstaff, Arizona

In summer, my aunt and uncle provide me with tree-fresh fruit from their peach orchard. My husband gets so excited when they have a bumper crop because he knows this dessert will be on our menu often.

Pastry for double-crust pie (9 inches)
      1 cup sugar
    1/4 cup all-purpose flour
      1 tablespoon quick-cooking tapioca
Dash salt
      1 cup whipping cream, *divided*
    1/4 teaspoon vanilla extract
      4 cups sliced fresh *or* frozen peaches,
        thawed
Additional sugar

Line a 9-in. pie plate with bottom pastry; trim pastry even with edge of plate. In a bowl, combine the sugar, flour, tapioca and salt; mix well. Set aside 2 tablespoons cream. Combine remaining cream with vanilla; add to the sugar mixture. Add peaches; toss to coat. Let stand for 15 minutes.

Pour peach mixture into crust. Roll out the remaining pastry; make a lattice top crust. Seal and flute edges. Brush with reserved cream; sprinkle with additional sugar.

Cover edges loosely with foil. Bake at 400° for 50-55 minutes or until golden brown and bubbly. Cool on a wire rack. Store pie in the refrigerator. **Yield:** 6-8 servings.

THIS TIP'S A PEACH

TO PEEL fresh peaches for a pie, plunge them into boiling water for 20 to 30 seconds, then into ice water. Once they're cool enough to handle, the peels come off easily.

 ▰▰▰▰▰▰▰▰▰▰▰

SWEETHEART SORBET
(Pictured above)

A warm reception always greets cool, smooth scoops of this lemony treat developed by our Test Kitchen. The not-too-sour, not-too-sweet confection you can serve for dessert is a refreshingly frosty finish.

　　1 cup sugar
　　1 cup water
　1/2 cup lemon juice
　　1 tablespoon grated lemon peel

In a bowl, combine all ingredients; whisk until sugar is dissolved. Pour into the cylinder of an ice cream freezer. Freeze according to manufacturer's directions. **Yield:** 2 cups.

▰▰▰▰▰▰▰▰▰▰▰

 ## APPLE BLACKBERRY PIE
(Pictured on page 108)

Dorian Lucas, Corning, California

After a blackberry-picking trip, my husband and I decided to include a few in an apple pie we were making. It was the best we'd ever tasted! We live near the mountains with our two children. Ingredients for fruit pies grow all around us.

　　2 cups all-purpose flour
　　1 teaspoon sugar
　　1 teaspoon salt
　　1 teaspoon ground cinnamon
　2/3 cup cold butter *or* margarine
　　4 to 6 tablespoons cold water
FILLING:
　　5 cups thinly sliced peeled tart apples
　　　(about 6 medium)
　　1 cup fresh blackberries

　1/2 cup packed brown sugar
4-1/2 teaspoons cornstarch
　　1 teaspoon ground cinnamon
　　1 teaspoon ground nutmeg

In a bowl, combine the flour, sugar, salt and cinnamon; cut in butter until crumbly. Gradually add water, tossing with a fork until dough forms a ball. Divide dough in half. Roll out one portion to fit a 9-in. pie plate; place pastry in plate and trim even with edge.

In a bowl, combine apples and blackberries. Combine the brown sugar, cornstarch, cinnamon and nutmeg; add to fruit mixture and toss to coat. Pour into crust. Roll out remaining pastry to fit top of pie; place over filling. Trim, seal and flute edges. Cut slits in pastry. Add decorative cutouts if desired. Cover edges loosely with foil.

Bake at 450° for 10 minutes. Reduce heat to 350°; remove foil. Bake 40-50 minutes longer or until lightly browned and filling is bubbly. Cool on a wire rack. Store in the refrigerator. **Yield:** 6-8 servings.

▰▰▰▰▰▰▰▰▰▰▰

CHERRY BLUEBERRY PIE
(Pictured below)

Betty Williams, Scotts, Michigan

Southwestern Michigan is noted for its fruit. I experimented and came up with this pie recipe that combines cherries and blueberries. It's especially good served warm with ice cream.

Pastry for a double-crust pie (9 inches)
　　2 cups pitted sweet cherries
　　2 cups fresh blueberries

3/4 cup sugar
1/4 cup all-purpose flour
1/8 teaspoon ground nutmeg
1 tablespoon butter *or* margarine
Additional sugar

Line a 9-in. pie plate with bottom crust; trim pastry even with edge. Set aside. In a bowl, gently combine cherries and blueberries. Combine the sugar, flour and nutmeg; stir into fruit. Let stand for 10 minutes. Pour into crust; dot with butter. Roll out remaining pastry; make a lattice crust. Seal and flute edges. Sprinkle with sugar. Cover edges of pastry loosely with foil.

Bake at 425° for 15 minutes. Reduce heat to 350°; bake 30-35 minutes longer or until pastry is golden brown and filling is bubbly. Cool on a wire rack. **Yield:** 6-8 servings.

GRAPE SHERBET

Sherry Rominger, Rogers, Arkansas

My husband, two daughters and I first enjoyed this re-freshing treat at our friends' house. They graciously shared the recipe after we all raved about it. The sherbet is always popular at ice cream socials.

1-3/4 cups grape juice
3 tablespoons lemon juice
1/2 cup sugar
1-3/4 cups half-and-half cream

In a large bowl, combine all ingredients. Pour into the cylinder of a 1-qt. ice cream freezer; freeze according to manufacturer's directions. Allow to ripen in ice cream freezer or in refrigerator freezer for 2-4 hours before serving. **Yield:** 1 quart.

SURPRISE CARROT CAKE
(Pictured above right)

Lisa Bowen, Little Britain, Ontario

A cousin gave me this recipe. It's a wonderful potluck pleaser with its "surprise" cream cheese center. My husband and our two young children love it, too! It's a great way to use up the overabundance of carrots from my garden.

3 eggs
1-3/4 cups sugar
3 cups shredded carrots
1 cup vegetable oil
2 cups all-purpose flour

2 teaspoons baking soda
2 teaspoons ground cinnamon
1 teaspoon salt
1/2 cup chopped pecans
FILLING:
1 package (8 ounces) cream cheese, softened
1/4 cup sugar
1 egg
FROSTING:
1 package (8 ounces) cream cheese, softened
1/4 cup butter *or* margarine, softened
2 teaspoons vanilla extract
4 cups confectioners' sugar

In a mixing bowl, beat eggs and sugar. Add carrots and oil; beat until blended. Combine the flour, baking soda, cinnamon and salt. Add to carrot mixture; mix well. Stir in pecans. Pour 3 cups batter into a greased and floured 10-in. fluted tube pan.

In a mixing bowl, beat cream cheese and sugar. Add egg; mix well. Spoon over batter. Top with remaining batter.

Bake at 350° for 55-60 minutes or until a tooth-pick inserted near the center comes out clean. Cool for 10 minutes before removing from pan to a wire rack to cool completely.

For frosting, in a small mixing bowl, beat the cream cheese, butter and vanilla until smooth. Gradually add confectioners' sugar. Frost cake. Store in the refrigerator. **Yield:** 12-16 servings.

Pies Made Pronto

WHAT'S the most time-consuming thing about making a pie? Rolling out the crust, of course! You don't need to get out your rolling pin at all to make any of these easy-to-assemble pies. But the scrumptious results will have folks thinking you spent hours in the kitchen.

━━━━━━━━━━

GLAZED BLACKBERRY PIE

(Pictured below)

Monica Gross, Downey, California

I use the first ripe berries of the season to make this fruity pie.

    5 cups fresh blackberries, *divided*
    1 pastry shell (9 inches), baked
    1 cup water, *divided*
  3/4 cup sugar
    3 tablespoons cornstarch
Red food coloring, optional
Whipped topping

Place 2 cups blackberries in pastry shell; set aside. In a saucepan, crush 1 cup berries. Add 3/4 cup water. Bring to a boil over medium heat, stirring constantly. Cook and stir for 2 minutes. Press berries

through a sieve. Set juice aside and discard pulp.

In a saucepan, combine the sugar and cornstarch. Stir in remaining water and reserved juice until smooth. Bring to a boil; cook and stir for 2 minutes or until thickened. Remove from the heat; stir in food coloring if desired. Pour half of the glaze over berries in pastry shell. Stir remaining berries into remaining glaze; carefully spoon over filling.

Refrigerate for 3 hours or until set. Garnish with whipped topping. Refrigerate leftovers. **Yield:** 6-8 servings.

━━━━━━━━━━

BLUEBERRY CREAM PIE

Diane Bullis, Grant, Michigan

This is a favorite pie with my family come blueberry season here in Michigan.

  1/2 cup sugar
  1/2 cup packed brown sugar
    3 tablespoons plus 1-1/2 teaspoons
      all-purpose flour
  1/4 teaspoon salt
  1/4 teaspoon ground nutmeg
    4 cups fresh *or* frozen blueberries, thawed,
      divided
    1 tablespoon butter *or* margarine
    1 tablespoon lemon juice
    1 pastry shell (9 inches), baked
TOPPING:
    2 cups whipped topping
    1 tablespoon sugar
  1/2 teaspoon vanilla extract

In a saucepan, combine the sugars, flour, salt and nutmeg. Add 2 cups blueberries, butter and lemon juice. Bring to a boil over medium-low heat, stirring constantly. Cook and stir for 2 minutes or until thickened. Refrigerate for 15 minutes. Stir in remaining berries.

Pour into the pastry shell. Refrigerate for 3 hours or until set. Combine whipped topping, sugar and vanilla; serve with the pie. Refrigerate leftovers. **Yield:** 6-8 servings.

LEMON PEAR PIE

Carolina Hofeldt, Lloyd, Montana

My husband loves all kinds of fruit, so he's a big fan of this fast-to-fix pie. The lemon and pear flavors taste fantastic together.

      2 eggs, lightly beaten
      1 cup sugar
  1/4 cup lemon juice
      1 tablespoon butter *or* margarine
      1 teaspoon grated lemon peel
      3 cans (15 ounces *each*) pear halves,
            drained and cubed
      1 unbaked pastry shell (9 inches)

In a saucepan, combine the first five ingredients. Cook and stir over low heat for 10 minutes or until thickened and bubbly. Remove from the heat; fold in pears. Pour into pastry shell.

Bake at 350° for 50-55 minutes or until crust is golden brown and filling is bubbly. Cool on a wire rack for 1 hour. Store pie in the refrigerator. **Yield:** 6-8 servings.

COCONUT PINEAPPLE PIE

Nancy Mendoza, Yakima, Washington

A breeze to prepare, this tropical-tasting pie is tops with whoever tries it.

  2-1/4 cups flaked coconut, *divided*
      2 tablespoons butter *or* margarine, melted
      1 can (20 ounces) crushed pineapple,
            undrained
    32 large marshmallows
      2 teaspoons rum *or* vanilla extract
  1/4 teaspoon salt
      1 cup whipping cream, whipped

In a bowl, combine 2 cups coconut and butter. Press into the bottom and up the sides of a greased 9-in. pie plate. Bake at 325° for 8-10 minutes or until golden brown. Cool on a wire rack. Toast the remaining coconut; set aside.

Drain pineapple, reserving 1/2 cup juice (discard remaining juice or refrigerate for another use); set pineapple aside. In a saucepan, combine marshmallows and reserved juice. Cook and stir

over medium heat until marshmallows are melted. Remove from the heat. Add pineapple, extract and salt; mix well. Refrigerate for 2 hours or until cool.

Fold in the whipped cream; spoon into prepared crust. Sprinkle with toasted coconut. Refrigerate for 2 hours or until set. Refrigerate leftovers. **Yield:** 8 servings.

APPLE GRAHAM PIE

Shirley Pochipinski, Prince Albert, Saskatchewan

I can whip up this pie in minutes using the microwave, so it's great for drop-in guests. People are always surprised I can serve them a slice so quickly.

      2 cups graham cracker crumbs (about 32
            squares)
  3/4 cup sugar, *divided*
  1/2 cup butter *or* margarine, melted
      4 cups sliced peeled tart apples (about 4
            medium)
      1 teaspoon ground cinnamon

In a bowl, combine the cracker crumbs, 1/4 cup sugar and butter until crumbly; press two-thirds onto the bottom and up the sides of an ungreased microwave-safe 9-in. pie plate. Set remaining crumb mixture aside.

In a bowl, toss apples with cinnamon and remaining sugar. Arrange in crust; sprinkle with reserved crumbs. Microwave, uncovered, on high for 8 minutes; rotate. Cook 7-8 minutes longer or until apples are tender. Cool on a wire rack. Store in the refrigerator. **Yield:** 6-8 servings.

Editor's Note: This recipe was tested in an 850-watt microwave.

WHICH PIES TO REFRIGERATE

REFRIGERATE pies containing dairy products or eggs. Pies made with eggs, milk, sour cream, whipped cream, whipped topping, yogurt or cream cheese should be refrigerated as soon as possible after they've been prepared or about 1 hour after baking.

ORANGE RHUBARB PIE

(Pictured below)

Lucille Boorsma, Delta, Colorado

I always remember rhubarb pie being too tart for my taste, so I started making adjustments until I came up with this recipe. Everyone who has tried it has told me they like it very much.

3-1/2 cups diced fresh *or* frozen rhubarb
  1/2 cup golden raisins
  1/2 cup chopped pecans
    1 tablespoon grated orange peel
1-1/2 cups sugar
  1/3 cup orange juice
    2 tablespoons quick-cooking tapioca
  1/4 teaspoon ground nutmeg
Pastry for double-crust pie (9 inches)
    2 tablespoons butter *or* margarine
    1 tablespoon milk
Additional sugar

In a large bowl, combine the rhubarb, raisins, pecans, orange peel, sugar, orange juice and tapioca. Let mixture stand for 30 minutes.

Line a 9-in. pie plate with bottom pastry; trim even with edge of plate. Pour filling into crust; dot with butter. Roll out remaining pastry to fit top of pie; place over filling. Trim, seal and flute edges; cut slits in top. Brush milk over pastry; sprinkle with sugar.

Cover edges loosely with foil. Bake at 400° for 30 minutes. Remove foil; bake 5 minutes longer

or until crust is golden brown and filling is bubbly. Cool on a wire rack. **Yield:** 6-8 servings.

UPSIDE-DOWN RASPBERRY CAKE

(Pictured above)

Joy Beck, Cincinnati, Ohio

This moist cake is great for any occasion. Pretty red berries peek out of every slice. I've received many compliments from family and friends.

1-1/2 cups fresh *or* frozen unsweetened
    raspberries,* *divided*
    1 cup butter *or* margarine, softened
    1 cup sugar
    3 eggs
    2 teaspoons lemon juice
    1 teaspoon vanilla extract
    2 cups all-purpose flour
1-1/2 teaspoons baking powder
  1/2 teaspoon salt
  2/3 cup milk
Confectioners' sugar

Line the bottom and sides of a 9-in. square baking pan with foil; coat with nonstick cooking spray. Place 1/2 cup raspberries in pan; set aside. In a mixing bowl, cream butter and sugar. Add eggs, lemon juice and vanilla; mix well. Combine flour, baking powder and salt; add to creamed mixture alternately with milk.

Fold in the remaining raspberries. Carefully spoon over berries in pan. Bake at 350° for 40-45 minutes or until a toothpick inserted near the center comes out clean. Cool for 10 minutes. Invert cake onto a serving platter; carefully remove foil. Cool completely. Dust with confectioners' sugar. **Yield:** 9 servings.

*Editor's Note: If using frozen raspberries, do not thaw before adding to batter.

BANANA CREAM PIE

Lila Case, Bella Vista, Arkansas

Being diabetic doesn't stop me from having "sweets". This pie is simply delicious.

> ✓ Uses less fat, sugar or salt. Includes Nutritional Analysis and Diabetic Exchanges.

1-1/2 cups cold fat-free milk
   1 package (1 ounce) sugar-free instant vanilla pudding mix
  1/3 cup fat-free sour cream
   1 carton (8 ounces) frozen reduced-fat whipped topping, thawed, *divided*
   3 medium firm bananas, sliced
   1 reduced-fat graham cracker crust (9 inches)

In a bowl, whisk milk and pudding mix for 2 minutes or until slightly thickened. Add sour cream; mix well. Fold in 1-1/2 cups whipped topping. Place half of the banana slices in the crust; top with half of the pudding mixture. Repeat layers. Spread with remaining whipped topping. Refrigerate for 4-6 hours before serving (pie will be soft set). Refrigerate leftovers. **Yield:** 8 servings.

Nutritional Analysis: One slice equals 260 calories, 7 g fat (5 g saturated fat), 1 mg cholesterol, 284 mg sodium, 42 g carbohydrate, 1 g fiber, 4 g protein. **Diabetic Exchanges:** 2 starch, 1 fruit.

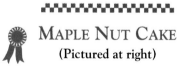

MAPLE NUT CAKE
(Pictured at right)

Emma Magielda, Amsterdam, New York

Our state is famous for its maple syrup. I like using maple syrup in desserts, like this cake, because it lends a distinct flavor.

  1/2 cup butter *or* margarine, softened
  1/2 cup sugar
   1 cup maple syrup
   2 eggs

2-1/4 cups cake flour
   3 teaspoons baking powder
   1 teaspoon salt
  1/2 cup milk
  1/2 cup chopped nuts
FROSTING:
   1 cup sugar
  1/2 cup maple syrup
   2 egg whites
   1 teaspoon corn syrup
  1/8 teaspoon salt
  1/4 teaspoon cream of tartar

In a bowl, cream the butter, sugar, syrup and eggs. Combine flour, baking powder and salt; add to the creamed mixture alternately with milk. Fold in nuts. Pour into two greased and floured 8-in. baking pans. Bake at 350° for 20-25 minutes or until a toothpick inserted near the center comes out clean. Cool for 10 minutes before removing from pans to wire racks to cool completely.

In a heavy saucepan or double boiler, combine the frosting ingredients. With a portable mixer, beat on low speed for 1 minute. Continue beating over low heat until frosting reaches 160°, about 8-10 minutes. Pour into a large mixing bowl. Beat on high until stiff peaks form, about 7 minutes. Frost between layers and over top and sides of cake. **Yield:** 12-14 servings.

Editor's Note: A stand mixer is recommended for beating the frosting after it reached 160°.

STRAWBERRY ICE

Kim Hammond, Watsonville, California

When we pick strawberries at a local farm, this is what many of the berries are used for.

　5　cups fresh *or* frozen unsweetened
　　　strawberries
2/3　cup sugar
2/3　cup water
1/4　cup lemon juice

Place the strawberries in a blender or food processor; cover and process until smooth. In a saucepan, heat sugar and water until sugar is dissolved; pour into blender. Add lemon juice; cover and process until combined.

　Pour into a shallow freezer container; cover and freeze for 4-6 hours or until almost frozen. Just before serving, whip mixture in a blender or food processor. **Yield:** 6 servings.

CARAMEL PECAN POUND CAKE

(Pictured above)

Rosella Day, Waycross, Georgia

My state is known for the delicious pecans it produces, so this recipe definitely represents Georgia. The pecan flavor comes through nicely in this cake.

　　1　cup butter (no substitutes), softened
2-1/4　cups packed brown sugar
　　1　cup sugar
　　5　eggs
　　3　teaspoons vanilla extract
　　3　cups all-purpose flour
　1/2　teaspoon baking powder
　1/2　teaspoon salt
　　1　cup milk
　　1　cup finely chopped pecans
Confectioners' sugar
Fresh fruit, optional

In a mixing bowl, cream butter. Gradually beat in sugars until light and fluffy. Add eggs, one at a time, beating well after each. Stir in vanilla. Combine the flour, baking powder and salt; add to the creamed mixture alternately with milk. Beat on low speed just until blended. Fold in pecans. Pour into a greased and floured 10-in. tube pan.

　Bake at 325° for 1-1/2 hours or until a toothpick inserted near the center comes out clean. Cool for 10 minutes before removing from pan to a wire rack to cool completely. Dust with confectioners' sugar. Serve with fruit if desired. **Yield:** 16 servings.

MINT CHOCOLATE CAKE

(Pictured below)

Virginia Horst, Mesa, Washington

My husband works for a mint farmer, so I'm always looking for recipes with mint in them, like this cake.

　　1　package (18-1/4 ounces) chocolate cake mix
FROSTING:
　1/2　cup butter *or* margarine, softened
　　2　cups confectioners' sugar
　　1　tablespoon water
　1/2　teaspoon peppermint extract
　　3　drops green food coloring

TOPPING:
- 1-1/2 cups milk chocolate chips
- 6 tablespoons butter *or* margarine, softened
- 1/4 teaspoon peppermint extract

Prepare cake batter according to package directions. Pour into a greased 15-in. x 10-in. x 1-in. baking pan. Bake at 350° for 25-30 minutes or until a toothpick inserted near the center comes out clean. Cool on a wire rack.

In a bowl, combine the frosting ingredients until smooth. Spread over cooled cake. For topping, in a microwave-safe bowl, melt chocolate chips and butter; stir in extract. Spread over frosting. Refrigerate until set. **Yield:** 20-24 servings.

BUTTERNUT SQUASH LAYER CAKE

(Pictured above right and on front cover)

Deanna Richter, Fenton, Iowa

The recipe for this lovely tall cake with its yummy old-fashioned frosting has been in our family a long time.

- 1/2 cup butter *or* margarine, softened
- 1 cup sugar
- 1 cup packed brown sugar
- 2 eggs
- 1 cup mashed cooked butternut squash
- 1 teaspoon maple flavoring
- 3 cups cake flour
- 4 teaspoons baking powder
- 1/4 teaspoon baking soda
- 1/2 cup milk
- 1 cup chopped walnuts

BROWN SUGAR FROSTING:
- 1-1/2 cups packed brown sugar
- 3 egg whites
- 6 tablespoons water
- 1/4 teaspoon cream of tartar
- 1/8 teaspoon salt
- 1 teaspoon vanilla extract

In a mixing bowl, cream the butter and sugars. Add eggs, one at a time, beating well after each addition. Add squash and maple flavoring; mix well. Combine flour, baking powder and baking soda; add to creamed mixture alternately with milk. Stir in walnuts. Pour into two greased and floured 9-in. round baking pans. Bake at 350° for 25-30 minutes or until a toothpick inserted near the center comes out clean. Cool 10 minutes before removing from pans to wire racks.

For frosting, combine the brown sugar, egg whites, water, cream of tartar and salt in a heavy saucepan. With a portable mixer, beat on low speed for 1 minute. Continue beating over low heat until a thermometer reads 160°, about 8-10 minutes. Pour frosting into a large mixing bowl; add vanilla. Beat on high speed until stiff peaks form, about 3 minutes. Spread between layers and over top and sides of cake. Refrigerate. **Yield:** 10-12 servings.

Editor's Note: A stand mixer is recommended for beating the frosting after it reaches 160°.

APPLE PIE ICE CREAM

Robin Lamb, Raleigh, North Carolina

As a mother of a young family, I appreciate recipes that youngsters really enjoy. This is certainly one of them.

- 1-1/4 cups sugar
- 1/4 cup all-purpose flour
- 1/4 teaspoon salt
- 4 cups milk
- 4 eggs, beaten
- 4 cups whipping cream
- 1 can (21 ounces) apple pie filling, chopped
- 3 tablespoons vanilla extract
- 1 teaspoon ground cinnamon

In a large saucepan, combine sugar, flour and salt; gradually stir in milk. Bring to a boil; cook and stir for 2 minutes or until thickened. Stir about 1 cup hot mixture into eggs; return all to the pan, stirring constantly. Cook and stir until the mixture reaches 160°. Remove from the heat; set the pan in ice and stir the mixture for 5-10 minutes.

Whisk in cream until blended. Add pie filling, vanilla and cinnamon. Cover and refrigerate overnight. Fill cylinder of ice cream freezer two-thirds full; freeze according to manufacturer's directions. Refrigerate remaining mixture until ready to freeze. **Yield:** 3 quarts.

Creating Decorative Crusts Is Easy...Easy As Pie, That Is!

A FOLD here and a twist there—with some simple but snappy finger work, you can easily turn out a pie that's as yummy to look at as it is to eat.

Eye-catching edges, cutout pieces of pastry trimming an otherwise plain upper crust and well-woven lattice tops all give pie crusts fancy finishing touches. And although they may look difficult, often these tasty decorations are easy to complete.

To help unravel the mystery behind making such appealing crusts, our Test Kitchen home economists have compiled simple-to-follow instructions on time-tested treatments, so you can create your own at home.

Pick up your rolling pin and roll out any of these beauties today. Your cutting-edge wizardry will surely earn a host of compliments from both family and friends!

SLICE UP SOME FUN

Before you create any of the decorative edges shown on these two pages, though you'll have to trim the dough so you have the right amount for an attractive edge. The edges can't be formed without enough dough—but too much dough will result in a thick edge that will lose its shape during baking.

Most of the treatments shown here require a built-up edge or a rolled edge. The pastry should be trimmed to 1/2 in. beyond the rim of the pie plate for a single-crust pie and 1 in. for a double-crust pie. This overhang is then turned under to form the built-up edge.

The other kind of edge, a flat edge, is made simply by trimming the pastry even with the edge of the pie plate.

(Keep in mind that the terms "rolled edge" and "flat edge" describe how the dough should be trimmed before the decorative edges are made.)

Now, embellish those edges with one of these fancy trims.

Ruffle Edge (below) is suitable for a single- or double-crust pie.

Make a rolled edge. Position your thumb and index finger about 1 in. apart on the edge of the crust, pointing out.

Position the index finger on your other hand between the two fingers and gently push the pastry toward the center in an upward direction. Continue around the edge.

Rope Edge (right) is suitable for a single- or double-crust pie.

Make a rolled edge. Then make a fist with one hand and press your thumb at an angle into the dough. Pinch some of the dough between your thumb and index finger.

Repeat at about 1/2-in. intervals around the crust. For a looser-looking rope, position your thumb at a wider angle and repeat at 1-in. intervals.

Braided Edge (below) is suitable for a single-crust pie. Make enough pastry for a double crust. Line a 9-in. pie plate with the bottom crust and shape a flat edge.

Roll remaining dough into a 10-in. x 8-in. rectangle. With a sharp knife, cut twelve 1/4-in.-wide strips. Gently braid three strips of dough. Brush edge of pastry with water. Place braid on edge of crust and press lightly to secure.

Repeat with remaining strips, attaching additional braids until entire edge is covered. Use foil to protect edges from overbrowning.

Cut Scalloped Edge

Cut Scalloped Edge (right) is suitable for a single-crust pie.

Make a flat edge. Hold a teaspoon or tablespoon upside down and roll the tip of the spoon around the edge of the pastry, cutting it. Remove and discard the cut pieces to create a scalloped look.

Remember—the larger the spoon, the bigger the scallops.

Leaf Trim

Leaf Trim (below) is suitable for a single-crust pie.

Make enough pastry for a double crust. Line a 9-in. pie plate with the bottom crust and make a flat edge. Roll out the remaining dough to 1/8-in. thickness.

Cut out leaf shapes, using 1-in. to 1-1/2-in. cookie cutters. With a sharp knife, score dough to create leaf veins. Brush bottom of each leaf with water.

Place one or two layers of leaves around the pastry edge. Press lightly to secure. Use foil to protect edges from overbrowning.

You can also use this technique with other cookie cutter designs, such as stars, hearts and apples. Vary them to suit the special occasion or season you are celebrating.

Lattice Top

Lattice Top (right) is suitable for a double-crust pie. Line a 9-in. pie plate with the bottom crust and trim pastry to 1 in. beyond edge of plate.

Roll out remaining dough into a 12-in. circle. With a fluted pastry wheel, pizza cutter or sharp knife, cut dough into 1/2-in.- to 1-in.-wide strips. Lay strips in rows about 1/2 in. to 3/4 in. apart. (Use longer strips for the center of the pie and shorter strips for the sides.)

Fold every other strip halfway back. Starting at the center, add strips at right angles, lifting every other strip as the cross strips are put down. Continue to add strips, lifting and weaving until lattice top is completed.

Trim strips even with pastry edge. Fold bottom crust up and over ends of strips. Finish by making a ruffle, rope or fluted edge.

Pastry Cutouts

Pastry Cutouts (below) are suitable for a single- or double-crust pie.

To make cutouts, roll out dough to 1/8-in. thickness. Cut out with 1-in. to 1-1/2-in. cookie cutters of desired shape. With a sharp knife, score designs (if desired) on cutouts.

For a single-crust pie, bake cutouts on an ungreased baking sheet at 400° for 6-8 minutes or until golden brown. Remove to wire rack to cool. Arrange over cooled filling on baked pie.

For a double-crust pie, brush bottom of each unbaked cutout with water and arrange over top crust of an unbaked pie. Press lightly to secure. Bake pie according to recipe.

Fluted Edge

Fluted Edge (right) is suitable for a single- or double-crust pie.

Make a rolled edge. Position your index finger on the edge of the crust, pointing out. Place the thumb and index finger of your other hand on the outside edge and pinch dough around the index finger to form a V shape. Continue around the edge.

As you can see, a decorative edge will lend an upper-crust look to any down-home dessert. In no time, you'll be able to bake up a picture-perfect pie that just might be too pretty to slice!

SPONGE CAKE WITH BLUEBERRY TOPPING

(Pictured below)

Frances Cooley, Coos Bay, Oregon

This recipe puts the blueberries grown in our area to good use. It's a great summertime dessert.

    6 eggs, *separated*
1-1/2 cups sugar
  3/4 cup orange juice
1-1/2 cups all-purpose flour
1-1/2 teaspoons baking powder
  1/4 teaspoon cream of tartar
BLUEBERRY TOPPING:
  1/2 cup sugar
    2 teaspoons cornstarch
    1 tablespoon grated orange peel
  1/2 cup orange juice
    2 cups fresh *or* frozen blueberries
SOUR CREAM TOPPING:
    2 cups (16 ounces) sour cream
    1 tablespoon confectioners' sugar
    1 teaspoon vanilla extract

In a large mixing bowl, beat egg yolks for 4-5 minutes or until thickened and light yellow. Gradually add sugar, beating for 1-2 minutes or until sugar is dissolved. Add orange juice; beat for 2-3 minutes or until mixture slightly thickens. Combine flour and baking powder; gradually add to yolk mixture and mix well.

In a small mixing bowl, beat egg whites and cream of tartar until stiff peaks form. Fold into egg yolk mixture until well blended. Pour into an ungreased 10-in. tube pan. Bake at 325° for 50-55 minutes or until cake springs back when lightly touched. Immediately invert pan to cool.

For blueberry topping, combine sugar, corn-starch and orange peel in a saucepan. Stir in orange juice until smooth. Bring to a boil; cook and stir for 2 minutes or until thickened. Remove from the heat. Stir in blueberries.

Combine sour cream, confectioners' sugar and vanilla. Remove cooled cake from pan; cut into slices. Serve with warm blueberry topping and sour cream topping. **Yield:** 12-16 servings.

PEANUT BUTTER LOVER'S CAKE

(Pictured above)

Teresa Mozingo, Camden, South Carolina

My family thrives on peanut butter, so they just love it when I make this recipe.

    3 eggs
1-2/3 cups sugar, *divided*
1-1/2 cups milk, *divided*
    3 squares (1 ounce *each*) unsweetened
      chocolate, finely chopped
  1/2 cup shortening
    1 teaspoon vanilla extract
    2 cups cake flour
    1 teaspoon baking soda
  1/2 teaspoon salt
PEANUT BUTTER FROSTING:
    2 packages (8 ounces *each*) cream cheese,
      softened
    1 can (14 ounces) sweetened condensed
      milk
1-1/2 cups peanut butter
  1/4 cup salted peanuts, chopped
    3 milk chocolate candy bars (1.55 ounces
      each), broken into squares

In a saucepan, whisk 1 egg until blended. Stir in 2/3 cup sugar, 1/2 cup milk and chocolate. Cook and stir over medium heat until chocolate is

melted and mixture just comes to a boil. Remove from the heat; cool to room temperature.

In a mixing bowl, cream shortening and remaining sugar. Add remaining eggs, one at a time, beating well after each. Beat in vanilla. Combine the flour, baking soda and salt; add to creamed mixture alternately with remaining milk. Add chocolate mixture; mix well.

Pour into three greased and floured 9-in. round baking pans. Bake at 325° for 25-30 minutes or until a toothpick comes out clean. Cool for 10 minutes before removing from pans to wire racks.

For frosting, in a mixing bowl, beat cream cheese until light and fluffy. Gradually add milk and peanut butter, beating well after each addition. Spread between layers and over top and sides of cooled cake. Sprinkle with peanuts. Garnish with candy bars. Store in the refrigerator. **Yield:** 12-14 servings.

FROSTY CHOCOLATE MOUSSE

Myra Innes, Auburn, Kansas

This is a wonderful dessert that whips up fast. It's very smooth and silky and complements any meal.

1-1/2 cups whipping cream
  1/2 cup sugar
  1/2 cup sifted baking cocoa
  1/2 teaspoon rum extract
  1/2 teaspoon vanilla extract

In a mixing bowl, combine all ingredients. Beat until mixture mounds softly. Spoon into dessert dishes. Freeze for at least 2 hours before serving. **Yield:** 4 servings.

WALNUT BLINTZ TORTE

(Pictured at right)

Suzan Stacey, Parsonsfield, Maine

This pretty torte is very popular at family gatherings. Everyone always asks for the recipe.

  2 tablespoons sugar
4-1/2 teaspoons cornstarch
  1 egg yolk
  1 cup milk
  1 teaspoon vanilla extract
CAKE BATTER:
  1/2 cup butter *or* margarine, softened
  1/2 cup sugar
  4 egg yolks

  1 teaspoon vanilla extract
  1 cup all-purpose flour
  1 teaspoon baking powder
  1/4 teaspoon salt
  5 tablespoons milk
MERINGUE:
  5 egg whites
  1 cup sugar
  2 cups chopped walnuts, *divided*

In a saucepan, combine sugar and cornstarch. Combine egg yolk and milk; add to pan. Bring to a gentle boil over medium-low heat, stirring constantly. Cook and stir for 2 minutes. Remove from the heat; stir in vanilla. Cover and refrigerate.

Meanwhile, in a mixing bowl, cream the butter and sugar. Add egg yolks and vanilla; mix well. Combine flour, baking powder and salt; add to creamed mixture alternately with milk. Spread into two greased and floured 9-in. round baking pans; set aside.

In a small mixing bowl, beat egg whites on medium speed until foamy. Gradually beat in sugar, a tablespoon at a time, on high until stiff glossy peaks form and sugar is dissolved. Fold in 1 cup nuts. Spread meringue evenly over batter. Sprinkle with remaining nuts. Bake at 325° for 35-40 minutes or until meringue is browned and crisp. Cool on wire racks for 10 minutes (the meringue will crack).

Carefully run a knife around edge of pans to loosen. Remove to wire racks; cool with meringue side up. To assemble, place one cake with meringue side up on a serving plate; carefully spread with custard. Top with remaining cake. Refrigerate until serving. **Yield:** 12-16 servings.

▰▰▰▰▰▰▰▰▰▰▰▰▰
CREAMY CANDY BAR DESSERT
(Pictured above)

Kathy Kittell, Lenexa, Kansas

Here's a dessert you'll have a hard time resisting until the end of the meal. It's every bit as yummy as it looks. One taste and you'll be smiling like a kid in a candy store—no matter what age you are!

    2 cups graham cracker crumbs (about 32
       squares)
    3 tablespoons sugar
  1/2 cup butter *or* margarine, melted
    1 jar (11-3/4 ounces) hot fudge ice cream
       topping
FILLING:
  1/2 cup cold milk
    2 packages (3.4 ounces *each*) instant
       vanilla *or* chocolate pudding
    2 cartons (16 ounces *each*) frozen
       whipped topping, thawed
    6 to 7 (2.07 ounces *each*) Snickers candy
       bars, chopped, *divided*

In a bowl, combine the crumbs and sugar; stir in butter. Press into an ungreased 13-in. x 9-in. x 2-in. dish. In a small saucepan, heat the fudge topping over low heat until warmed; pour evenly over crust. Cool.

In a mixing bowl, beat the milk, pudding mix and whipped topping for 2-3 minutes or until stiff, scraping sides of bowl often. Stir in three-fourths of the candy bar pieces. Pour over crust. Sprinkle with remaining candy bar pieces. Cover and refrigerate for 2-3 hours or overnight. Refrigerate leftovers. **Yield:** 15 servings.

▰▰▰▰▰▰▰▰▰▰▰▰▰
GEORGIA PECAN CAKE
(Pictured below)

Carolyn Griffin, Macon, Georgia

This recipe came from my mother and has always been a hit with our family. One taste and you'll see why.

    1 cup butter *or* margarine, softened
    2 cups sugar
    4 eggs
    3 cups all-purpose flour
  3/4 teaspoon salt
  1/2 teaspoon baking soda
  1/2 teaspoon baking powder
    1 cup buttermilk
    1 teaspoon vanilla extract
  1/2 teaspoon lemon extract
    1 cup chopped pecans

In a mixing bowl, cream butter and sugar. Add the eggs, one at a time, beating well after each addition. Combine the flour, salt, baking soda and baking powder; set 1/4 cup aside. Add the remaining dry ingredients to the creamed mixture alternately with buttermilk. Stir in the extracts. Toss pecans with the reserved flour mixture; fold into batter.

Pour into a greased and floured 10-in. tube pan. Bake at 325° for 60-70 minutes or until a toothpick inserted near the center comes out clean. Cool for 10 minutes before removing from pan to a wire rack. **Yield:** 12-16 servings.

Cakes, Pies & Desserts

MOIST CHOCOLATE CAKE

Linda Dorion, Nanoose Bay, British Columbia

Family and friends like to gather in my kitchen for slices of this scrumptious cake.

  1 cup butter *or* margarine, softened
  1 cup quick-cooking oats
1/2 cup baking cocoa
  2 cups boiling water
  3 cups packed brown sugar
  2 teaspoons vanilla extract
  4 eggs
  2 cups all-purpose flour
  2 teaspoons baking powder
  2 teaspoons baking soda
1/2 teaspoon salt
  1 can (16 ounces) *or* 2 cups chocolate
    frosting

Place the butter, oats and cocoa in a mixing bowl; add boiling water and stir until butter is melted. Add brown sugar and vanilla; mix well. Add eggs, one at a time, beating well after each addition. Combine the flour, baking powder, baking soda and salt; add to oat mixture just until combined.

Pour into a greased 13-in. x 9-in. x 2-in. baking pan. Bake at 375° for 30-35 minutes or until a toothpick inserted near the center comes out clean. Cool completely on a wire rack. Frost with chocolate frosting. **Yield:** 12-16 servings.

CRUSTLESS PEAR PIE

Eunice Gutbrod, Greenfield, Wisconsin

Having an abundance of pears one summer, I came up with this pleasing pie using that fresh fruit.

✓ Uses less fat, sugar or salt. Includes Nutritional Analysis and Diabetic Exchanges.

  4 cups sliced peeled pears
1/2 cup sugar
  1 tablespoon cornstarch
1/4 teaspoon ground cinnamon
1/4 teaspoon ground ginger
1/4 teaspoon ground nutmeg
  2 tablespoons chopped almonds
3/4 cup all-purpose flour
1/3 cup packed brown sugar
1/2 teaspoon baking powder
1/8 teaspoon salt
1/4 cup cold butter *or* stick margarine

In a bowl, combine the pears, sugar, cornstarch, cinnamon, ginger and nutmeg; toss to coat. Trans-

fer to a 9-in. pie plate coated with nonstick cooking spray. Sprinkle with almonds.

In a bowl, combine the flour, brown sugar, baking powder and salt; cut in butter until crumbly. Sprinkle over the top. Bake at 350° for 40-45 minutes or until golden. Cool on a wire rack. Store in the refrigerator. **Yield:** 8 servings.

Nutritional Analysis: One slice equals 242 calories, 7 g fat (4 g saturated fat), 16 mg cholesterol, 114 mg sodium, 44 g carbohydrate, 3 g fiber, 2 g protein. **Diabetic Exchanges:** 1 starch, 2 fruit, 1 fat.

PUMPKIN CRUNCH PARFAITS

(Pictured above)

Lorraine Darocha, Berkshire, Massachusetts

Here's a fun dessert that your youngsters can help make. It's a great treat for Halloween or Thanksgiving.

   3/4 cup cold milk
    1 package (3.4 ounces) instant vanilla
      pudding mix
    2 cups whipped topping
    1 cup cooked *or* canned pumpkin
  1/2 teaspoon pumpkin pie spice
    1 cup chopped pecans
1-1/2 cups crushed gingersnaps (about 32
      cookies)
Additional whipped topping

In a mixing bowl, beat milk and pudding mix on low speed for 2 minutes. Stir in whipped topping, pumpkin and pumpkin pie spice; mix well. Fold in pecans. Spoon half of the mixture into parfait glasses; top with half of the gingersnap crumbs. Repeat layers. Top with additional whipped topping. **Yield:** 6 servings.

FANTASTIC FRUIT PIES are
perfect for everyday appetites
and special occasions alike.

SLICE OF HEAVEN. Clockwise from bottom left: Dutch Apricot Pie (p. 128), Sweet Apple Pie (p. 125), Fluffy Strawberry Meringue Pie (p. 124), Glazed Pineapple Pie (p. 125) and Very Lemony Meringue Pie (p. 128).

DUTCH APRICOT PIE

(Pictured on page 126)

Joanne Hutmacher, Lemoore, California

I freeze several bagfuls of apricots when they are in season, thinking of this pie all the while. At holiday time, there's nothing like a luscious taste of summer.

　　3/4 cup sugar
　　2 tablespoons quick-cooking tapioca
　　4 cups sliced fresh apricots (about 16)
　　1 tablespoon lemon juice
Pastry for single-crust pie (9 inches)
TOPPING:
　　2/3 cup all-purpose flour
　　1/2 cup sugar
　　1/2 cup chopped pecans, toasted
　　1/4 cup butter *or* margarine, melted

In a bowl, combine sugar and tapioca; mix well. Add apricots and lemon juice; toss to coat. Let stand for 15 minutes. Line a 9-in. pie plate with pastry. Trim pastry to 1/2 in. beyond edge of plate; flute edges. Pour filling into crust.

In a small bowl, combine flour, sugar and pecans. Stir in butter. Sprinkle over filling. Cover edges loosely with foil. Bake at 350° for 15 minutes. Remove foil; bake 25-30 minutes longer or until crust is golden brown and filling is bubbly. Cool on a wire rack. Store in the refrigerator. **Yield:** 6-8 servings.

VERY LEMONY MERINGUE PIE

(Pictured on page 127)

Betty Bradley, Sebring, Florida

As a winter resident of Florida, I have access to juicy tree-fresh lemons. They're at their zesty best in this mouth-watering family pie recipe.

1-1/4 cups sugar
　　1/3 cup cornstarch
　　1 cup cold water
　　3 egg yolks
　　1 cup lemon juice
　　3 tablespoons butter *or* margarine
　　1 pastry shell (9 inches), baked
MERINGUE:
　　1 tablespoon cornstarch
　　1/3 cup cold water
　　3 egg whites
　　1 teaspoon vanilla extract
Dash salt
　　6 tablespoons sugar

In a saucepan, combine sugar and cornstarch. Stir in water until smooth. Cook and stir over medium heat until thickened and bubbly. Reduce heat; cook and stir 2 minutes longer. Remove from heat. Stir a small amount of hot filling into egg yolks. Return all to pan, stirring constantly. Bring to a gentle boil; cook and stir 2 minutes longer.

Remove from the heat. Add lemon juice and butter; stir until butter is melted and mixture is blended. Pour hot filling into pastry shell.

In a saucepan, combine cornstarch and water until smooth. Cook and stir over medium-low heat until mixture is thickened, about 2 minutes. Remove from the heat. In a mixing bowl, beat egg whites, vanilla and salt until foamy. Gradually beat in sugar, 1 tablespoon at a time, on medium speed until soft peaks form and sugar is dissolved. Gradually beat in cornstarch mixture, 1 tablespoon at a time, on high until stiff peaks form.

Spread evenly over hot filling, sealing edges to crust. Bake at 325° for 18-20 minutes or until meringue is golden. Cool on a wire rack for 1 hour. Refrigerate pie for at least 3 hours before serving. Refrigerate leftovers. **Yield:** 6-8 servings.

RED RASPBERRY MOUSSE DESSERT

(Pictured below)

Edna Hoffman, Hebron, Indiana

When I need a light and refreshing finish to a special meal, I make this fluffy, fruity mousse. Ladyfingers add an elegant look to this pretty dessert.

　　2 packages (3 ounces *each*) raspberry gelatin
1-3/4 cups boiling water
　　2 packages (10 ounces *each*) frozen sweetened raspberries, thawed
　　2 cups whipping cream, whipped
　　23 ladyfingers

Patriotic Fruit Pizza

HERE's a pie-in-the-sky idea from our Test Kitchen—a dessert pizza you decorate like a high-flyin' flag! It's simple to make, so you can quickly raise one for the Fourth of July or a summer picnic.

PATRIOTIC PIZZA

- 1 cup all-purpose flour
- 1/2 cup confectioners' sugar
- 1/2 cup cold butter *or* margarine
- 2 packages (8 ounces *each*) cream cheese, softened
- 1 cup sugar
- 1 teaspoon vanilla extract
- 1/2 teaspoon lemon juice

- 2 cups halved fresh strawberries
- 1/2 cup fresh *or* frozen blueberries

In a bowl, combine the flour and confectioners' sugar; cut in butter until crumbly. Press onto a greased 12-in. pizza pan. Bake at 325° for 10-15 minutes or until lightly browned. Let cool.

Meanwhile, in a mixing bowl, beat the cream cheese and sugar. Add vanilla and lemon juice, mixing until smooth. Spread 1 cup over the crust. Set the remaining cream cheese mixture aside.

Arrange five rows of strawberries on top of the pizza to create red stripes. Place the blueberries in the upper left corner.

Cut a hole in the corner of a plastic or pastry bag; insert a star pastry tip #21. Fill the bag with the reserved cream cheese mixture. Pipe a zigzag pattern between the rows of strawberries for the white stripes. **Yield:** 1 pizza.

Fresh mint and raspberries and additional whipped cream, optional

In a large bowl, dissolve gelatin in boiling water. Stir in raspberries. Refrigerate until partially thickened. Fold in whipped cream.

Arrange the ladyfingers with rounded side out around the sides of an ungreased 9-in. springform pan. Carefully spoon the raspberry mixture into pan. Cover and refrigerate until firm. Garnish with mint, raspberries and whipped cream if desired. **Yield:** 12 servings.

RAISIN CARROT CAKE

Joyce Donald, Star City, Saskatchewan

This lightened-up moist cake is a favorite with my husband and son.

✓ Uses less fat, sugar or salt. Includes Nutritional Analysis and Diabetic Exchanges.

- 2 egg whites
- 3/4 cup sugar
- 1/2 cup unsweetened applesauce
- 1/4 cup canola oil
- 1-1/2 cups finely shredded carrots
- 1/2 cup reduced-fat vanilla yogurt
- 1/4 cup water
- 1 cup all-purpose flour, *divided*
- 1 cup whole wheat flour
- 2 teaspoons ground cinnamon
- 1-1/2 teaspoons baking soda
- 1/4 teaspoon salt
- 1/4 teaspoon ground nutmeg
- 1/4 teaspoon ground cloves
- 3/4 cup raisins
- 1-1/2 teaspoons confectioners' sugar

In a mixing bowl, beat egg whites until foamy. Add sugar, applesauce and oil; mix well. Stir in the carrots, yogurt and water. Set aside 1 tablespoon all-purpose flour. Combine the whole wheat flour, cinnamon, baking soda, salt, nutmeg, cloves and remaining all-purpose flour; add to batter and mix just until moistened. Toss raisins with reserved flour; stir into batter.

Pour into a 9-in. square baking pan coated with nonstick cooking spray. Bake at 325° for 50-55 minutes or until a toothpick comes out clean. Cool on a wire rack. Sprinkle with confectioners' sugar. **Yield:** 9 servings.

Nutritional Analysis: One piece equals 279 calories, 7 g fat (1 g saturated fat), 1 mg cholesterol, 306 mg sodium, 52 g carbohydrate, 4 g fiber, 5 g protein. **Diabetic Exchanges:** 2-1/2 starch, 1 fruit, 1 fat.

SUGAR-FREE CHOCOLATE ECLAIRS

(Pictured below)

Dorothy Longhurst, Sandy, Utah

Family and friends are in for a treat when you serve them these luscious eclairs. No one can even tell they're sugar free.

✓ **Uses less fat, sugar or salt. Includes Nutritional Analysis and Diabetic Exchanges.**

    1/2 cup water
    1/4 cup butter (no substitutes)
    1/2 cup all-purpose flour
      2 eggs
VANILLA FILLING:
 1-1/4 cups cold fat-free milk
    1/4 teaspoon vanilla extract
      1 package (1 ounce) sugar-free instant
        vanilla pudding mix
      1 cup fat-free whipped topping
CHOCOLATE TOPPING:
 1-1/2 cups cold fat-free milk
      1 package (1.4 ounces) sugar-free instant
        chocolate pudding mix

In a saucepan, bring water and butter to a boil. Add flour all at once, stirring until a smooth ball forms. Remove from the heat; let stand for 5 minutes. Add eggs, one at a time, beating well after each addition. Continue beating until mixture is smooth and shiny. Transfer to a resealable plastic bag; seal.

Cut a 1-in. hole in one corner of bag. Pipe eight 3-1/2-in. logs onto an ungreased baking sheet. Bake at 450° for 10 minutes. Reduce heat to 400°; bake 15-20 minutes longer or until golden brown. Transfer to a wire rack. Immediately cut a slit in each to allow steam to escape; cool. Split and set the tops aside. Remove soft dough from the inside with a fork.

For filling, in a mixing bowl, beat milk, vanilla and pudding mix on low speed for 2 minutes or until thickened. Fold in whipped topping; set aside. In another mixing bowl, beat milk and chocolate pudding mix for 2 minutes or until thickened. Spoon vanilla filling into eclairs; replace tops. Spread with chocolate topping. **Yield:** 8 eclairs.

Nutritional Analysis: One eclair equals 170 calories, 7 g fat (4 g saturated fat), 70 mg cholesterol, 418 mg sodium, 19 g carbohydrate, trace fiber, 6 g protein. **Diabetic Exchanges:** 1-1/2 starch, 1 fat.

EASY RHUBARB DESSERT

(Pictured above)

Mildred Mesick, Richmond, New York

This is a very tasty and attractive dessert. It's great served warm with ice cream.

      4 cups sliced fresh *or* frozen rhubarb
      1 package (3 ounces) raspberry gelatin
    1/3 cup sugar
      1 package (18-1/4 ounces) yellow *or*
        white cake mix
      1 cup water
    1/3 cup butter *or* margarine, melted
Ice cream, optional

Place rhubarb in a greased 13-in. x 9-in. x 2-in. baking dish. Sprinkle with the gelatin, sugar and cake mix. Pour water evenly over dry ingredients; drizzle with butter. Bake at 350° for 1 hour or until rhubarb is tender. Serve with ice cream if desired. **Yield:** 16-20 servings.

APPLE CRISP

Kelly Pember, Wheeler, Wisconsin

I love apples! This crisp featuring that fruit is always a hit with my family.

6 cups sliced peeled apples
1 cup sugar
3/4 cup all-purpose flour
1 teaspoon ground cinnamon
1/2 cup cold butter *or* margarine
Ice cream, optional

Place the apples in a greased 9-in. square baking dish. In a bowl, combine the sugar, flour and cinnamon; cut in butter until crumbly. Sprinkle over apples. Bake at 375° for 45-50 minutes or until golden brown and bubbly around the edges. Serve with ice cream if desired. **Yield:** 8 servings.

BERRY RHUBARB SAUCE

Pat Burnley, Lancaster, Pennsylvania

When those first tender shoots start turning our backyard rhubarb patches pink, I know spring is really here. This rhubarb sauce is a favorite.

4 cups chopped fresh *or* frozen rhubarb
(1/2-inch pieces)
1/2 cup sugar
1/4 cup red raspberry preserves
Ice cream, pound cake *or* fresh fruit, optional

In a saucepan, bring rhubarb and sugar to a boil, stirring occasionally. Reduce heat; simmer, uncovered, until rhubarb is softened, about 6 minutes. Stir in preserves; heat through. Serve over ice cream, pound cake or fresh fruit. **Yield:** about 2 cups.

STRAWBERRY SUNSHINE CAKE

(Pictured at right)

Rosemary Binette, Les Cedres, Quebec

With fluffy whipped topping frosting and a fresh strawberry filling and garnish, this impressive three-layer sponge cake is a scrumptious summer dessert. For best results, be sure to slice it with a serrated knife.

1 cup egg whites (about 8)
1/2 teaspoon cream of tartar
1/2 teaspoon salt
1-1/2 cups sugar, *divided*
5 egg yolks
2 tablespoons water
1/2 teaspoon *each* almond, lemon and
vanilla extracts
1 cup all-purpose flour
FILLING:
1 package (3 ounces) strawberry gelatin
1 cup boiling water
1/2 cup ice water
1 pint fresh strawberries, sliced
1 carton (8 ounces) frozen whipped
topping, thawed, *divided*
Additional strawberries for garnish

In a large mixing bowl, beat egg whites, cream of tartar and salt until soft peaks form. Gradually add 1 cup sugar, a tablespoon at a time, beating until stiff peaks form; set aside.

In another bowl, beat egg yolks until slightly thickened, about 5 minutes. Gradually add remaining sugar, beating until thick and lemon-colored. Blend in water and extracts. Sift flour over batter; beat until smooth. Fold in egg whites just until blended.

Spoon into an ungreased 10-in. tube pan. Cut through batter with a knife to remove air pockets; smooth the top. Bake at 325° for 50-55 minutes or until cake springs back when lightly touched. Immediately invert pan; cool completely.

In a bowl, dissolve gelatin in boiling water. Add ice water and stir. Place bowl in ice water for about 5 minutes or until slightly thickened. Fold in strawberries and 1/2 cup whipped topping.

Run a knife around sides of cake to remove. Split horizontally into three layers; place bottom layer on a serving plate. Spread with half of the gelatin mixture. Repeat. Top with remaining cake layer. Frost top and sides with remaining whipped topping. Garnish with strawberries. Refrigerate leftovers. **Yield:** 12-16 servings.

Cooking for Two

Satisfy hearty appetities with these small-serving recipes that won't leave you with a week's worth of leftovers.

ORANGE CHICKEN SALAD

(Pictured at left)

Stephanie Bishop, Winston-Salem, North Carolina

The refreshing taste of orange makes this chicken salad different from all the others I've tried over the years.

2 cups cubed cooked chicken
1/2 cup diced celery
1/2 cup diced green pepper
1 tablespoon finely chopped onion
1/2 cup mayonnaise
1 tablespoon orange juice
1/8 teaspoon grated orange peel
1/8 teaspoon salt
Lettuce leaves, optional

In a bowl, combine the chicken, celery, green pepper and onion. Add mayonnaise, orange juice and peel and salt; mix well. Cover and refrigerate until serving. Serve on lettuce if desired. **Yield:** 2 servings.

BUTTERMILK SCONES

(Pictured at left)

Ruth LeBlanc, Nashua, New Hampshire

I was happy to discover this scone recipe. The small quantity is just what I was looking for in my quest for recipes for two.

1 cup all-purpose flour
2 tablespoons plus 1/2 teaspoon sugar, divided
1 teaspoon baking powder
1/8 teaspoon baking soda
1/4 cup cold butter *or* margarine
1/3 cup buttermilk
3 tablespoons raisins *or* dried currants
1/4 teaspoon grated lemon *or* orange peel
1/8 teaspoon ground cinnamon

In a bowl, combine the flour, 2 tablespoons sugar, baking powder and baking soda. Cut in butter until mixture resembles coarse crumbs. Stir in the buttermilk, raisins and lemon peel until a soft dough forms. Turn onto a lightly floured surface; knead gently 5-6 times or until no longer sticky.

On a lightly greased baking sheet, pat dough into a 5-in. circle about 3/4 in. thick. Score the top, making six wedges. Combine cinnamon and remaining sugar; sprinkle over the top. Bake at 375° for 23-25 minutes or until golden brown. Break into wedges. Serve warm. **Yield:** 6 scones.

OLD-FASHIONED CHOCOLATE SODA

(Pictured at left)

Dawn Sams, Grayslake, Illinois

We enjoy making this old-fashioned soda fountain specialty at home. It's a favorite treat for my grandchildren.

6 tablespoons chocolate syrup
2 tablespoons whipped cream in a can
2-1/2 cups cold carbonated water
4 scoops ice cream of your choice

For each serving, place 3 tablespoons chocolate syrup in a 16-oz. glass. Stir in 1 tablespoon of whipped cream and 1-1/4 cups water until foamy. Add two scoops of ice cream. **Yield:** 2 servings.

CHILLED ASPARAGUS SALAD

(Pictured at left)

Kathy Willis, Pryor, Oklahoma

This salad is easy to prepare, and the cool tangy change from eating asparagus as a hot side dish makes one sit up and take notice.

1/2 pound fresh asparagus, trimmed
1/2 cup water
2 tablespoons ranch salad dressing
2 tablespoons shredded cheddar cheese
2 tablespoons slivered almonds, toasted

Place asparagus in a skillet; add water. Bring to a boil. Reduce heat; cover and simmer for 3-4 minutes or until crisp-tender. Rinse in cold water; drain well. Cover and refrigerate for at least 1 hour or until chilled.

To serve, drizzle asparagus with salad dressing. Sprinkle with cheese and almonds. **Yield:** 2 servings.

SKILLET CHICKEN

(Pictured above)

Wandalean Reagan, Baltimore, Maryland

I found this basic recipe in a package of chicken breasts purchased from the grocery store. I made changes because my husband and I like more sauce than the original recipe provided.

　　2　boneless skinless chicken breast halves
　　1　tablespoon butter *or* margarine
　1/2　cup chopped onion
　　1　can (14-1/2 ounces) diced tomatoes, undrained
　　1　tablespoon Worcestershire sauce
　1/2　teaspoon ground mustard
　1/2　teaspoon salt
　1/8 to 1/4　teaspoon pepper
Hot cooked rice

In a skillet, brown chicken in butter. Add onion; saute until tender. Stir in the tomatoes, Worcestershire sauce, mustard, salt and pepper. Bring to a boil over medium heat. Reduce heat; cover and simmer for 15 minutes or until chicken juices run clear. Serve over rice. **Yield:** 2 servings.

PEANUTTY CARROTS

Ursula Ogden, Laurelville, Ohio

Even people who think they don't like carrots will eat and enjoy this dish. When I was working as housekeeper and cook for a lawyer years ago, he was so pleased with this recipe that he insisted I cook it whenever he entertained. He called it the "specialty of the house".

　　2　cups julienned carrots
　1/2　cup water
　1/4　teaspoon salt
　　2　tablespoons chopped salted peanuts
　　1　tablespoon butter *or* margarine
　　2　teaspoons sugar
Pepper to taste

In a saucepan, bring carrots, water and salt to a boil. Reduce heat; cover and cook for 10 minutes or until carrots are crisp-tender. Drain. Add the peanuts, butter, sugar and pepper; toss to coat. **Yield:** 2 servings.

GLAZED STRAWBERRY SUNDAES

(Pictured below)

Claudette Mogle, Federal Way, Washington

I have had a lifelong affinity for anything strawberry. This recipe came from a friend many years ago, but I adapted it to suit our particular tastes. It's quick and easy to prepare but is an impressive dessert to serve company. For variety, I've also used fresh peaches or nectarines with equally delicious results.

1-1/3 cups halved fresh strawberries
3 tablespoons butter *or* margarine
4 teaspoons sugar
1/4 teaspoon grated lime peel
1/4 teaspoon orange extract
Vanilla *or* chocolate ice cream

In a skillet over medium heat, cook and stir the strawberries in butter for 1 minute. Add the sugar, lime peel and orange extract. Cook 1-2 minutes longer or until mixture is heated through. Serve over vanilla or chocolate ice cream. **Yield:** 2 servings.

ZUCCHINI WITH PECANS

Wanda Penton, Amite, Louisiana

I came across this vegetable recipe in my grandmother's collection a number of years ago. At first, I only cooked it for Sunday dinners or special occasions. But my family enjoyed it so much, I make it all the time now. Toasted pecans add a nice crunch to this simple-to-make side dish.

1-1/2 cups julienned zucchini
1 teaspoon olive *or* vegetable oil
1/4 teaspoon garlic salt
Dash pepper
2 tablespoons chopped pecans, toasted

In a skillet, saute zucchini in oil for 5 minutes or until crisp-tender. Sprinkle with garlic salt, pepper and pecans. Serve immediately. **Yield:** 2 servings.

FRENCH SALAD DRESSING

Carolyn Ozment, Gaylesville, Alabama

This simple dressing has served me well for many years. Using this basic recipe, I can easily make simple variations, usually with ingredients I have on hand. As a result, I have always made my own salad dressings. It's delicious served over a variety of different salad greens.

1/4 cup vegetable oil
2 tablespoons vinegar
3/4 teaspoon salt
1 garlic clove, minced
Dash pepper
Salad greens

In a jar with a tight-fitting lid, combine the oil, vinegar, salt, garlic and pepper; shake well. Serve over salad greens. **Yield:** about 1/3 cup.

CARAMEL DUMPLING PUDDING
(Pictured above)

Marianne Ryan, Lyons, Colorado

I found this recipe handwritten into an old cookbook of my mom's, who was born in 1897. We like to eat this old-fashioned dessert warm, topped with cream, ice cream or whipped cream.

1 cup water
3/4 cup packed brown sugar, *divided*
1 tablespoon butter *or* margarine
1 teaspoon vanilla extract
1/2 cup all-purpose flour
1/2 teaspoon baking powder
Pinch *each* nutmeg and salt
1/4 cup evaporated milk
1/2 cup raisins
1/4 cup chopped walnuts
Ice cream

In a small saucepan over medium heat, bring water and 1/2 cup brown sugar to a boil. Remove from the heat; stir in butter and vanilla until butter is melted. Pour into a greased 1-qt. baking dish; set aside.

In a bowl, combine the flour, baking powder, nutmeg, salt and milk just until blended. Stir in the remaining brown sugar. Fold in raisins and walnuts. Drop by spoonfuls over the top of the sauce. Bake, uncovered, at 350° for 30 minutes or until bubbly and golden brown. Spoon into dishes. Top with ice cream. **Yield:** 2 servings.

Pork Chops with Tomatoes and Peppers

(Pictured at right)

Esther Lux, Lead, South Dakota

My mother created delicious dishes based on whatever was in the refrigerator or on the shelf. This recipe is one she tried, and it became our traditional Sunday dinner. She increased the ingredients proportionately to the number of people she invited after church.

- 2 bone-in pork loin chops (3/4 inch thick)
- 1 tablespoon butter *or* margarine
- 1/4 teaspoon salt
- 1/8 teaspoon pepper
- 4 thin onion slices
- 4 thin green pepper rings
- 4 thin fresh tomato slices
- 1/8 teaspoon dried basil
- 1/8 teaspoon dried thyme
- Additional pepper

In a skillet, brown pork chops in butter on each side. Season with salt and pepper. Layer with onion, green pepper and tomato. Sprinkle with basil, thyme and additional pepper. Reduce heat; cover and cook for 20 minutes or until meat juices run clear. **Yield:** 2 servings.

Scalloped Potatoes

(Pictured at right)

Marilyn MacIntyre, Rome, New York

After our two children became adults and left home, I continued to cook meals as usual. Soon we became tired of having to eat the same leftovers several days in a row, so I sat down and came up with this pared-down recipe.

- 4-1/2 teaspoons all-purpose flour
- 3/4 cup milk
- 1/4 teaspoon salt
- Dash pepper
- 2 medium baking potatoes, peeled and thinly sliced
- 1/2 cup thinly sliced onion
- 1/2 cup soft bread crumbs
- 1 tablespoon butter *or* margarine, melted

In a saucepan, combine flour, milk, salt and pepper until smooth. Bring to a boil; cook and stir for 1-2 minutes or until thickened. In a greased 1-qt. baking dish, layer half of the potatoes, onion and white sauce. Repeat layers. Toss bread crumbs and butter; sprinkle over top. Cover and bake at 375° for 50-55 minutes or until potatoes are tender. **Yield:** 2 servings.

Refreshing Fruit Salad

(Pictured at right)

Annette Hemsath, Sutherlin, Oregon

I keep cans of fruit in the refrigerator so they'll be cold whenever we want to be refreshed with this salad. My husband loves it.

- 1 can (11 ounces) mandarin oranges, drained
- 1 can (8 ounces) pineapple chunks, drained
- 1 medium ripe banana, sliced
- 1/2 cup halved seedless grapes
- 3 tablespoons mayonnaise
- 3 tablespoons sour cream
- 1 tablespoon honey
- 1/4 cup chopped walnuts
- 1/4 cup flaked coconut, optional

In a bowl, combine the fruit. In another bowl, combine the mayonnaise, sour cream and honey. Pour over fruit and toss to coat. Cover and refrigerate. Just before serving, stir in walnuts and coconut if desired. **Yield:** 2 servings.

Mini Zucchini Bread

(Pictured at right)

Ruth Lear, Bradenton, Florida

I've made this bread many times and have given it as gifts for Christmas. The molasses makes it darker than most zucchini breads but gives it a rich flavor.

- 2 eggs
- 3/4 cup sugar
- 1/2 cup vegetable oil
- 1-1/2 teaspoons molasses
- 1-1/2 teaspoons vanilla extract
- 1 cup shredded zucchini
- 1-1/2 cups all-purpose flour
- 1 teaspoon baking soda
- 1/2 teaspoon salt
- 1/2 teaspoon ground cinnamon
- 1/4 teaspoon baking powder
- 1/2 cup chopped pecans

In a mixing bowl, beat the eggs, sugar, oil, molasses and vanilla. Add zucchini; mix well. Combine the flour, baking soda, salt, cinnamon and baking powder; stir into zucchini mixture just until moistened. Stir in nuts.

Transfer to two greased and floured 5-3/4-in. x 3-in. x 2-in. loaf pans. Bake at 350° for 38-42 minutes or until a toothpick inserted near the center comes out clean. Cool for 10 minutes before removing from pans to a wire rack. **Yield:** 2 loaves.

I'm a creative cook, so I came up with this simple recipe based on how I remember my grandma making this dish when I was young.

- 1/4 cup chopped onion
- 1/4 cup chopped green pepper
- 2 garlic cloves, minced
- 2 tablespoons olive *or* vegetable oil
- 4 eggs

Salt and pepper to taste

- 1/2 cup cubed fully cooked ham
- 1/4 cup grated Parmesan cheese

In a 6-in. broiler-proof skillet, saute the onion, green pepper and garlic in oil. Reduce heat to medium. In a bowl, beat eggs, salt and pepper. Add egg mixture and ham to vegetables.

As eggs set, lift edges, letting uncooked portion flow underneath. When eggs are nearly set, sprinkle with cheese. Broil 4-5 in. from the heat for 1-2 minutes or until eggs are completely set. **Yield:** 2 servings.

FRENCH VEAL CHOPS
(Pictured above)

Betty Biehl, Mertztown, Pennsylvania

I have been cooking for just my husband and me for the last 30 years. I come up with new recipes for two all the time. This recipe works well when you've had a busy day and can't spend much time cooking, but you still want a very special meal.

- 2 veal chops (1 inch thick)
- 1/2 teaspoon salt

Dash pepper

- 1 tablespoon vegetable oil
- 1/2 cup chopped onion
- 2 tablespoons butter *or* margarine, divided
- 1/4 cup chicken broth
- 1/3 cup dry bread crumbs
- 2 tablespoons grated Parmesan cheese

Sprinkle veal chops with salt and pepper. In a skillet, brown chops on both sides in oil. Sprinkle onion into a greased shallow baking dish; dot with 1 tablespoon butter. Top with chops; drizzle with broth. Melt remaining butter; toss with bread crumbs and Parmesan cheese. Sprinkle over top.

Bake, uncovered, at 350° for 30-35 minutes or until meat is no longer pink and a meat thermometer reads 160°. **Yield:** 2 servings.

PARMESAN HAM FRITTATA

T. Lentini, Rogue River, Oregon

This egg dish is true to my Italian heritage. Italians make frittatas with many combinations of ingredients.

CHEESY POTATOES
(Pictured below)

Jessica Ryan, Victoria, Texas

I created this recipe a few years ago for a fifth-grade school project. I love being in the kitchen with my mom and helping her with meal preparations. My whole family was impressed with the few additions I made to these potatoes to make them extra tasty.

2 medium potatoes, peeled and cut into
   1/2-inch cubes
1/2 cup water
1/2 cup shredded cheddar *or* Swiss cheese
1 tablespoon butter *or* margarine
1/2 teaspoon seasoned salt
Crumbled cooked bacon

In a saucepan over medium heat, bring potatoes and water to a boil. Reduce heat; simmer, uncovered, for 10 minutes or until potatoes are tender. Drain. Stir in cheese, butter and seasoned salt. Cook for 2-3 minutes or until the cheese and butter are melted. Sprinkle with bacon. **Yield:** 2 servings.

GRANDMA'S DATE BARS

Marilyn Reid, Cherry Creek, New York

These nicely textured bars are delicious. My great-grandmother made these bars, and the recipe has come down through the generations. Now my children are making them.

1 cup sugar
1 cup all-purpose flour
1 teaspoon baking powder
1/2 teaspoon salt
1 cup chopped dates
1 cup chopped walnuts
3 eggs, well beaten
Confectioners' sugar

In a bowl, combine the first seven ingredients. Transfer to a greased 8-in. square baking pan. Bake at 350° for 25 minutes or until a toothpick inserted near the center comes out clean. Cool on a wire rack. Dust with confectioners' sugar. Cut into squares. **Yield:** 16 servings.

SPICY TOMATO COOLER

Susan Zambito, New Orleans, Louisiana

The blend of flavors in this recipe creates a very refreshing drink. I often serve it for breakfast, but in warm weather, it suits any time of day.

1 can (12 ounces) V8 *or* tomato juice,
   chilled
1/4 cup beef broth
1/4 teaspoon pepper
1/8 teaspoon celery salt
1/8 teaspoon Worcestershire sauce
Dash hot pepper sauce, optional

In a small pitcher, combine the first five ingredients. Add hot pepper sauce if desired. Serve over ice if desired. **Yield:** 2 servings.

BAKED PEARS
(Pictured above)

Betty Schledorn, Ocala, Florida

This dessert is versatile—you can serve it warm or cold and for any size group. Chilled pears can be dressed up with a dollop of whipped topping, fruit-filled yogurt or ice cream.

2 medium ripe pears, peeled and halved
4 teaspoons butter *or* margarine
1 teaspoon lemon juice
2 teaspoons sugar
1/4 teaspoon ground cinnamon
4 teaspoons orange marmalade

Place pear halves, cut side up, in a shallow 1-qt. baking dish. Place butter in the center of each; drizzle with lemon juice. Combine sugar and cinnamon; sprinkle over pears. Top with marmalade. Cover and bake at 350° for 15-20 minutes or until heated through. **Yield:** 2 servings.

THE PERFECT SIZE

DO YOU dine alone or cook for just yourself and one other person? There are appliances available that are suitable for your lifestyle, such as toaster ovens, countertop grills and mini coffeemakers and food processors.

Cooking for Two

DILLED SOLE WITH ALMONDS

(Pictured at left)

Bonnie Baumgardner, Sylva, North Carolina

I make this attractive and delicious dish fairly often because I can have it ready in less than half an hour. The seasonings blend for a nice flavor.

 2 tablespoons cornmeal
 1/4 teaspoon salt
 1/8 teaspoon lemon-pepper seasoning
 2 sole, flounder *or* other whitefish fillets
 (about 3/4 pound)
 2 tablespoons butter *or* margarine, *divided*
 1/4 teaspoon dill weed
 3 tablespoons slivered almonds

In a shallow dish, combine the first three ingredients. Coat both sides of fillets with mixture. In a skillet, melt 1 tablespoon butter; stir in the dill. Add fillets; cook for 2-3 minutes on each side or until fish flakes easily with a fork. Remove and keep warm.

Add almonds and remaining butter to the skillet; cook and stir for 4 minutes or until lightly browned. Sprinkle over fish. **Yield:** 2 servings.

LEMON BASIL CARROTS

(Pictured at left)

Donna Smith, Palisade, Colorado

I discovered that the subtle taste of lemon really enhances the flavor of carrots. This recipe is a winner!

1-1/2 cups sliced carrots
 1 tablespoon butter *or* margarine
 1 tablespoon lemon juice
 1/2 teaspoon garlic salt, optional
 1/2 teaspoon dried basil
Dash pepper

In a saucepan, cook carrots in a small amount of water until tender. Drain and set aside. In the same pan, melt butter; stir in lemon juice, garlic salt if desired, basil and pepper. Return carrots to the pan and heat through. **Yield:** 2 servings.

SIMPLY FUDGY BROWNIES

(Pictured at left)

Marjorie Hoyt, Center Conway, New Hampshire

I don't know where I got this recipe, but I've had it for over 30 years. Adding chocolate chips was my idea. When my children were in school, I found out they were selling these brownies to their friends!

 1/4 cup baking cocoa
 1/2 cup vegetable oil
 2 eggs
 1 cup sugar
 1 teaspoon vanilla extract
 3/4 cup all-purpose flour
 1/8 teaspoon salt
 1/2 cup chopped walnuts
 1/2 cup milk chocolate chips

In a small bowl, combine cocoa and oil until smooth. In another bowl, beat eggs. Add the sugar, vanilla and cocoa mixture; mix well. Stir in flour and salt just until moistened. Fold in walnuts.

Pour into a greased 8-in. square baking pan; sprinkle with chocolate chips. Bake at 325° for 30 minutes or until a toothpick comes out clean. Cool on a wire rack. **Yield:** 16 brownies.

BANANA TOFFEE CREAM

(Pictured below)

Betty Ferguson, Edmonton, Alberta

I spotted this recipe in a magazine about 40 years ago. I recall when my preschool daughter and I were planning her upcoming birthday party, I asked her what kind of cake she wanted. She replied, "I don't want a cake…I want that 'brickle stuff'."

 1/2 cup whipping cream, whipped
 1/2 cup English toffee bits *or* almond
 brickle chips
 1 large ripe banana, sliced

Combine the whipped cream, toffee bits and banana. Spoon into parfait glasses or dishes. Cover and refrigerate until serving. **Yield:** 2 servings.

BANANA APPLE MUFFINS

Alice Muradliyan, Covina, California

This recipe makes just half a dozen light tasty muffins that stay moist. They're flavorful whether served plain, with butter and jam or dipped in cinnamon-sugar right out of the oven.

     3/4 cup old-fashioned oats
     1/2 cup all-purpose flour
       3 tablespoons sugar
       1 teaspoon baking powder
     1/4 teaspoon salt
     1/4 teaspoon ground allspice
     1/4 teaspoon ground cinnamon
       1 egg
     1/3 cup milk
       1 tablespoon vegetable oil
     1/2 cup grated peeled tart apple
     1/4 cup mashed ripe banana

In a bowl, combine the first seven ingredients. In another bowl, beat the egg, milk and oil. Stir into dry ingredients just until moistened. Fold in apple and banana. Fill greased muffin cups about three-fourths full.

Bake at 375° for 25-30 minutes or until a toothpick comes out clean. Cool for 5 minutes before removing from pan to a wire rack. **Yield:** 6 muffins.

APPLE FRITTERS

(Pictured above)

John Robbins, Springdale, Pennsylvania

This is an old Southern recipe. When we got home from a trip through the South years ago, I found the recipe among the brochures I brought back. I've been making theses fritters ever since.

       1 cup cake flour
     3/4 teaspoon baking powder
     1/4 teaspoon salt
       1 egg
     1/3 cup milk
     3/4 cup chopped peeled tart apple
       4 teaspoons butter *or* margarine, melted
       1 tablespoon sugar
       1 tablespoon orange juice
       2 teaspoons grated orange peel
     1/4 teaspoon vanilla extract
Oil for frying
Confectioners' sugar

In a bowl, combine the flour, baking powder and salt. In another bowl, beat egg and milk. Add the apple, butter, sugar, orange juice, peel and vanilla; mix well. Stir into dry ingredients just until moistened.

In an electric skillet or deep-fat fryer, heat 1/4 in. of oil to 375°. Drop batter by rounded tablespoons into oil. Fry until golden brown on both sides. Drain on paper towels. Dust with confectioners' sugar. Serve warm. **Yield:** 2-3 servings.

CHICKEN SALAD ON A TORTILLA

Shirley Banks, Westfield, Iowa

I started to fix fajitas for our supper one evening and ended up turning it into a salad instead. My husband was impressed with the concoction. Whenever I serve it for a quick lunch to unexpected company, they often request the recipe.

     1/2 pound boneless skinless chicken
           breasts, cut into thin strips
       2 flour tortillas (8 inches), warmed
     1/4 cup mayonnaise
       2 cups torn lettuce
       1 large tomato, cut into wedges
       4 to 6 thin slices red onion
       1 medium carrot, grated
     1/2 cup shredded cheddar cheese
Salsa, optional

In a skillet coated with nonstick cooking spray, cook chicken until no longer pink. To assemble, place tortillas on serving plates. Spread with mayonnaise. Top with lettuce, chicken, tomato, onion, carrot and cheese. Serve with salsa if desired. **Yield:** 2 servings.

Orange Gelatin Cups

Mrs. John Eaton, Palm Harbor, Florida

My mother used gelatin in so many good dishes, and as I got older, I did the same. This recipe is one I created. It's a refreshing accompaniment to any meal.

- 1 package (3 ounces) orange gelatin
- 1 cup boiling water
- 1 cup applesauce
- 1 can (11 ounces) mandarin oranges, drained

In a small bowl, dissolve gelatin in boiling water. Stir in applesauce. Pour into four dessert dishes. Add oranges. Cover and refrigerate for 2 hours or until set. **Yield:** 4 servings.

Crispy Potato Pancakes

(Pictured below)

Nancy Salinas, Grand Rapids, Minnesota

Here's a potato pancake that doesn't take much time to make and is just right for two people. Weekends become our time to relax and enjoy life, and this is one of our favorite treats.

- 2 medium potatoes, peeled
- 1 egg
- 1/3 cup chopped onion
- 1 tablespoon all-purpose flour

- 1/2 teaspoon salt
- 1/4 teaspoon pepper
- 1/4 teaspoon garlic powder
- Vegetable oil

Finely grate potatoes; drain any liquid. Place potatoes in a bowl. Add egg, onion, flour, salt, pepper and garlic powder; mix well. In a large skillet, heat 1/8 in. of oil over medium heat. Drop batter by 1/4 cupfuls; press lightly to flatten. Fry until golden brown on both sides. Serve immediately. **Yield:** 2 servings.

Cherry Cappuccino Sundaes

(Pictured above)

J.A. Rogg, Philadelphia, Pennsylvania

Most of my favorite recipes come from Reiman Publications, but this one I adapted from our local newspaper. It's a luscious beverage that's always a hit.

- 1/2 cup milk
- 3/4 cup pitted sweet cherries
- 1/2 teaspoon honey
- 1/4 teaspoon almond extract
- Coffee *or* cappuccino ice cream
- 2 tablespoons grated semisweet chocolate

In a blender, combine the first four ingredients; cover and process until blended. Serve over ice cream. Sprinkle with grated chocolate if desired. **Yield:** 2 servings.

BROCCOLI FETTUCCINE

(Pictured at right)

Dorothy Elliott, DeKalb, Illinois

This simple recipe is one of my favorites. The flavor is great, and it can be prepared in a very short time. Sometimes I add shrimp for a change and to make a heartier meal.

        4 ounces uncooked fettuccine
        2 cups broccoli florets
        3 tablespoons chopped green onions
        1 teaspoon vegetable oil
        1 can (14-1/2 ounces) stewed tomatoes
    1/4 to 1/2 teaspoon dried oregano
    1/2 teaspoon dried thyme
    1/4 teaspoon pepper
        2 teaspoons cornstarch
    1/4 cup water
        2 teaspoons grated Parmesan cheese

Cook fettuccine according to package directions. Meanwhile, in a skillet, stir-fry the broccoli and onions in oil for 3 minutes. Add the tomatoes, oregano, thyme and pepper. Bring to a boil. Reduce heat; simmer, uncovered, for 6 minutes.

Combine cornstarch and water until smooth; stir into skillet. Bring to a boil; cook for 1 minute. Drain fettuccine; top with broccoli mixture. Sprinkle with Parmesan cheese. **Yield:** 2 servings.

ONION 'N' TOMATO TOPPED MUFFINS

(Pictured at right)

Fran Skalisky, Sebeka, Minnesota

The idea of onion muffins came from a friend of ours who ate onion sandwiches every day. I felt they needed some extra flavor, so I experimented and came up with some simple additions.

        2 English muffins, split and toasted
        2 tablespoons butter *or* margarine
        4 sweet onion slices
        4 tomato slices
        1 cup (4 ounces) shredded mozzarella cheese
    1/2 teaspoon dried basil

Spread muffin halves with butter; top each with an onion slice, tomato slice, 1/4 cup cheese and basil. Broil 4 in. from the heat for 3-4 minutes or until the cheese is melted. Serve immediately. **Yield:** 2 servings.

SUMMER SQUASH BAKE

(Pictured at right)

Sue Joyce, Winston-Salem, North Carolina

My daughter-in-law created this recipe and shared it with me. I was delighted, since my husband and I were cutting down on fried foods and that's the way I had always prepared squash. This recipe is versatile…it can easily be adjusted to serve for a family dinner.

        1 pound yellow summer squash, chopped
    1/4 cup water
    1/4 cup chopped onion
    1/2 teaspoon salt
        1 egg, beaten
    1/4 cup dry bread crumbs
        2 tablespoons butter *or* margarine, melted
Pepper to taste
    1/2 cup shredded cheddar cheese

In a saucepan, combine the squash, water, onion and salt. Bring to a boil. Reduce heat; cover and simmer for 15-20 minutes or until squash is tender. Remove from the heat; cool.

Stir in the egg, bread crumbs, butter and pepper. Transfer to a greased 1-qt. baking dish; sprinkle with cheese. Bake, uncovered, at 350° for 30 minutes or until heated through and the cheese is melted. **Yield:** 2 servings.

CHIVE-ONION VEGETABLE DIP

Margie Wampler, Butler, Pennsylvania

When my dear friend served this dip at a party years ago, it was a great hit…so simple and versatile. I have served it with crackers, potato chips, vegetables and party rye bread.

    3/4 cup ricotta cheese
        3 tablespoons sour cream
        1 tablespoon milk
    1/4 teaspoon garlic salt
    1/8 teaspoon salt
Dash pepper
        1 tablespoon chopped green onion
        1 tablespoon snipped chives
Assorted raw vegetables

In a blender, combine the first six ingredients; cover and process until smooth. Stir in onion and chives. Cover and refrigerate for at least 1 hour. Serve with assorted raw vegetables. **Yield:** about 1 cup.

SPAGHETTI 'N' MEAT SAUCE

(Pictured at right)

Carolyn Ozment, Gaylesville, Alabama

This recipe has been a mainstay in our family. I began making it about 50 years ago. It is easily doubled or tripled, and the results are always delicious.

    1/2 pound ground beef
    1/4 cup chopped onion
      1 can (8 ounces) tomato sauce
      1 medium tomato, seeded and chopped
      1 teaspoon Worcestershire sauce
    1/2 to 1 teaspoon salt
    1/2 teaspoon Italian seasoning
    1/4 teaspoon pepper
Hot cooked spaghetti

In a skillet, cook beef and onion over medium heat until meat is no longer pink; drain. Add the tomato sauce, tomato, Worcestershire sauce, salt, Italian seasoning and pepper. Bring to a boil. Reduce heat; cover and simmer for 10 minutes or until heated through. Serve over spaghetti. **Yield:** 2 servings.

CREAM OF POTATO SOUP

(Pictured below)

Ruth Ann Stelfox, Raymond, Alberta

This soup is comfort food, especially welcome when the temperatures take a plunge. I serve this often...it's a simple supper that can be prepared in a short time.

      2 medium potatoes, peeled and diced
      1 cup water
      2 tablespoons chopped onion
      2 tablespoons butter *or* margarine
      2 tablespoons all-purpose flour
      3 cups milk
    1/2 teaspoon salt
    1/8 teaspoon celery salt
Dash pepper
Paprika and minced fresh parsley

Place the potatoes and water in a saucepan; bring to a boil over medium-high heat. Cover and cook until tender; drain and set aside.

In the same pan, saute onion in butter until tender. Stir in flour until blended. Gradually stir in milk. Bring to a boil; cook and stir for 2 minutes or until thickened. Reduce heat; add the potatoes, salt, celery salt and pepper. Cook for 2-3 minutes or until heated through. Garnish with parsley and paprika. **Yield:** 2 servings.

MINI APPLE PIE

Edna Hoffman, Hebron, Indiana

I like to try new recipes when apples are in season, and this one was a keeper. Golden Delicious apples are our favorite.

    1/4 cup golden raisins
    1/3 cup apple juice
      2 large Golden Delicious apples (about 1 pound), peeled and sliced
      2 tablespoons sugar
      2 tablespoons brown sugar
      1 tablespoon all-purpose flour
    1/4 teaspoon ground cinnamon
Pastry for a single-crust pie (9 inches)

In a saucepan over medium heat, cook raisins in apple juice for 5 minutes. Add apples; cook, uncovered, for 8-10 minutes or until tender. Remove from the heat; cool. Combine the sugars, flour and cinnamon; add to apple mixture.

On a floured surface, roll out half of the pastry to fit a 20-oz. baking dish. Place pastry in dish; trim to edge of dish. Add filling.

Roll out the remaining pastry to fit top of pie; place over filling. Trim, seal and flute edges. Cut slits in pastry. Bake at 400° for 35-40 minutes or until golden brown and bubbly. Cool on a wire rack. **Yield:** 2 servings.

WHIPPED CREAM BISCUITS

Linda Murrow, Aurora, Colorado

Since there is no shortening to cut in, these light, airy biscuits are quick and easy to make. Time the baking so that they're out of the oven when you sit down to eat.

1 cup all-purpose flour
1-1/2 teaspoons baking powder
1/4 teaspoon salt
1/2 cup whipping cream, whipped

In a bowl, combine the flour, baking powder and salt. Stir in cream. Turn dough onto a floured surface; knead 10 times. Roll to 3/4-in. thickness; cut with a 2-1/4-in. round biscuit cutter. Place on an ungreased baking sheet. Bake at 425° for 10 minutes or until lightly browned. Serve warm. **Yield:** 5 biscuits.

SPICED COFFEE WITH CREAM

Alpha Wilson, Roswell, New Mexico

This recipe was a wonderful discovery made 50 years ago. I serve it to company or as a treat for my husband and me.

1/4 cup evaporated milk
2-1/4 teaspoons confectioners' sugar
1/4 teaspoon ground cinnamon
1/8 teaspoon vanilla extract
1 cup hot strong brewed coffee
Ground nutmeg
2 cinnamon sticks

Pour milk into a small mixing bowl; place mixer beaters in the bowl. Cover and freeze for 30 minutes or until ice crystals begin to form.

Add the sugar, cinnamon and vanilla; beat until thick and fluffy. Pour about 1/2 cup into each cup. Add coffee; sprinkle with nutmeg. Serve immediately; garnish with cinnamon sticks if desired. **Yield:** 2 servings.

ROSEMARY-GARLIC CHICKEN AND VEGGIES

(Pictured below)

Robert Dessell, Pensacola, Florida

I enjoy cooking, and this has become a signature entree. My wife asks me to make it once a week. It's a simple dish to prepare, and the colorful vegetables make it attractive.

1/2 cup chopped sweet yellow pepper
1/2 cup chopped sweet red pepper
1 small onion, cut into wedges
1 small zucchini, halved and cut into 1/2-inch slices
2 tablespoons olive *or* vegetable oil, *divided*
2 boneless skinless chicken breast halves
2 garlic cloves, sliced
2 sprigs fresh rosemary

Place the peppers, onion and zucchini in a greased 1-qt. baking dish; drizzle with 1 tablespoon oil and toss to coat. In a skillet, brown chicken in remaining oil; place over vegetables. Top with garlic and rosemary. Bake, uncovered, at 400° for 20-25 minutes or until meat juices run clear. **Yield:** 2 servings.

Western Omelet Sandwich

(Pictured at left)

Jackie Kelly, Maple Shade, New Jersey

I created this recipe for my son, who has a ravenous appetite. It's a simple combination of ingredients that imparts the best of flavors.

  1/2 cup chopped onion
  1/2 cup diced green pepper
    1 tablespoon butter *or* margarine
    1 cup diced fully cooked ham
    1 tablespoon minced fresh parsley
    4 eggs
Salt and pepper to taste
    4 slices bread, toasted and buttered

In a large skillet over medium heat, saute onion and green pepper in butter until tender. Add ham and parsley. Beat eggs; pour into skillet. As eggs set, lift edges, letting uncooked portion flow underneath. When eggs are completely set, remove from the heat. Cut into wedges; serve on toast. **Yield:** 2 servings.

Macaroni 'n' Cheese for Two

(Pictured at left)

Mrs. O. Lick, Boyne Falls, Michigan

The sour cream and cheese gives this macaroni dish a distinctive taste of its own.

  1/3 cup sour cream
  1/3 cup milk
    1 cup (4 ounces) shredded sharp
      cheddar cheese
  3/4 cup elbow macaroni, cooked and
      drained
    2 tablespoons chopped onion, optional
Paprika

In a bowl, combine the sour cream and milk. Stir in the cheese, macaroni and onion if desired. Transfer to a greased 2-1/2-cup baking dish; sprinkle with paprika. Cover and bake at 325° for 25 minutes or until heated through. **Yield:** 2 servings.

Creamy Hot Cocoa

(Pictured at left)

Sara Swyers, Fayetteville, Georgia

Hot cocoa made school days memorable for me. Mom had it ready when I came home. It was a special time
for her and me to be together. Her tasty recipe is not overly sweet, but it's oh, so comforting.

    4 teaspoons sugar
    2 teaspoons baking cocoa
1-1/3 cups boiling water
  2/3 cup evaporated milk
  1/4 teaspoon vanilla extract
    2 tablespoons marshmallow creme

Divide sugar, cocoa and water between two mugs; stir until dissolved. Stir in milk, vanilla and marshmallow creme; mix well. Serve immediately. **Yield:** 2 servings.

Tropical Banana Splits

(Pictured below)

Ruth Peterson, Jenison, Michigan

When we kids were growing up, this was a special treat because my mother didn't make it that often.

    2 small bananas, sliced
    1 can (8-1/4 ounces) tropical fruit salad,
      chilled and drained
  1/2 cup whipped topping
  1/4 cup chopped walnuts

Place bananas in two dessert dishes; top with fruit salad. Garnish with a dollop of whipped topping and sprinkle with nuts. **Yield:** 2 servings.

SHRIMP DIJONNAISE

(Pictured at right)

Wanda Penton, Franklinton, Louisiana

This is a very easy dish to prepare for two. After the shrimp have marinated, dinner can be on the table in minutes! It's a refreshing departure from meat, and the mixture of flavors is delicious.

   1/2 cup lemon juice
   1/4 cup butter *or* margarine, melted
     2 tablespoons vegetable oil
     2 tablespoons Dijon mustard
     1 tablespoon Worcestershire sauce
     3 garlic cloves, minced
   3/4 pound uncooked large shrimp, peeled and deveined

In a large resealable plastic bag, combine the lemon juice, butter, oil, mustard, Worcestershire sauce and garlic. Add shrimp; seal bag and turn to coat. Refrigerate for 4 hours, turning occasionally. Drain and discard marinade. Broil shrimp 4 in. from the heat for 4 minutes or until pink. **Yield:** 2 servings.

COLORFUL FRIED RICE

(Pictured at right)

Linda Rae Lee, San Francisco, California

This recipe was given to me by a dear friend many years ago. The variety of ingredients makes it very colorful, and preparation is simple. I serve it often.

   1-1/2 cups cold cooked rice
     2 green onions, chopped
     1 small carrot, diced
   1/4 cup fresh *or* frozen peas, thawed
     4 teaspoons soy sauce
     1 tablespoon minced fresh parsley
     1 tablespoon vegetable oil
     1 egg, beaten
   Salt and pepper to taste

In a skillet, cook and stir the rice, onions, carrot, peas, soy sauce and parsley in oil until onions are tender and rice is heated through. Add egg; cook and stir until egg is completely set. Season with salt and pepper. **Yield:** 2 servings.

WARM SPINACH SALAD

(Pictured at right)

Helen Ward O'Key, Torrington, Connecticut

In addition to being a very tasty side-dish salad, this is one of my favorites to have for lunch. It makes just the right amount for two portions, so I can treat myself and a loved one to it as well.

     2 onion slices, separated into rings
   1/4 teaspoon garlic powder
     1 tablespoon butter *or* margarine
     1 cup sliced fresh mushrooms
     4 cups torn fresh spinach
   Salt to taste
     2 tablespoons raspberry vinaigrette dressing *or* vinaigrette of your choice
   1/2 cup salad croutons

In a skillet, saute onion and garlic powder in butter until onion is tender. Add mushrooms; cover and cook for 1 minute or until tender. Add spinach; sprinkle with salt and vinaigrette. Cover and cook for 1 minute or until spinach is wilted. Serve warm with croutons. **Yield:** 2 servings.

PEARS IN SPICED RAISIN SAUCE

(Pictured at right)

Davida Nicholson, Washington, Iowa

Because it's so easy to make, we enjoy this dessert often. I usually make extra, as it keeps well.

     1 can (8 ounces) sliced pears
   1/4 cup raisins
     1 teaspoon cornstarch
   1/4 teaspoon ground cinnamon
   1/8 teaspoon salt, optional
   1/8 teaspoon ground ginger
     3 tablespoons orange juice
   Vanilla ice cream

Drain pears, reserving 1/4 cup juice (discard remaining juice or save for another use); set the pears aside. In a saucepan, combine raisins and reserved juice. Bring to a boil. Reduce heat; cover and simmer for 5 minutes.

In a bowl, combine the cornstarch, cinnamon, salt if desired and ginger; stir in orange juice until smooth. Add to raisin mixture. Bring to a boil; cook and stir for 1-2 minutes or until thickened. Reduce heat. Add pears; cook and stir until heated through. Serve over ice cream. **Yield:** 2 servings.

FRUITFUL IDEAS

USE leftover canned fruit as a topping for pound cake or ice cream.

Freeze extra fruit juice in ice cube trays. These flavored ice cubes taste fabulous in lemon-lime soda or fruit punch.

Meals in Minutes

A hot home-cooked meal is just minutes away with these recipes that can be made in half an hour or less.

Shortcut Supper Saves Time in The Kitchen

SPEEDING tasty meals to the table is child's play for Carly Carter of Nashville, Tennessee. In fact, she could probably write the book on it.

"In addition to my number one job as a wife and mother, I write articles on children and family life," she shares. "I love to cook—so a favorite topic of mine is fun and family time in the kitchen."

It's evident by the fast-to-fix fare featured here that Carly's recipes are every bit as good as her words.

"One night, while trying to tend to both dinner and our son, Clarke, I opted to use frozen vegetables in my chicken stir-fry," Carly says. "Not wanting to stand watch over the stovetop, I baked the entree in the oven. Guests say Chicken Stir-Fry Bake tastes like it's hot from the skillet.

"As a switch from commercial dressing, I whisk together my own sweet and tangy honey-mustard concoction to complement the salad greens. I refrigerate any leftover dressing to use later in the week."

Instant pudding is the "secret ingredient" that makes Chocolate Fudge Mousse such a breeze to prepare. "It's so much quicker and easier to whip up than a traditional mousse. But it's equally fluffy and luscious, so it even satisfies my husband David's rather large sweet tooth," she says.

"Since our son is an early bird—he's always up at 4 a.m.—I often make this entire meal in the morning and refrigerate it. Then at dinnertime, it's just a matter of baking the main course and serving."

Between meals, Carly gardens and knits...and keeps her fingers flying across her computer keyboard. Who knows what novel ideas she'll come up with next for shortcuts in the kitchen?

CHICKEN STIR-FRY BAKE

- 2 cups uncooked instant rice
- 1 can (8 ounces) sliced water chestnuts, drained
- 2 cups cubed cooked chicken
- 1 package (16 ounces) frozen stir-fry vegetables, thawed
- 1 can (14-1/2 ounces) chicken broth
- 1/4 cup soy sauce
- 1 garlic clove, minced
- 1/2 to 3/4 teaspoon ground ginger

Place rice in an 11-in. x 7-in. x 2-in. baking dish. Layer with water chestnuts, chicken and vegetables. Combine remaining ingredients; pour over top. Cover and bake at 375° for 25 minutes or until rice is tender. **Yield:** 4 servings.

HONEY-MUSTARD TOSSED SALAD

- 1/4 cup buttermilk
- 1/4 cup sour cream
- 2 tablespoons Dijon mustard
- 2 tablespoons honey
- 1-1/2 teaspoons dried minced onion
- 1 teaspoon dried parsley flakes
- Torn salad greens and tomato wedges

In a small bowl, whisk together the first six ingredients. Serve over salad. **Yield:** 3/4 cup dressing.

CHOCOLATE FUDGE MOUSSE

- 2 cups cold milk
- 1 package (3.9 ounces) instant chocolate pudding mix
- 1/4 cup hot fudge ice cream topping
- 3 cups whipped topping

In a bowl, whisk milk and pudding mix for 2 minutes. Stir in fudge topping. Fold in whipped topping. Chill until serving. **Yield:** 6 servings.

Fast-to-Fix Fare Is Pretty and Palate Pleasing

THE FAIREST FARE of all, in the opinion of Aleta Beane, is almost always the simplest. Indeed, her collection of quick-and-easy recipes is a thing of beauty.

"As a home-based hair stylist, I usually plan cooking around my customers' hair appointments," she shares from Benton, Kentucky. Luckily, this active grandmother of three also has a flair for getting a head start on mealtime.

Judging by the fast favorites featured here, Aleta doesn't cut corners on flavor.

"My sweet and savory Apricot Lamb Chops are a speedy one-skillet entree," she says. "On evenings my husband, Teddy, comes home late from selling farm equipment, I can hurry them right to the table.

"You can substitute pork chops for the lamb," says Aleta. "Apple juice or slices complement the pork nicely.

"Purchased salad greens and a bottled dressing make Veggie Spinach Salad a breeze to toss together. I also like to add grated mozzarella cheese."

Dessert lovers enjoy Aleta's pleasing Puffed Pancakes. "The fruit-filled pastries offer a bite of summertime in any season," she affirms.

On the run when it comes to hobbies, too, Aleta raises, trains, sells and exhibits Tennessee Walking horses. Of course, for this versatile lady, "fancy footwork" comes naturally—whether in the salon, the showring or the kitchen!

APRICOT LAMB CHOPS

12 lamb loin chops (1 inch thick)
1/4 teaspoon salt
1/4 teaspoon garlic powder
2 tablespoons Dijon-mayonnaise blend
2 tablespoons brown sugar
1/2 cup apricot nectar
2 tablespoons minced fresh mint
2/3 cup dried apricot halves, cut into 1/4-inch strips

Sprinkle lamb chops with salt and garlic powder. Rub each side of chops with Dijon-mayonnaise blend and sprinkle with brown sugar. In a large nonstick skillet coated with nonstick cooking spray, brown chops on both sides over medium-high heat.

Add apricot nectar and mint. Reduce heat; cover and simmer for 12-15 minutes. Add apricots. Simmer, uncovered, 5 minutes longer or until meat reaches desired doneness and sauce is slightly thickened. Serve sauce over lamb. **Yield:** 6 servings.

VEGGIE SPINACH SALAD

3 cups torn fresh spinach
3 cups torn red leaf lettuce
1 cup broccoli florets
1 cup cauliflowerets
1 small carrot, sliced
1/4 cup raisins
1 bacon strip, cooked and crumbled
1/2 cup ranch salad dressing

In a bowl, toss the spinach, lettuce, broccoli, cauliflower, carrot, raisins and bacon. Serve with the dressing. **Yield:** 6 servings.

PUFFED PANCAKES

6 teaspoons butter (no substitutes)
3 eggs
1/2 cup milk
2 tablespoons vegetable oil
1/4 teaspoon almond extract
1/2 cup all-purpose flour
1/4 cup orange marmalade
1 teaspoon lemon juice
1 pint fresh strawberries, sliced
1 medium firm banana, sliced
1/2 cup whipped topping
2 tablespoons orange juice concentrate
1 tablespoon brown sugar

Divide butter between six 10-oz. custard cups. Place on a 15-in. x 10-in. x 1-in. baking pan. Heat in a 400° oven until butter is melted. In a bowl, beat eggs; add milk, oil and extract. Add flour; beat until smooth. Divide among custard cups. Bake for 12-15 minutes or until golden brown and puffy.

In a small saucepan, melt marmalade; stir in lemon juice. Toss with fruit. Combine whipped topping, orange juice concentrate and sugar. Serve fruit over pancakes; top with topping. **Yield:** 6 servings.

Three Cooks Share Their Speedy Standbys

BETWEEN back-to-school busyness and gardens ripe for the picking, autumn doesn't leave much extra time to spend in the kitchen. Hearty, fast-to-fix meals come in handy then.

The menu here combines recipes from three taste- and time-conscious cooks.

Mexican Chicken and Rice is shared by Cindy Gage of Blair, Nebraska. "With two teen athletes and a rodeoing husband to cheer on, I've found that ready-in-minutes recipes are a necessity at our house," the full-time nurse reports.

"On days I get home late from the hospital, I'm glad this main dish comes together easily in one skillet. Sometimes, I make it ahead in the morning and refrigerate. It's so quick to just sprinkle on the cheese and reheat it for dinner."

It's a toss-up which ingredient tickles the taste buds most in this attractive Apple Spinach Salad. The mix of refreshing mint, lemon, fruit and greens blends perfectly.

"Adding sunflower kernels is such a speedy way to give this salad extra protein and fiber," says Louise Barnum, an active great-grandmother from Edwardsburg, Michigan.

"For simple serving alternatives, replace the apple slices with pears, or tuck in chicken or tuna to make a well-dressed entree," she suggests.

Peachy Angel Food Cake makes a deliciously lasting impression in a flash. "Drop-in dinner guests don't have to go without dessert when you have this snappy recipe to turn to," says Betty Jean Nichols of Eugene, Oregon.

"For a fun change of pace, top it with ice cream, custard or frozen yogurt, then sprinkle toasted almonds on top."

MEXICAN CHICKEN AND RICE

2 pounds boneless skinless chicken breasts, cut into 1-inch pieces
1 medium green pepper, chopped
1 small onion, chopped
2 tablespoons vegetable oil
1 can (8-3/4 ounces) whole kernel corn, drained
1 cup chicken broth
1 cup salsa
1/2 to 1 teaspoon salt
1/2 to 1 teaspoon chili powder, optional
1/4 teaspoon pepper
1-1/2 cups uncooked instant rice
1/2 to 1 cup shredded cheddar cheese

In a large skillet, saute the chicken, green pepper and onion in oil until chicken is no longer pink and vegetables are crisp-tender. Add the corn, broth, salsa, salt, chili powder if desired and pepper; bring to a boil.

Stir in the rice; cover and remove from the heat. Let stand for 5 minutes. Fluff with a fork. Sprinkle with cheese. Cover and let stand for 2 minutes or until cheese is melted. **Yield:** 6 servings.

APPLE SPINACH SALAD

1/3 cup vegetable oil
2 tablespoons lemon juice
1 tablespoon thinly sliced green onion
1 teaspoon sugar
1-1/2 teaspoons chopped fresh mint *or* 1/2 teaspoon dried mint flakes
1/4 teaspoon salt
Dash pepper
1 package (10 ounces) fresh spinach, torn
2 medium apples, thinly sliced
1 small cucumber, halved and thinly sliced
2 tablespoons sunflower kernels, toasted

In a jar with a tight-fitting lid, combine the oil, lemon juice, green onion, sugar, mint, salt and pepper; shake well. In a salad bowl, combine the spinach, apples and cucumber. Drizzle with dressing; toss to coat. Sprinkle with sunflower kernels. **Yield:** 6 servings.

PEACHY ANGEL FOOD CAKE

1 prepared angel food loaf cake (10-1/2 ounces)
2 cups canned sliced peaches, drained
3/4 cup whipping cream, whipped
Ground nutmeg, optional

Cut six serving-size pieces from cake (save remaining cake for another use). Place cake on individual plates. Top with peaches and whipped cream; sprinkle with nutmeg if desired. **Yield:** 6 servings.

Fast and Flavorful Meal Is Full of Kid Appeal

SPEEDING MEALS to the table is kid stuff for Heidi Wilcox of Lapeer, Michigan. As a mother and home-based day care provider, she plans menus for many that are ready in mere minutes.

"Besides my daughter, Brittany, and son, Joe, I feed six other youngsters. That's no small challenge," Heidi shares. "I count on easy meals that I can prepare as I'm reciting stories, refereeing games and supervising naps.

"Since kids tend to tell time with their tummies, they know exactly when lunch should be served," she adds. Within 30 minutes of the first "I'm hungry!" from one of her young charges, Heidi has a nutritious meal ready and on the table.

"One of the gang's favorite sandwiches is my Open-Faced Tuna Burger. The kids prefer the zesty salad dressing to a mayonnaise base," she notes. "Bits of pimiento add color. And serving the tuna on a toasted bun means no soggy bread.

"Try substituting flaked chicken for tuna in the sandwich, or French dressing instead of ranch," Heidi suggests.

"Sauteed Green Beans are seasoned with some of my favorite herbs. I've found that basil, oregano and parsley are great flavor accents for canned, frozen or fresh beans. I've taken this delicious side along to last-minute potlucks as well."

To make Heidi's side dish even heartier, add crumbled bacon or small chunks of ham to the green beans.

A "berry" tasty way to put sparkle into her menu is with zippy Fruit Punch, a recipe Heidi's mom dreamed up.

"Kids love this pretty red beverage," Heidi reports. "I often have a pitcher in the fridge ready to pour, except for the ginger ale. I've found that mixing it in right before serving gives it the proper fizz! It's so colorful, I traditionally serve it to my family during the holidays.

"I think involving kids in the kitchen is a wonderful way to teach them the importance of helping others," says Heidi, adding that her day care "chefs" help stir up many of her quick recipes. "It's amazing how much better food tastes to children when they've had a hand in making it, too."

OPEN-FACED TUNA BURGERS

    3 slices bread, crust removed, cubed
  1/2 cup evaporated milk
4-1/2 teaspoons ranch salad dressing mix
    2 cans (6 ounces *each*) tuna, drained and flaked
    1 jar (2 ounces) chopped pimientos, drained
    4 hamburger buns, split and toasted

In a bowl, soak bread cubes in evaporated milk; let stand for 5 minutes. Stir in the salad dressing mix, tuna and pimientos. Spoon about 1/4 cup onto each bun half. Place on a baking sheet. Broil 6 in. from the heat for 4 minutes or until golden brown. **Yield:** 4 servings.

SAUTEED GREEN BEANS

    1 package (9 ounces) frozen cut green beans, thawed
    2 tablespoons butter *or* margarine
    1 teaspoon dried minced onion
  1/4 teaspoon salt
  1/4 teaspoon *each* dried basil, oregano and parsley flakes

In a large skillet, saute beans in butter for 4-5 minutes. Add the onion and seasonings. Reduce heat; cook and stir for 5 minutes or until heated through. **Yield:** 4 servings.

FRUIT PUNCH

    1 quart white grape juice, chilled
    1 quart cranberry-raspberry juice, chilled
    1 liter ginger ale, chilled

In a punch bowl or large pitcher, combine all ingredients. Serve immediately. **Yield:** 3 quarts.

MAKE SANDWICHES SPECIAL

SURPRISE kids with sandwiches in the shape of animals or other fun objects. It's as simple as using animal-shaped cookie cutters.

You can also replace regular white bread with fun alternatives such as tortillas, croissants, bagels, biscuits, English muffins or hot dog buns.

The Best of Country Cooking 2003

Our Most Memorable Meals

Remember the favorite foods you grew up with? These memorable meals are full of that old-fashioned flavor.

Breakfast Dishes Are a Great Way To Start the Day

IT'S SAID breakfast is the most important meal of the day. It will also be the most memorable when these four dishes are on the menu.

Ann Thomas of Telford, Pennsylvania shares the recipe for Golden Pancakes. "My mother made these delicious pancakes way back in the Depression years," Ann recalls. "She beat the batter by hand, but I use my blender."

"Onion Brunch Squares can be prepared ahead of time," explains Danna Givot of San Diego, California. "So it's ideal for busy mornings. Just pop it in the oven while you start your day."

Linda Tucker's mother-in-law gave her the recipe for Saucy Fruit Medley. "We love it for breakfast," says this Farmington, Missouri cook, "but it also makes a refreshing dessert in summer."

Danish Coffee Cake was passed down to Lee Deneau of Lansing, Michigan as well. "My mother made this tender, flaky pastry as part of a special breakfast on Sundays or holidays," Lee shares.

GOLDEN PANCAKES

6 eggs
1 cup cream-style cottage cheese
1/2 cup all-purpose flour
1/4 cup milk
1/4 cup vegetable oil
1/2 teaspoon vanilla extract
1/4 teaspoon salt

In a blender, combine all ingredients. Cover and process on the highest speed for 1 minute. Pour batter by 1/4 cupfuls onto a greased hot griddle. Turn when bubbles form on top; cook until second side is golden brown. **Yield:** about 14 pancakes.

ONION BRUNCH SQUARES

2 large onions, chopped
2 tablespoons butter *or* margarine
1 tablespoon all-purpose flour
1/2 cup sour cream
1/2 teaspoon salt
1/2 teaspoon caraway seeds, optional
3 eggs, lightly beaten
3 bacon strips, cooked and crumbled
1 tube (8 ounces) refrigerated crescent rolls

In a skillet, saute onions in butter until tender; cool. Meanwhile, in a bowl, combine the flour, sour cream, salt and caraway seeds if desired until blended. Add eggs and mix well. Stir in bacon and reserved onions.

Unroll crescent roll dough into an ungreased 9-in. square baking pan. Press seams together to seal; press dough 1 in. up the sides of pan. Pour onion mixture into crust. Bake at 375° for 25-30 minutes or until a knife inserted near the center comes out clean. **Yield:** 9 servings.

SAUCY FRUIT MEDLEY

1 can (21 ounces) cherry pie filling
1 can (15 ounces) fruit cocktail, drained
2 medium navel oranges, peeled and sectioned
1 medium grapefruit, peeled and sectioned
1 medium tart apple, peeled and diced
1 cup strawberry-cranberry *or* raspberry-cranberry juice
1/2 cup chopped pecans, optional

In a large bowl, combine all ingredients. Cover and refrigerate for at least 1 hour before serving. **Yield:** 8-10 servings.

DANISH COFFEE CAKE

1 cup cold butter (no substitutes), *divided*
2 cups all-purpose flour, *divided*
2 tablespoons plus 1 cup water, *divided*
1/4 teaspoon salt
3 eggs

ICING:
2 tablespoons butter (no substitutes), softened
1-1/2 cups confectioners' sugar
1-1/2 teaspoons vanilla extract
1 to 2 tablespoons water
1/2 cup chopped walnuts

In a bowl, cut 1/2 cup cold butter into 1 cup flour until mixture resembles coarse crumbs. Sprinkle with 2 tablespoons water; toss with a fork until mix-

ture forms a ball. Divide into thirds. On a floured surface, roll each portion into a 9-in. x 6-in. rectangle. Place on greased baking sheets; set aside.

In a saucepan, bring salt and remaining butter and water to a boil. Add remaining flour all at once; stir until a smooth ball forms. Remove from the heat; let stand for 5 minutes. Add eggs, one at a time, beating well after each. Continue beating until mixture is smooth and shiny. Spread over the dough.

Bake at 400° for 30 minutes or until puffed and golden brown. Cool for 10 minutes before removing from pans to wire racks.

For icing, combine butter, confectioners' sugar, vanilla and enough water to achieve desired consistency. Spread over warm coffee cakes. Sprinkle with walnuts. Store in the refrigerator. **Yield:** 3 coffee cakes.

Country Cooks Get Creative with Their Cooking

SPENDING TIME in the kitchen coming up with new recipes is a joy for country cooks, especially when the results are as delicious as the hearty meal featured here.

"When a friend gave me some ground turkey to use up, I looked for an inventive way to prepare it," says Patricia Eckard of Singers Glen, Virginia. "I found this recipe while scouring through my collection. My family loves it because of the stuffing inside. For variety, I sometimes use cheese on top instead of bacon."

Peppered Green Beans are attractive to serve alongside any main entree. The recipe comes from Chet Sioda of Tacoma, Washington, who says, "I like the tangy taste of these green beans. Red pepper and onion add extra color and flavor."

Louisiana Sweet Potato Casserole is a hand-me-down from Aline Fazzio's mother. "My dad used to plant a lot of sweet potatoes, so Mother became quite creative in preparing them," says Aline from her home in Houma, Louisiana. "It's our annual holiday dish with turkey and trimmings, but when I have a yen for something sweet, I reach into my file for this recipe."

Joyce Mart of Wichita, Kansas can serve up Berry Cheesecake Parfaits in no time. "Impressive and delicious, they seem to be just the right touch after a full meal. I also recommend them as a great midnight snack."

STUFFED TURKEY ROLL

    1 egg, lightly beaten
  1/2 cup quick-cooking oats
  1/2 teaspoon salt
  1/8 teaspoon pepper
    1 pound ground turkey
  1/4 cup chopped onion
  1/4 cup chopped celery
    3 tablespoons butter or margarine
    2 tablespoons water
  1/2 teaspoon rubbed sage
  1/4 teaspoon ground thyme
    2 cups seasoned stuffing cubes
    2 bacon strips, halved

In a bowl, combine the egg, oats, salt and pepper. Crumble turkey over mixture and mix well. Pat into a 12-in. x 9-in. rectangle on a piece of heavy-duty foil; set aside.

In a saucepan, saute onion and celery in butter until tender. Remove from the heat. Stir in water, sage and thyme. Add stuffing; mix well. Spoon over turkey to within 1 in. of edges. Roll up, jelly-roll style, starting with a short side and peeling away foil while rolling.

Place loaf, seam side down, in a greased 9-in. x 5-in. x 3-in. loaf pan. Place bacon strips over top. Bake, uncovered, at 325° for 60-70 minutes or until meat is no longer pink and a meat thermometer reads 165°. **Yield:** 4 servings.

PEPPERED GREEN BEANS

    1 medium sweet red pepper, julienned
    1 medium onion, julienned
    1 tablespoon olive or vegetable oil
    1 package (16 ounces) frozen cut green beans
    2 tablespoons cider vinegar
  1/8 teaspoon crushed red pepper flakes, optional
Salt and pepper to taste

In a skillet, saute red pepper and onion in oil until crisp-tender. Add beans; cook and stir for 10-12 minutes or until heated through. Remove from the heat; drain. Stir in vinegar, pepper flakes if desired, salt and pepper. **Yield:** 6-8 servings.

LOUISIANA SWEET POTATO CASSEROLE

    4 eggs, beaten
    1 cup sugar
    1 cup milk
  1/4 cup butter or margarine, melted
    3 tablespoons all-purpose flour
  1/4 teaspoon each salt, ground cinnamon, nutmeg and allspice
    3 cups shredded uncooked sweet potatoes

In a bowl, combine the eggs, sugar, milk and butter. Combine the flour, salt, cinnamon, nutmeg and allspice; stir into the egg mixture with sweet potatoes. Transfer to a greased 8-in. square baking dish.

Bake, uncovered, at 350° for 40-45 minutes or until a knife inserted near the center comes out clean. **Yield:** 6-8 servings.

2 cups fresh raspberries *or* other berries
1/2 cup graham cracker crumbs (8 squares)

❧❧❧❧❧❧❧❧❧❧❧❧❧

BERRY CHEESECAKE PARFAITS

**1 package (8 ounces) cream cheese,
softened**
2 to 4 tablespoons sugar
1/2 cup vanilla yogurt

In a mixing bowl, beat the cream cheese and sugar until smooth. Stir in yogurt. In parfait glasses or bowls, alternate layers of raspberries, cream cheese mixture and cracker crumbs. Serve immediately or refrigerate for up to 8 hours. **Yield:** 4 servings.

The Best of Country Cooking 2003

Meat-and-Potatoes Meal Satisfies Hearty Appetites

IF YOUR FAMILY and friends are fans of meat and potatoes, look no further than this palate-pleasing meal.

"I enjoy preparing Steak Over Potatoes since it is one of the easiest hearty meals I serve," says Dennis Robinson of Laurel, Montana. "The chicken gumbo soup adds a unique flavor to the rest of the ingredients."

Joanie Elbourn of Gardner, Massachusetts has been eating Buttery Carrots 'n' Onions since she was a child.

"My mother always served this attractive side dish for all her special dinners," recalls Joanie. "Now I do, too. Even my guests who normally aren't too fond of carrots ask for the recipe. The added sweetness from the honey and sugar is a pleasant surprise."

The longer the dressing for Salad with Tomato-Green Pepper Dressing is refrigerated, the more flavorful it becomes. "The bright red-orange color is a sharp contrast to salad greens," says Virginia Broten, who shares the recipe. "At my Pinewood, Minnesota house, it's everybody's favorite salad topping."

Dollie Ainley of Doniphan, Missouri has had the recipe for Crisp Lemon Sugar Cookies for about 40 years. "And in that time, I've made a few changes," Dollie notes. "These cookies are my husband's favorites, so I bake them for him nearly every week.

"One of my daughter's friends still remembers having these special treats when she stopped in on her way home from school. They're scrumptious served with a glass of cold milk."

STEAK OVER POTATOES

2-1/2   pounds beef round steak
  1   can (10-3/4 ounces) condensed cream of onion soup, undiluted
  1   can (10-1/2 ounces) condensed chicken gumbo soup, undiluted
1/4   teaspoon pepper
  8   baking potatoes

Cut steak into 3-in. x 1/4-in. strips; place in a bowl. Stir in soups and pepper. Transfer to a greased 2-1/2-qt. baking dish. Cover and bake at 350° for 30 minutes.

Add potatoes to the oven. Bake for 1-1/2 hours or until meat and potatoes are tender. Serve steak over potatoes. **Yield:** 8 servings.

BUTTERY CARROTS 'N' ONIONS

  1   pound carrots, cut into 1/4-inch slices
1-1/4   cups water, *divided*
  1   teaspoon chicken bouillon granules
  3   medium onions, sliced and separated into rings
  2   tablespoons butter *or* margarine
  1   tablespoon all-purpose flour
  1   teaspoon salt
  1   teaspoon honey
1/4   teaspoon sugar
Dash pepper

In a saucepan, combine carrots, 1/2 cup water and bouillon. Bring to a boil. Reduce heat; cover and cook for 5 minutes or until carrots are crisp-tender. Drain, reserving cooking liquid. Set carrots aside and keep warm.

In a large skillet, saute onions in butter for 10 minutes. Sprinkle with flour; stir until blended. Stir in the salt, honey, sugar, pepper and reserved cooking liquid until blended. Add remaining water; bring to a boil. Reduce heat; simmer, uncovered, for 10 minutes. Stir in carrots; heat through. **Yield:** 8-10 servings.

SALAD WITH TOMATO-GREEN PEPPER DRESSING

  1   can (10-3/4 ounces) condensed tomato soup, undiluted
3/4   cup sugar
2/3   cup cider vinegar
1/2   cup vegetable oil
  1   large green pepper, cut into chunks
1/2   medium onion, cut into chunks
  1   garlic clove, halved
  1   teaspoon ground mustard
1/2   teaspoon salt
1/2   teaspoon paprika
Salad greens and vegetables of your choice

In a blender, combine the first 10 ingredients; cover and process until smooth. Serve over tossed

salad. Store leftovers in the refrigerator; shake before using. **Yield:** 4 cups dressing.

🔲🔲🔲🔲🔲🔲🔲🔲🔲🔲🔲
CRISP LEMON SUGAR COOKIES

1/2 cup butter *or* margarine, softened
1/2 cup butter-flavored shortening
  1 cup sugar
  1 egg
  1 tablespoon milk
  2 teaspoons lemon extract
  1 teaspoon vanilla extract

2-1/2 cups all-purpose flour
  3/4 teaspoon salt
  1/2 teaspoon baking soda
Additional sugar

In a mixing bowl, cream butter, shortening and
sugar. Beat in egg, milk and extracts. Combine the
flour, salt and baking soda; gradually add to
creamed mixture.

  Shape into 1-in. balls or drop by rounded teaspoonfuls 2 in. apart onto ungreased baking
sheets. Flatten with a glass dipped in sugar. Bake
at 400° for 9-11 minutes or until edges are lightly browned. Immediately remove to wire racks to
cool. **Yield:** about 6-1/2 dozen.

Tasty Dinner Made Up of Family Favorites

THE SATISFYING SUPPER featured here is sure to win your family's stamp of approval...the recipes already rate No. 1 in the homes of the four cooks who shared them!

As a stay-at-home mom with two small children, Kelly Ritter of Douglasville, Georgia is always looking for quick and easy recipes that can be prepared ahead of time. "I also don't like to heat up my oven during our hot Georgia summers," notes Kelly.

"I adapted the recipe for Slow-Cooker Salmon Loaf from one I found in an old cookbook of my grandma's."

"Until you try Cottage Cheese Potato Rolls, you will not believe how good they are!" declares Salem, Oregon resident Corky Huffsmith. "Our three kids and their families all live nearby, so we often have family dinners. These rolls are a favorite."

Seasoned Beans and Tomatoes are back on the menu again at John Wasnock's family gatherings in Medina, New York. "For years, Grandma Wasnock had served them on Christmas Day," John recalls.

"We forgot about the recipe until my aunt served this dish at her daughter's wedding. That's when we found out the recipe came from a homemade cookbook my aunt received at her own wedding shower."

Maribelle Culver's recipe for Creamy Citrus Sherbet was handwritten in a booklet that came with her family's first refrigerator in the 1940s. "I was young at the time, but I can still remember the iceman delivering blocks of ice.

"Since finding the booklet among my mother's things, I make this refreshing dessert often," Maribelle says from her Grand Rapids, Michigan home.

SLOW-COOKER SALMON LOAF

2 eggs, lightly beaten
2 cups seasoned stuffing croutons
1 cup chicken broth
1 cup grated Parmesan cheese

1/4 teaspoon ground mustard
1 can (14-3/4 ounces) salmon, drained, bones and skin removed

In a bowl, combine the first five ingredients. Add salmon and mix well. Transfer to a slow cooker coated with nonstick cooking spray. Gently shape mixture into a loaf. Cover and cook on low for 4-6 hours or until a meat thermometer reads 160°. **Yield:** 6 servings.

COTTAGE CHEESE POTATO ROLLS

1 cup boiling water
1/2 cup mashed potato flakes
1 package (1/4 ounce) active dry yeast
1/4 cup warm water (110° to 115°)
1/4 cup sugar
1 teaspoon salt
2 eggs
2 tablespoons vegetable oil
1 cup small-curd cottage cheese
4 to 4-1/2 cups all-purpose flour
Sesame seeds, optional

In a bowl, combine the boiling water and potato flakes; mix well. Cool for 10 minutes. Meanwhile, in a mixing bowl, dissolve yeast in warm water. Beat in the sugar, salt, 1 egg and oil until blended. Stir cottage cheese into the potatoes; add to yeast mixture and mix well. Beat in 3 cups flour until smooth. Stir in enough remaining flour to form a soft dough.

Turn dough onto a floured surface; knead until smooth and elastic, about 6-8 minutes. Place in a greased bowl, turning once to grease top. Cover and let rise in a warm place until doubled, about 1 hour.

Punch dough down. Turn onto a lightly floured surface. Divide into 24 pieces; shape each into a ball. Place 3 in. apart on greased baking sheets. Cover and let rise until doubled, about 45 minutes. Beat remaining egg; brush over dough. Sprinkle with sesame seeds if desired. Bake at 350° for 16-18 minutes or until golden brown. Remove from pans to wire racks. **Yield:** 2 dozen.

SEASONED BEANS AND TOMATOES

1 medium onion, diced
2 tablespoons vegetable oil
2 cups fresh *or* frozen green beans, thawed

1 can (14-1/2 ounces) diced tomatoes,
   undrained
2 tablespoons sugar
1/4 teaspoon salt
1/4 teaspoon ground cloves
1/8 teaspoon pepper

In a skillet, saute onion in oil until tender. Stir
in the remaining ingredients. Bring to a boil. Reduce heat; cook, uncovered, over medium-low
heat until beans are tender. Serve with a slotted
spoon. **Yield:** 4-6 servings.

CREAMY CITRUS SHERBET

2 cups sugar
1-1/2 cups orange juice
5 tablespoons lemon juice
4 cups milk

In a large bowl, combine sugar and juices. Gradually add milk. Pour into a 2-qt. freezer container.
Freeze for 1 hour, then stir every 30 minutes until
slushy. Freeze overnight. **Yield:** about 2 quarts.

Easy Yet Elegant Dinner Great for Serving Guests

DINNER GUESTS will think you spent hours in the kitchen preparing this impressive spread, when really, it's simple to prepare.

"Chicken with Peach Stuffing is my favorite kind of recipe...something that tastes good, yet requires little preparation," says Theresa Stewart of New Oxford, Pennsylvania.

Ruth Ann Stelfox's cousin shared the recipe for Mustard Salad Dressing after she liked its mild, delicious taste. "It's so easy to whisk up," says Ruth Ann, who lives in Raymond, Alberta.

Wanting to make a colorful vegetable for Christmas dinner one year, Joan Sieck of Rensselaer, New York put together Squash Rings with Green Beans. "It was a big hit with our guests," Joan says.

Las Vegas, Nevada native June Nehmer discovered Orange Meringue Pie while vacationing in Florida one year. "I made a few changes and added lime juice for extra tartness," June details. "It's colorful, refreshing and looks so pretty on the plate."

CHICKEN WITH PEACH STUFFING

   1 can (15-1/4 ounces) sliced peaches
   4 boneless skinless chicken breast halves
   2 tablespoons vegetable oil
   2 tablespoons butter *or* margarine
   1 tablespoon brown sugar
   1 tablespoon cider vinegar
1/8 teaspoon ground allspice
   3 cups instant chicken-flavored stuffing mix

Drain peaches, reserving juice; set the peaches aside. Add enough water to juice to measure 1 cup; set aside.

In a skillet, brown chicken on both sides in oil. Gradually stir in the peach juice mixture, butter, brown sugar, vinegar and allspice. Bring to a boil. Reduce heat; cover and simmer for 5 minutes or until chicken juices run clear.

Stir in stuffing mix and peaches. Cover and remove from the heat. Let stand for 5 minutes or until liquid is absorbed. **Yield:** 4 servings.

MUSTARD SALAD DRESSING

1/2 cup mayonnaise *or* salad dressing
   2 tablespoons sugar
   1 tablespoon white vinegar
1-1/2 teaspoons prepared mustard
Salad greens and vegetables of your choice

In a bowl, whisk the mayonnaise, sugar, vinegar and mustard until well blended. Cover and refrigerate until serving. Serve with salad. **Yield:** 1 cup.

SQUASH RINGS WITH GREEN BEANS

   2 medium acorn squash (about 2 pounds *each*)
3/4 teaspoon salt, *divided*
1/4 teaspoon pepper, *divided*
1/4 cup plus 2 tablespoons butter *or* margarine, *divided*
1/2 cup packed brown sugar
   2 tablespoons water
   1 pound fresh green beans, cut into 1-1/2-inch pieces
1/4 teaspoon dried basil
1/4 teaspoon dried rosemary, crushed

Cut squash into 1-in. slices; discard seeds and ends. Arrange slices in a single layer in a greased 15-in. x 10-in. x 1-in. baking pan. Sprinkle with 1/4 teaspoon salt and 1/8 teaspoon pepper. Cover and bake at 350° for 40 minutes.

Meanwhile, in a saucepan, combine 1/4 cup butter, brown sugar and water; bring to a boil. Brush over the squash. Bake, uncovered, for 15 minutes or until tender, basting frequently.

Place beans in a saucepan and cover with water; bring to a boil. Cook for 10 minutes or until tender; drain. Add basil, rosemary, and remaining butter, salt and pepper. Spoon into squash rings. **Yield:** 6 servings.

ORANGE MERINGUE PIE

1-1/2 cups graham cracker crumbs (about 24 squares)
1/4 cup sugar
1/3 cup butter *or* margarine, melted
FILLING:
   1 cup sugar
1/4 cup cornstarch
1/4 teaspoon salt
   1 cup orange juice
1/2 cup water

        3 egg yolks, well beaten
        2 tablespoons lime juice
        4 teaspoons grated orange peel
        1 tablespoon butter *or* margarine
MERINGUE:
        3 egg whites
    1/8 teaspoon cream of tartar
        6 tablespoons sugar

In a bowl, combine the cracker crumbs and sugar; stir in butter. Press onto the bottom and up the sides of a 9-in. pie plate. Bake at 375° for 8-10 minutes or until lightly browned. Cool.

For filling, combine the sugar, cornstarch and salt in a saucepan. Whisk in orange juice and water until smooth. Cook and stir over medium heat until thickened and bubbly. Reduce heat;

cook and stir 2 minutes longer.

Remove from the heat. Gradually stir 1 cup hot filling into egg yolks; return all to the pan, stirring constantly. Bring to a gentle boil; cook and stir for 2 minutes. Remove from the heat; stir in the lime juice, orange peel and butter. Pour hot filling into pie crust.

For the meringue, beat egg whites in a mixing bowl until foamy. Add cream of tartar; beat on medium speed until soft peaks form. Gradually beat in sugar, 1 tablespoon at a time, on high until stiff peaks form. Spread over hot filling, sealing edges to crust.

Bake at 350° for 12-15 minutes or until golden. Cool on a wire rack for 1 hour; refrigerate for 1-2 hours before serving. Refrigerate leftovers. **Yield:** 6-8 servings.

Cold Weather Calls For Down-Home Comfort Food

CHASE AWAY THE CHILL of winter with this heart-warming meal.

Hardin, Montana resident Jeanne Davis has used the Beef Rouladen recipe for years and relies on it when she has company. "It's a main dish that can be prepared ahead and makes a hearty meal when cold weather sets in," Jeanne says.

Living in Florida during the winter, Patty Kile can pick fresh grapefruit right on her property. "Greens 'n' Grapefruit Salad is a refreshing side dish with any meal," notes Patty, who lives in Greentown, Pennsylvania the rest of the year.

"I love brussels sprouts!" declares Lynne Howard of Annandale, Virginia. "I created the recipe for Bacon-Topped Brussels Sprouts myself, but I'm always looking for other ways to prepare them."

The recipe for Strawberry Schaum Torte was handed down to Diane Krisman from her German grandmother. "She took great pride in serving this delicate dessert," says Diane, from Hales Corners, Wisconsin. "Whenever I make it, I'm filled with warm memories of childhood."

BEEF ROULADEN

2 cups sliced onions
4 tablespoons vegetable oil, *divided*
6 bacon strips
6 beef round *or* sirloin tip steaks (about 1/4 pound *each*)
1/2 teaspoon salt
1/4 teaspoon pepper
1 tablespoon Dijon mustard
6 dill pickle spears
3/4 cup all-purpose flour
1-1/3 cups water
4 teaspoons beef bouillon granules
1 teaspoon dried thyme
1 bay leaf
1 tablespoon butter *or* margarine, melted
Hot cooked noodles

In a large skillet, saute onions in 2 tablespoons of oil until tender; remove with a slotted spoon and set aside. In the same skillet, cook bacon for 3-4 minutes or until partially cooked but not crisp. Remove and set aside.

Pound steaks to 1/4-in. thickness; sprinkle with salt and pepper. Spread with mustard and top with sauteed onions. Place a pickle at one short end and a bacon strip lengthwise on top. Roll up jelly-roll style; secure with toothpicks. Set aside 1 tablespoon flour for thickening. Coat the roll-ups with remaining flour.

In the skillet, heat remaining oil over medium heat; brown roll-ups on all sides. Add water, bouillon, thyme and bay leaf. Bring to a boil. Reduce heat; cover and simmer for 30 minutes or until beef is tender.

Remove roll-ups and keep warm. Combine butter and reserved flour; add to the pan juices. Bring to a boil; cook and stir for 2 minutes or until thickened. Discard bay leaf and toothpicks. Serve beef and gravy over noodles. **Yield:** 6 servings.

GREENS 'N' GRAPEFRUIT SALAD

4 cups torn salad greens
2 tablespoons chopped red onion
1 medium grapefruit, peeled and sectioned
1/2 cup sliced fresh mushrooms
1/2 cup sliced water chestnuts
DRESSING:
1/2 cup mayonnaise *or* salad dressing
1/4 cup Catalina salad dressing
1/4 cup sesame seeds, toasted
2 tablespoons sugar
2 tablespoons cider vinegar

In a bowl, combine the greens, onion, grapefruit, mushrooms and water chestnuts. In a small bowl, whisk together dressing ingredients. Drizzle over salad; serve immediately. **Yield:** 4-6 servings.

BACON-TOPPED BRUSSELS SPROUTS

1 package (16 ounces) frozen brussels sprouts
2 tablespoons butter *or* margarine, melted
1/2 teaspoon garlic salt
1/4 teaspoon onion powder
1/4 teaspoon dried oregano
1/2 pound sliced bacon, cooked and crumbled

Cook brussels sprouts according to package directions; drain. Add butter, garlic salt, onion pow-

der and oregano; toss. Place in a serving dish. Top with bacon. **Yield:** 4-6 servings.

🔳🔳🔳🔳🔳🔳🔳🔳🔳🔳🔳

STRAWBERRY SCHAUM TORTE

   8 egg whites (about 1 cup)
   2 cups sugar
   1 tablespoon white vinegar
   1 teaspoon vanilla extract
 1/4 teaspoon salt
Sliced fresh strawberries
Whipped cream

In a large mixing bowl, beat the egg whites on high speed until soft peaks form. Reduce speed to medium. Add sugar, 2 tablespoons at a time, beating until stiff and glossy peaks form. Beat in the vinegar, vanilla and salt.

Spread into a greased 10-in. springform pan. Bake at 300° for 65-70 minutes or until lightly browned. Remove to a wire rack to cool (the meringue will fall). Serve with strawberries and whipped cream. Store leftovers in the refrigerator. **Yield:** 10-12 servings.

Editor's Note: This recipe requires a stand mixer.

The Best of Country Cooking 2003

General Recipe Index

A

APPETIZERS & SNACKS
Cold Appetizers
    Fruit Kabobs with Citrus Dip, 157
    Picnic Stuffed Eggs, 5
Dips and Spreads
    Black Bean Salsa, 8
    Cheddar Cheese Carrot, 9
    Chive-Onion Vegetable Dip, 144
    ✓Curry Carrot Dip, 6
    Emerald Isle Dip, 9
    Fiesta Cheese Ball, 10
    Garden Salsa, 7
    Herbed Garlic Cheese Spread, 5
    Salmon Cheese Spread, 8
Hot Appetizers
    Cheesy Sausage Nachos, 5
    Fourth of July Pizza, 6
    New Haven Clam Pizza, 10
Snack Mix
    Fruit 'n' Nut Trail Mix, 11

APPLES
Apple Blackberry Pie, 110
Apple Cabbage Slaw, 157
Apple Crisp, 131
Apple Fritters, 142
Apple Graham Pie, 113
Apple Pie Ice Cream, 117
Apple Spinach Salad, 161
Apple Tossed Salad, 48
Banana Apple Muffins, 142
Blue Cheese Apple Salad, 62
Cranberry Apple Cider, 7
Golden Apple Potato Salad, 62
Maple Apple Rings, 76
Mini Apple Pie, 146
Pork Chops with Onions and Apples, 37
Sweet Apple Pie, 125

APRICOTS
✓Apricot Cranberry Bread, 87
Apricot Lamb Chops, 154
Apricot Scones, 86
Dutch Apricot Pie, 128

ARTICHOKES
Artichokes Au Gratin, 78
Zesty Broccoli and Artichokes, 67

ASPARAGUS
Chilled Asparagus Salad, 133
Chilled Marinated Asparagus, 51
Early-Bird Asparagus Supreme, 77

AVOCADOS
Citrusy Avocado Crab Salad, 60
Orange-Avocado Tossed Salad, 54

B

BANANAS
Banana Apple Muffins, 142
✓Banana Cream Pie, 115
Banana Toffee Cream, 141
Tropical Banana Splits, 149

BARS & BROWNIES
Brownies from Heaven, 96
Cheesecake Diamonds, 96
Choco-Cloud Brownies, 94
Chocolate Chip Cheesecake Bars, 95
Cranberry Walnut Bars, 103
Grandma's Date Bars, 139
Pumpkin Spice Bars, 102
Raspberry Citrus Bars, 97
Simply Fudgy Brownies, 141

BEANS
Black Bean Salsa, 8
Peppered Green Beans, 166
Saucy Green Bean Bake, 78
Sauteed Green Beans, 162
Seasoned Beans and Tomatoes, 170
Squash Rings with Green Beans, 172
White Bean and Pasta Soup, 60

BEEF & CORNED BEEF (*also see* *Ground Beef*)
Barbecued Beef Brisket, 35
Beef Rouladen, 174
Beefy Tomato Rigatoni, 39
Busy Day Beef Stew, 13
✓Down-Home Pot Roast, 15
Emerald Isle Dip, 9
French Veal Chops, 138
Italian Beef Sandwiches, 20
Marinated Beef Tenderloin, 17
Pineapple Beef Stir-Fry, 26
Roast Beef Sandwich Roll, 24
Savory Vegetable Beef Stew, 41
Slow-Cooked Coffee Pot Roast, 38
Slow-Cooked Rump Roast, 20
Steak Over Potatoes, 168
Sweet 'n' Sour Pot Roast, 13
Sweet Beef Stew, 43
Vegetable Beef Soup, 58
Yankee Pot Roast, 42

BEVERAGES
Citrus Grape Drink, 11
Citrus Quencher, 5
Cranberry Apple Cider, 7
Creamy Hot Cocoa, 149
Fruit Punch, 162
Mint Iced Tea Cooler, 7
Mock Eggnog, 8
Old-Fashioned Chocolate Soda, 133
Peppermint Hot Chocolate, 11
Spiced Coffee with Cream, 147
Spicy Tomato Cooler, 139

BISCUITS & SCONES
Apricot Scones, 86
Buttermilk Scones, 133
Whipped Cream Biscuits, 147

BLACKBERRIES
Apple Blackberry Pie, 110
Glazed Blackberry Pie, 112

BLUE-RIBBON RECIPES
Appetizers
    Fiesta Cheese Ball, 10
    New Haven Clam Pizza, 10
    Picnic Stuffed Eggs, 5
Breads and Rolls
    Almond-Filled Butterhorns, 84
    Buttermilk Pan Rolls, 89
    Cheddar-Chili Bread Twists, 86
    Chocolate Chip Carrot Bread, 85
    Garlic Parmesan Breadsticks, 84
Cakes, Pies and Desserts
    Apple Blackberry Pie, 110
    Cherry Blueberry Pie, 110
    Dutch Apricot Pie, 128
    Fluffy Strawberry Meringue Pie, 124
    Frosty Chocolate Mousse, 121
    Glazed Pineapple Pie, 125
    Maple Nut Cake, 115
    Peaches 'n' Cream Pie, 109
    Peanut Butter Lover's Cake, 120
    Raspberry Meringue Pie, 109
    Sponge Cake with Blueberry
        Topping, 120
    Surprise Carrot Cake, 111
    Sweet Apple Pie, 125
    Very Lemony Meringue Pie, 128
    Walnut Blintz Torte, 121
Cookies and Bars
    Chocolate Chip Cheesecake Bars, 95
    Chocolate Meringues, 100
    Chocolate Surprise Cookies, 96
    Cinnamon Snaps, 91
    Fruit-Filled Spritz Cookies, 100
    Sour Cream Chocolate Cookies, 91
    Swedish Butter Cookies, 91
    Toffee Malted Cookies, 101
    White Chocolate Oatmeal Cookies, 97
Main Dishes
    Broccoli Ham Quiche, 24
    Busy Day Beef Stew, 13
    Cheese-Stuffed Pork Roast, 25
    Chicken Carrot Fried Rice, 33

Chicken Roll-Ups with Cherry
    Sauce, 14
Glazed Holiday Pork Roast, 13
Italian Beef Sandwiches, 20
Marinated Beef Tenderloin, 17
Meatball Stroganoff with Noodles, 40
Meaty Chili Lasagna, 42
Mexican Chicken Manicotti, 37
Pepperoni Pasta Bake, 43
Ravioli with Shrimp Tomato Sauce, 31
Roast Pork with Raspberry Sauce, 16
Shrimp Patty Sandwiches, 17
Slow-Cooked Rump Roast, 20
Sourdough Cheeseburgers, 22
Spaghetti 'n' Meatballs, 36
Spicy Chicken Linguine, 32
Stuffed Pork Tenderloin, 21
Sweet 'n' Sour Pot Roast, 13
Trout Baked in Cream, 44

Side Dishes
Candied Sweet Potatoes, 72
Confetti Carrot Fritters, 70
Loaded Mashed Potatoes, 67
Oven-Roasted Carrots, 73
Rich 'n' Cheesy Macaroni, 69
Scalloped Carrots, 68
Sweet Potato Bake, 70
Zesty Broccoli and Artichokes, 67

Soups and Salads
Cranberry Orange Vinaigrette, 61
Cream Cheese Chicken Soup, 50
Creamy Carrot Parsnip Soup, 53
Festive Tossed Salad, 51
Layered Ham and Spinach Salad, 47
Pickled Carrots, 50
Spicy Potato Salad, 49
Spinach Salad with Spicy Honey
    Dressing, 64
White Bean and Pasta Soup, 60

BLUEBERRIES
Blueberry Cream Pies, 112
Cherry Blueberry Pie, 110
Patriotic Pizza, 129
Sponge Cake with Blueberry Topping, 120

BREADS (also see Biscuits & Scones;
Coffee Cakes; Muffins; Rolls; Pancakes;
Yeast Breads)
Apple Fritters, 142
✓Apricot Cranberry Bread, 87
Cheddar-Chili Bread Twists, 86
Chocolate Chip Carrot Bread, 85
Cranberry Cheese Bread, 83
Garlic Parmesan Breadsticks, 84
Holiday Fruitcake, 89
Light Candied Fruitcake, 81
Mini Zucchini Bread, 136
Veggie French Bread, 158

BROCCOLI & CAULIFLOWER
Broccoli Chowder, 54
Broccoli Fettuccine, 144
Broccoli Ham Quiche, 24
Broccoli Noodle Supreme, 76
Broccoli Slaw, 63
Broccoli Supreme, 72
Cheddar Cauliflower, 69
Creamy Cauliflower Salad, 52
Zesty Broccoli and Artichokes, 67

C

CABBAGE & SAUERKRAUT
Apple Cabbage Slaw, 157
✓Beef Cabbage Stromboli, 35
Cheddar Cabbage Casserole, 79
Grape and Cabbage Salad, 65
No-Fuss Pork and Sauerkraut, 39
✓Raspberry Cabbage Salad, 49
Slow-Cooked Cabbage Rolls, 29

CAKES & TORTES
Butternut Squash Layer Cake, 117
Caramel Pecan Pound Cake, 116
Georgia Pecan Cake, 122
Maple Nut Cake, 115
Mint Chocolate Cake, 116
Moist Chocolate Cake, 123
Peachy Angel Food Cake, 161
Peanut Butter Lover's Cake, 120
✓Raisin Carrot Cake, 129
Raspberry-Almond Jelly Roll, 124
Sponge Cake with Blueberry Topping, 120
Strawberry Sunshine Cake, 131
Surprise Carrot Cake, 111
Upside-Down Raspberry Cake, 114
Walnut Blintz Torte, 121

CANDIES
Almond Rock Candy, 107
Buckeyes, 95
Cherry Swirl Fudge, 103
Double Chocolate Fudge, 94
Orange Truffles, 101
Reindeer Treats, 103
Sunflower Fudge, 93
Terrific Toffee, 106

CARROTS
Buttery Carrots 'n' Onions, 168
Carrots and Pineapple, 74
Cheddar Cheese Carrot, 9
Chicken Carrot Fried Rice, 33
Chocolate Chip Carrot Bread, 85
Confetti Carrot Fritters, 70
Creamy Carrot Parsnip Soup, 53
✓Curry Carrot Dip, 6
Flavorful Carrots, 75
Honey-Mustard Carrots, 75
Lemon Basil Carrots, 141
Microwave Carrot Casserole, 74
Nutty Carrot Salad, 53
Oven-Roasted Carrots, 73
Peanutty Carrots, 134
Pickled Carrots, 50
✓Raisin Carrot Cake, 129
Sauteed Carrots, 75
Scalloped Carrots, 68
Surprise Carrot Cake, 111

CASSEROLES
Main Dishes
Beefy Tomato Rigatoni, 39
Cheesy Zucchini Bake, 34
Chicken Stir-Fry Bake, 153
Pepperoni Pasta Bake, 43
Spinach Cheese Strata, 44
Side Dishes
Artichokes Au Gratin, 78
Broccoli Supreme, 72
Cheddar Cabbage Casserole, 79
Cheesy Eggplant Bake, 73
Loaded Mashed Potatoes, 67
Louisiana Sweet Potato Casserole, 166
Macaroni 'n' Cheese for Two, 149
Rich 'n' Cheesy Macaroni, 69
Saucy Green Bean Bake, 78
Scalloped Carrots, 68
Scalloped Potatoes, 136
Summer Squash Bake, 144
Sweet Potato Bake, 70

CHEESE
Berry Cheesecake Parfaits, 167
Blue Cheese Apple Salad, 62
Cheddar Cabbage Casserole, 79
Cheddar Cauliflower, 69
Cheddar Cheese Carrot, 9
Cheddar-Chili Bread Twists, 86
✓Cheese-Stuffed Potatoes, 79
Cheese-Stuffed Pork Roast, 25
Cheesecake Diamonds, 96
Cheesy Chicken Corn Soup, 48
Cheesy Eggplant Bake, 73
Cheesy Potatoes, 138
Cheesy Sausage Nachos, 5
Cheesy Tuna Noodles, 27
✓Cheesy Turkey Burgers, 33
Cheesy Vegetable Soup, 54
Cheesy Zucchini Bake, 34
Chocolate Chip Cheesecake Bars, 95
Cottage Cheese Potato Rolls, 170
Cranberry Cheese Bread, 83
Cream Cheese Chicken Soup, 50
Creamy Fettuccine, 29
Creamy Parmesan Sauce, 68
Fancy Mac 'n' Cheese, 158
Fiesta Cheese Ball, 10
Garlic Parmesan Breadsticks, 84
Herbed Garlic Cheese Spread, 5

✓*Recipe includes Nutritional Analysis
and Diabetic Exchanges*

CHEESE (*continued*)
Macaroni 'n' Cheese for Two, 149
Parmesan Ham Frittata, 138
Rich 'n' Cheesy Macaroni, 69
Salmon Cheese Spread, 8
Sourdough Cheeseburgers, 22
Spinach Cheese Strata, 44
Swiss Cheese Potato Pancakes, 72

CHERRIES
Cherry Blueberry Pie, 110
Cherry Cappuccino Sundaes, 143
Cherry Swirl Fudge, 103
Chicken Roll-Ups with Cherry Sauce, 14

CHICKEN & FOWL
Cheesy Chicken Corn Soup, 48
Chicken Carrot Fried Rice, 33
Chicken Fajita Salad, 55
Chicken French Bread Pizza, 20
✓Chicken Lasagna, 23
Chicken Roll-Ups with Cherry Sauce, 14
Chicken Salad on a Tortilla, 142
Chicken Stir-Fry Bake, 153
Chicken with Peach Stuffing, 172
Cornish Hens with Veggies, 26
Cream Cheese Chicken Soup, 50
Flower Garden Soup, 64
Fruited Chicken, 29
Grilled Italian Chicken, 30
Hearty Chicken Vegetable Soup, 58
Jalapeno Grilled Chicken, 22
Mexican Chicken and Rice, 161
Mexican Chicken Manicotti, 37
Orange Chicken Salad, 133
Pasta Jambalaya, 21
Rosemary-Garlic Chicken and
    Veggies, 147
Skillet Chicken, 134
Southwestern Chicken Barley Soup, 55
Spicy Chicken Linguine, 32
Tropical Glazed Chicken Strips, 32

CHOCOLATE
Brownies from Heaven, 96
Buckeyes, 95
Cherry Swirl Fudge, 103
Choco-Cloud Brownies, 94
✓Chocolate Cappuccino Cookies, 107
Chocolate Chip Carrot Bread, 85
Chocolate Chip Cheesecake Bars, 95
Chocolate Chunk Shortbread, 105
Chocolate Fudge Mousse, 153
Chocolate Meringues, 100
Chocolate Surprise Cookies, 96
Creamy Candy Bar Dessert, 122
Creamy Hot Cocoa, 149
Double Chocolate Fudge, 94
Frosty Chocolate Mousse, 121
Mint Chocolate Cake, 116
Moist Chocolate Cake, 123

Old-Fashioned Chocolate Soda, 133
Orange Truffles, 101
Peppermint Hot Chocolate, 11
Simply Fudgy Brownies, 141
Sour Cream Chocolate Cookies, 91
✓Sugar-Free Chocolate Eclairs, 130
Sunflower Fudge, 93
Terrific Toffee, 106
White Chocolate Oatmeal Cookies, 97

COCONUT
Coconut Pineapple Pie, 113
Easy Macaroons, 104

COFFEE CAKES
Cranberry Swirl Coffee Cake, 87
Danish Coffee Cake, 165
Strawberry Rhubarb Coffee Cake, 81

COLESLAW
Apple Cabbage Slaw, 157
Broccoli Slaw, 63
Grape and Cabbage Salad, 65

CONDIMENTS
Creamy Parmesan Sauce, 68
Homemade Cajun Seasoning, 69
South Liberty Hall Relish, 70

COOKIES (*also see Bars & Brownies*)
✓Chocolate Cappuccino Cookies, 107
Chocolate Chunk Shortbread, 105
Chocolate Meringues, 100
Chocolate Surprise Cookies, 96
Cinnamon Snaps, 91
Crisp Lemon Sugar Cookies, 169
Crispy Butter Cookies, 106
Easy Macaroons, 104
Fruit-Filled Spritz Cookies, 100
✓Honey Spice Cookies, 95
Molasses Butterballs, 105
No-Fuss Peanut Butter Cookies, 104
Orange Drop Cookies, 105
Peanut Butter 'n' Jelly Cookies, 105
Peppermint Candy Cookies, 93
Popcorn Cookies, 93
Santa Sugar Cookies, 102
Sour Cream Chocolate Cookies, 91
Star Sandwich Cookies, 106
Strawberry-Nut Pinwheel Cookies, 100
Swedish Butter Cookies, 91
Toffee Malted Cookies, 101
White Chocolate Oatmeal Cookies, 97

CORN
Cheesy Chicken Corn Soup, 48
✓Corn and Peppers, 68
Corn and Sausage Soup, 63

CRANBERRIES
✓Apricot Cranberry Bread, 87
Cranberry Apple Cider, 7

Cranberry Cheese Bread, 83
Cranberry Gelatin Mold, 52
Cranberry Orange Vinaigrette, 61
Cranberry Swirl Coffee Cake, 87
Cranberry Walnut Bars, 103

D

DESSERTS (*also see specific kinds*)
Apple Crisp, 131
Baked Pears, 139
Banana Toffee Cream, 141
Berry Cheesecake Parfaits, 167
Berry Rhubarb Sauce, 131
Creamy Candy Bar Dessert, 122
Easy Rhubarb Dessert, 130
Fruit Kabobs with Citrus Dip, 157
Patriotic Pizza, 129
Pears in Spiced Raisin Sauce, 150
Red Raspberry Mousse Dessert, 128
Sparkling Melon, 158
Strawberry Schaum Torte, 175
✓Sugar-Free Chocolate Eclairs, 130

DIPS & SPREADS (*also see Salsas*)
Cheddar Cheese Carrot, 9
Chive-Onion Vegetable Dip, 144
✓Curry Carrot Dip, 6
Emerald Isle Dip, 9
Fiesta Cheese Ball, 10
Fruit Kabobs with Citrus Dip, 157
Herbed Garlic Cheese Spread, 5
Salmon Cheese Spread, 8

E

EGGS
Broccoli Ham Quiche, 24
Parmesan Ham Frittata, 138
Picnic Stuffed Eggs, 5
Spinach Cheese Strata, 44
Western Omelet Sandwich, 149

F

FISH & SEAFOOD
Cheesy Tuna Noodles, 27
Citrusy Avocado Crab Salad, 60
Crab Pasta Salad, 52
Dilled Sole with Almonds, 141
Linguine with Garlic Clam Sauce, 44
New Haven Clam Pizza, 10
Open-Faced Tuna Burgers, 162
Pasta Jambalaya, 21
Ravioli with Shrimp Tomato Sauce, 31
Salmon Cheese Spread, 8
Salmon Stuffed Peppers, 14
Sesame Dill Fish, 157
Shrimp Dijonnaise, 150
Shrimp Patty Sandwiches, 17
Slow-Cooker Salmon Loaf, 170
Trout Baked in Cream, 44

General Recipe Index

FRUIT (also see specific kinds)
Citrus Quencher, 5
Citrusy Avocado Crab Salad, 60
Creamy Citrus Sherbet, 171
Fruit 'n' Nut Trail Mix, 11
Fruit-Filled Spritz Cookies, 100
Fruit Kabobs with Citrus Dip, 157
Fruit Punch, 162
Fruit-Stuffed Pork Roast, 27
Fruited Chicken, 29
Glazed Holiday Pork Roast, 13
Greens 'n' Grapefruit Salad, 174
Holiday Breakfast Braid, 88
Holiday Fruitcake, 89
Light Candied Fruitcake, 81
Refreshing Fruit Salad, 136
Saucy Fruit Medley, 164
Sparkling Melon, 158
Sunshine Fruit Salad, 62
Tropical Banana Splits, 149
Tropical Glazed Chicken Strips, 32

G

GRAPES
Citrus Grape Drink, 11
Grape and Cabbage Salad, 65
Grape Sherbet, 111

GRILLED & BROILED RECIPES
Barbecued Beef Brisket, 35
Barbecued Turkey Slices, 40
✓Cheesy Turkey Burgers, 33
Fancy Mac 'n' Cheese, 158
Grilled Italian Chicken, 30
Jalapeno Grilled Chicken, 22
Onion 'n' Tomato Topped Muffins, 144
Open-Faced Tuna Burgers, 162
Parmesan Ham Frittata, 138
Pork Chops with Onions and Apples, 37
Shrimp Dijonnaise, 150

GROUND BEEF
✓Beef Cabbage Stromboli, 35
Meatball Stroganoff with Noodles, 40
Meaty Chili Lasagna, 42
Slow-Cooked Cabbage Rolls, 29
Slow-Cooked Tamale Casserole, 33
Sourdough Cheeseburgers, 22
Spaghetti 'n' Meat Sauce, 146
✓Turkey 'n' Beef Loaf, 30

H

HAM & BACON
Bacon-Topped Brussels Sprouts, 174
Broccoli Ham Quiche, 24
Ham Loaf with Mustard Sauce, 28
Ham with Vegetables, 45
Layered Ham and Spinach Salad, 47
Parmesan Ham Frittata, 138

Split Pea Soup, 59
Western Omelet Sandwich, 149

I

ICE CREAM & SHERBET
Apple Pie Ice Cream, 117
Cherry Cappuccino Sundaes, 143
Creamy Citrus Sherbet, 171
Glazed Strawberry Sundaes, 134
Grape Sherbet, 111
Strawberry Ice, 116
Sweetheart Sorbet, 110
Tropical Banana Splits, 149

L

LAMB
Apricot Lamb Chops, 154

LEMON
Crisp Lemon Sugar Cookies, 169
Lemon Basil Carrots, 141
Lemon Pear Pie, 113
Very Lemony Meringue Pie, 128

M

MEAT LOAVES & MEATBALLS
Ham Loaf with Mustard Sauce, 28
Meatball Stroganoff with Noodles, 40
Spaghetti 'n' Meatballs, 36
✓Turkey 'n' Beef Loaf, 30

MEAT PIE & PIZZAS
Chicken French Bread Pizza, 20
Fourth of July Pizza, 6
New Haven Clam Pizza, 10
Turkey Potpie, 16

MICROWAVE RECIPIES
Apple Graham Pie, 113
Bow Tie Turkey Bake, 27
Cheddar Cauliflower, 69
Cheesy Tuna Noodles, 27
Cherry Swirl Fudge, 103
Microwave Carrot Casserole, 74
Microwave Scalloped Potatoes, 76
Orange Truffles, 101

MINT
Mint Chocolate Cake, 116
Mint Iced Tea Cooler, 7
Peppermint Candy Cookies, 93
Peppermint Hot Chocolate, 11

MUFFINS
Banana Apple Muffins, 142
California Orange Muffins, 83
Tropical Muffins, 82

N

NUTS & PEANUT BUTTER
Almond-Filled Butterhorns, 84
Buckeyes, 95
Caramel Pecan Pound Cake, 116
Chocolate Surprise Cookies, 96
Cranberry Walnut Bars, 103
Dilled Sole with Almonds, 141
Fruit 'n' Nut Trail Mix, 11
Georgia Pecan Cake, 122
Maple Nut Cake, 115
No-Fuss Peanut Butter Cookies, 104
Nutty Carrot Salad, 53
Peanut Butter 'n' Jelly Cookies, 105
Peanut Butter Lover's Cake, 120
Peanutty Carrots, 134
Raspberry-Almond Jelly Roll, 124
Reindeer Treats, 103
Strawberry-Nut Pinwheel Cookies, 100
Walnut Blintz Torte, 121
Zucchini with Pecans, 135

O

OATS
Oatmeal Yeast Bread, 82
White Chocolate Oatmeal Cookies, 97

ONIONS
Buttery Carrots 'n' Onions, 168
Chive-Onion Vegetable Dip, 144
Onion 'n' Tomato Topped Muffins, 144
Onion Brunch Squares, 164
Pork Chops with Onions and Apples, 37

ORANGE
California Orange Muffins, 83
Cranberry Orange Vinaigrette, 61
Orange-Avocado Tossed Salad, 54
Orange Chicken Salad, 133
Orange Drop Cookies, 105
Orange Gelatin Cups, 143
Orange Meringue Pie, 172
Orange Rhubarb Pie, 114
Orange Sweet Potatoes, 78
Orange Truffles, 101
Pork with Orange Sauce, 38
Raspberry Citrus Bars, 97

OVEN ENTREES (also see Casseroles;
Meat Loaves & Meatballs; Meat Pie &
Pizza; Microwave Recipes)
Cheese-Stuffed Pork Roast, 25
Chicken Roll-Ups with Cherry Sauce, 14
Cornish Hens with Veggies, 26
Country-Style Ribs, 23
French Veal Chops, 138
Fruit-Stuffed Pork Roast, 27

✓ *Recipe includes Nutritional Analysis and Diabetic Exchanges*

OVEN ENTREES (continued)
Glazed Holiday Pork Roast, 13
Glazed Pork Tenderloin, 39
Marinated Beef Tenderloin, 17
Mexican Chicken Manicotti, 37
Onion Brunch Squares, 164
Roast Pork with Raspberry Sauce, 16
Rosemary-Garlic Chicken and
        Veggies, 147
Salmon Stuffed Peppers, 14
✓ Southwestern Pork Roast, 25
Steak Over Potatoes, 168
Stuffed Pork Tenderloin, 21
Stuffed Turkey Roll, 166
Sweet 'n' Sour Pot Roast, 13
Tropical Glazed Chicken Strips, 32
Trout Baked in Cream, 44

P

PANCAKES
Golden Pancakes, 164
Puffed Pancakes, 154

PASTA & NOODLES
✓ Angel Hair Pasta Salad, 53
Beefy Tomato Rigatoni, 39
Bow Tie Turkey Bake, 27
Broccoli Fettuccine, 144
Broccoli Noodle Supreme, 76
Cheesy Tuna Noodles, 27
✓ Chicken Lasagna, 23
Crab Pasta Salad, 52
Creamy Fettuccine, 29
Fancy Mac 'n' Cheese, 158
Linguine with Garlic Clam Sauce, 44
Macaroni 'n' Cheese for Two, 149
Meatball Stroganoff with Noodles, 40
Meaty Chili Lasagna, 42
Mexican Chicken Manicotti, 37
Pasta Jambalaya, 21
Pepperoni Pasta Bake, 43
Ravioli with Shrimp Tomato Sauce, 31
Rich 'n' Cheesy Macaroni, 69
Spaghetti 'n' Meat Sauce, 146
Spaghetti 'n' Meatballs, 36
Spicy Chicken Linguine, 32
Sun Kernel Delight, 50
Vegetable Pasta Salad, 62
✓ Vegetarian Lasagna, 31
White Bean and Pasta Soup, 60

PEACHES
Chicken with Peach Stuffing, 172
Peach Cream Pie, 125
Peaches 'n' Cream Pie, 109
Peachy Angel Food Cake, 161

PEARS
Baked Pears, 139
✓ Crustless Pear Pie, 123

Lemon Pear Pie, 113
Pears in Spiced Raisin Sauce, 150

PEPPERS
Cheddar-Chili Bread Twists, 86
✓ Corn and Peppers, 68
Jalapeno Grilled Chicken, 22
Meaty Chili Lasagna, 42
Peppered Green Beans, 166
Pork Chops with Tomatoes and
        Peppers, 136
Salad with Tomato-Green Pepper
        Dressing, 168
Salmon Stuffed Peppers, 14

PIES
Apple Blackberry Pie, 110
Apple Graham Pie, 113
✓ Banana Cream Pie, 115
Blueberry Cream Pies, 112
Cherry Blueberry Pie, 110
Coconut Pineapple Pie, 113
✓ Crustless Pear Pie, 123
Dutch Apricot Pie, 128
Fluffy Strawberry Meringue Pie, 124
Glazed Blackberry Pie, 112
Glazed Pineapple Pie, 125
Lemon Pear Pie, 113
Mini Apple Pie, 146
Orange Meringue Pie, 172
Orange Rhubarb Pie, 114
Peach Cream Pie, 125
Peaches 'n' Cream Pie, 109
Raspberry Meringue Pie, 109
Sweet Apple Pie, 125
Very Lemony Meringue Pie, 128

PINEAPPLE
Carrots and Pineapple, 74
Coconut Pineapple Pie, 113
Glazed Pineapple Pie, 125
Pineapple Beef Stir-Fry, 26
Tropical Muffins, 82

PORK (also see Ham & Bacon; Sausage)
Barbecued Pork Chop Supper, 28
Cheese-Stuffed Pork Roast, 25
Country-Style Ribs, 23
Fruit-Stuffed Pork Roast, 27
Glazed Holiday Pork Roast, 13
Glazed Pork Tenderloin, 39
No-Fuss Pork and Sauerkraut, 39
Pork Chops with Onions and Apples, 37
Pork Chops with Tomatoes and
        Peppers, 136
✓ Pork Veggie Stir-Fry, 41
Pork with Orange Sauce, 38
Roast Pork with Raspberry Sauce, 16
✓ Southwestern Pork Roast, 25
Stroganoff-Style Pork Chops, 34
Stuffed Pork Tenderloin, 21

POTATOES & SWEET POTATOES
Candied Sweet Potatoes, 72
✓ Cheese-Stuffed Potatoes, 79
Cheesy Potatoes, 138
Cottage Cheese Potato Rolls, 170
Cream of Potato Soup, 146
Crispy Potato Pancakes, 143
Golden Apple Potato Salad, 62
Italian Potato Salad, 60
Loaded Mashed Potatoes, 67
Louisiana Sweet Potato Casserole, 166
Microwave Scalloped Potatoes, 76
Orange Sweet Potatoes, 78
Potato Rolls, 88
Scalloped Potatoes, 136
Spicy Potato Salad, 49
Steak Over Potatoes, 168
Sweet Potato Bake, 70
Swiss Cheese Potato Pancakes, 72

PRESSURE COOKER RECIPES
Ham with Vegetables, 45
Sweet Beef Stew, 43

PUDDING & MOUSSE
Caramel Dumpling Pudding, 135
Chocolate Fudge Mousse, 153
Frosty Chocolate Mousse, 121
Pumpkin Crunch Parfaits, 123

PUMPKIN
Pumpkin Crunch Parfaits, 123
Pumpkin Spice Bars, 102

R

RAISINS & DATES
Grandma's Date Bars, 139
Pears in Spiced Raisin Sauce, 150
✓ Raisin Carrot Cake, 129

RASPBERRIES
Berry Cheesecake Parfaits, 167
Berry Rhubarb Sauce, 131
Raspberry-Almond Jelly Roll, 124
✓ Raspberry Cabbage Salad, 49
Raspberry Citrus Bars, 97
Raspberry Meringue Pie, 109
Red Raspberry Mousse Dessert, 128
Roast Pork with Raspberry Sauce, 16
Upside-Down Raspberry Cake, 114

RHUBARB
Berry Rhubarb Sauce, 131
Easy Rhubarb Dessert, 130
Orange Rhubarb Pie, 114
Strawberry Rhubarb Coffee Cake, 81

RICE & BARLEY
Chicken Carrot Fried Rice, 33
Colorful Fried Rice, 150
Mexican Chicken and Rice, 161

Patchwork Rice Pilaf, 77
Southwestern Chicken Barley Soup, 55
Wild Rice Waldorf, 65

ROLLS
Almond-Filled Butterhorns, 84
Buttermilk Pan Rolls, 89
Cottage Cheese Potato Rolls, 170
Glazed Crescent Rolls, 85
Potato Rolls, 88

S

SALADS & DRESSINGS (also see Coleslaw)
Dressings
    Cranberry Orange Vinaigrette, 61
    French Salad Dressing, 135
    Maple-Dijon Salad Dressing, 65
    Mustard Salad Dressing, 172
    Poppy Seed Dressing, 47
    Tomato Soup Salad Dressing, 61
Fruit and Gelatin Salads
    Blue Cheese Apple Salad, 62
    Christmas Gelatin Ring, 48
    Cranberry Gelatin Mold, 52
    Orange Gelatin Cups, 143
    Refreshing Fruit Salad, 136
    Saucy Fruit Medley, 164
    Sunshine Fruit Salad, 62
Green Salads
    Apple Spinach Salad, 161
    Apple Tossed Salad, 48
    Festive Tossed Salad, 51
    Greens 'n' Grapefruit Salad, 174
    Honey-Mustard Tossed Salad, 153
    Orange-Avocado Tossed Salad, 54
    ✓Raspberry Cabbage Salad, 49
    Salad with Tomato-Green Pepper Dressing, 168
    Spinach Salad with Spicy Honey Dressing, 64
    Veggie Spinach Salad, 154
    Warm Spinach Salad, 150
Main-Dish Salads
    Chicken Fajita Salad, 55
    Chicken Salad on a Tortilla, 142
    Citrusy Avocado Crab Salad, 60
    Layered Ham and Spinach Salad, 47
    Orange Chicken Salad, 133
Pasta and Rice Salads
    ✓Angel Hair Pasta Salad, 53
    Crab Pasta Salad, 52
    Sun Kernel Delight, 50
    Vegetable Pasta Salad, 62
    Wild Rice Waldorf, 65
Potato Salads
    Golden Apple Potato Salad, 62
    Italian Potato Salad, 60
    Spicy Potato Salad, 49
Vegetable Salads
    Chilled Asparagus Salad, 133
    Chilled Marinated Asparagus, 51
    Cool Cucumber Salad, 59
    Creamy Cauliflower Salad, 52
    Fiesta Vegetable Salad, 61
    Nutty Carrot Salad, 53
    Pickled Carrots, 50
    Vegetable Salad Medley, 64

SALSAS
Black Bean Salsa, 8
Garden Salsa, 7

SANDWICHES
✓Beef Cabbage Stromboli, 35
✓Cheesy Turkey Burgers, 33
Fried Green Tomato Sandwiches, 36
Italian Beef Sandwiches, 20
Onion 'n' Tomato Topped Muffins, 144
Open-Faced Tuna Burgers, 162
Roast Beef Sandwich Roll, 24
Shrimp Patty Sandwiches, 17
Sourdough Cheeseburgers, 22
Western Omelet Sandwich, 149

SAUSAGE
Cheesy Sausage Nachos, 5
Corn and Sausage Soup, 63
Pasta Jambalaya, 21
Pepperoni Pasta Bake, 43
Spaghetti 'n' Meatballs, 36
White Bean and Pasta Soup, 60

SIDE DISHES (also see Casseroles)
Acorn Squash with Spinach Stuffing, 79
Bacon-Topped Brussels Sprouts, 174
Broccoli Noodle Supreme, 76
Buttery Carrots 'n' Onions, 168
Candied Sweet Potatoes, 72
Carrots and Pineapple, 74
Cheddar Cauliflower, 69
✓Cheese-Stuffed Potatoes, 79
Cheesy Potatoes, 138
Colorful Fried Rice, 150
Confetti Carrot Fritters, 70
✓Corn and Peppers, 68
Crispy Potato Pancakes, 143
Early-Bird Asparagus Supreme, 77
Flavorful Carrots, 75
Honey-Mustard Carrots, 75
Lemon Basil Carrots, 141
Maple Apple Rings, 76
Okra Medley, 67
Orange Sweet Potatoes, 78
Oven-Roasted Carrots, 73
Patchwork Rice Pilaf, 77
Peanutty Carrots, 134
Peppered Green Beans, 166
Sauteed Carrots, 75
Sauteed Green Beans, 162
Seasoned Beans and Tomatoes, 170
Squash Rings with Green Beans, 172
Sweet-Sour Beets, 77
Swiss Cheese Potato Pancakes, 72
Zesty Broccoli and Artichokes, 67
Zucchini with Pecans, 135

SKILLET & STOVETOP SUPPERS
Apricot Lamb Chops, 154
Beef Rouladen, 174
Broccoli Fettuccine, 144
Chicken Carrot Fried Rice, 33
Chicken with Peach Stuffing, 172
Creamy Fettuccine, 29
Dilled Sole with Almonds, 141
✓Down-Home Pot Roast, 15
Linguine with Garlic Clam Sauce, 44
Meatball Stroganoff with Noodles, 40
Mexican Chicken and Rice, 161
Pasta Jambalaya, 21
Pineapple Beef Stir-Fry, 26
Pork Chops with Tomatoes and Peppers, 136
✓Pork Veggie Stir-Fry, 41
Pork with Orange Sauce, 38
Ravioli with Shrimp Tomato Sauce, 31
Sesame Dill Fish, 157
Skillet Chicken, 134
Spaghetti 'n' Meat Sauce, 146
Stroganoff-Style Pork Chops, 34
Yankee Pot Roast, 42

SLOW COOKER RECIPES
Barbecued Pork Chop Supper, 28
Fruited Chicken, 29
Italian Beef Sandwiches, 20
No-Fuss Pork and Sauerkraut, 39
Slow-Cooked Cabbage Rolls, 29
Slow-Cooked Coffee Pot Roast, 38
Slow-Cooked Rump Roast, 20
Slow-Cooked Tamale Casserole, 33
Slow-Cooker Salmon Loaf, 170

SOUPS & CHILI
Broccoli Chowder, 54
Cheesy Chicken Corn Soup, 48
Cheesy Vegetable Soup, 54
Corn and Sausage Soup, 63
Cream Cheese Chicken Soup, 50
Cream of Potato Soup, 146
Creamy Carrot Parsnip Soup, 53
Flower Garden Soup, 64
Hearty Chicken Vegetable Soup, 58
Hearty Vegetable Soup, 47
Roasted Veggie Chili, 58
Southwestern Chicken Barley Soup, 55
Split Pea Soup, 59
Vegetable Beef Soup, 58
White Bean and Pasta Soup, 60

✓*Recipe includes Nutritional Analysis and Diabetic Exchanges*

SPINACH
Acorn Squash with Spinach Stuffing, 79
Apple Spinach Salad, 161
Layered Ham and Spinach Salad, 47
Spinach Cheese Strata, 44
Spinach Salad with Spicy Honey
    Dressing, 64
✓Vegetarian Lasagna, 31
Veggie Spinach Salad, 154
Warm Spinach Salad, 150

SQUASH & ZUCCHINI
Acorn Squash with Spinach Stuffing, 79
Butternut Squash Layer Cake, 117
Cheesy Zucchini Bake, 34
Mini Zucchini Bread, 136
Squash Rings with Green Beans, 172
Summer Squash Bake, 144
Zucchini with Pecans, 135

STEWS
Busy Day Beef Stew, 13
Savory Vegetable Beef Stew, 41
Sweet Beef Stew, 43

STRAWBERRIES
Fluffy Strawberry Meringue Pie, 124
Glazed Strawberry Sundaes, 134
Patriotic Pizza, 129
Strawberry Ice, 116
Strawberry-Nut Pinwheel Cookies, 100
Strawberry Rhubarb Coffee Cake, 81
Strawberry Schaum Torte, 175
Strawberry Sunshine Cake, 131

T

TIPS
Appliances suitable for single cooking, 139
Carrot tips, 71
Cooking vegetables, 75
Creating decorative pie crusts, 118
Cutting pizza, 11
Fruit ideas, 150
Helpful cookie hints, 92
Making sandwiches special, 160
Peeling peaches, 109
Reliable roast hints, 45
Which pies to refrigerate, 113

TOMATOES
Beefy Tomato Rigatoni, 39
Fried Green Tomato Sandwiches, 36
Onion 'n' Tomato Topped Muffins, 144
Pork Chops with Tomatoes and
    Peppers, 136
Salad with Tomato-Green Pepper
    Dressing, 168
Seasoned Beans and Tomatoes, 170
Spicy Tomato Cooler, 139
Tomato Bread, 82

TURKEY
Barbecued Turkey Slices, 40
Bow Tie Turkey Bake, 27
✓Cheesy Turkey Burgers, 33
Stuffed Turkey Roll, 166
✓Turkey 'n' Beef Loaf, 30
Turkey Potpie, 16

V

VEGETABLES (*also see specific kinds*)
Bacon-Topped Brussels Sprouts, 174
Cheesy Eggplant Bake, 73
Cheesy Vegetable Soup, 54
Chive-Onion Vegetable Dip, 144
Cool Cucumber Salad, 59
Cornish Hens with Veggies, 26
Fiesta Vegetable Salad, 61
Flower Garden Soup, 64
Garden Salsa, 7
Ham with Vegetables, 45
Hearty Chicken Vegetable Soup, 58
Hearty Vegetable Soup, 47
✓Pork Veggie Stir-Fry, 41
Roasted Veggie Chili, 58
Rosemary-Garlic Chicken and
    Veggies, 147
Savory Vegetable Beef Stew, 41
Sweet-Sour Beets, 77
Vegetable Beef Soup, 58
Vegetable Pasta Salad, 62
Vegetable Salad Medley, 64
Veggie French Bread, 158
Veggie Spinach Salad, 154

Y

YEAST BREADS (*also see Coffee Cakes; Rolls*)
Holiday Breakfast Braid, 88
Oatmeal Yeast Bread, 82
Tomato Bread, 82

Alphabetical Recipe Index

A

Acorn Squash with Spinach Stuffing, 79
Almond-Filled Butterhorns, 84
Almond Rock Candy, 107
✓Angel Hair Pasta Salad, 53
Apple Blackberry Pie, 110
Apple Cabbage Slaw, 157
Apple Crisp, 131
Apple Fritters, 142
Apple Graham Pie, 113
Apple Pie Ice Cream, 117
Apple Spinach Salad, 161
Apple Tossed Salad, 48
✓Apricot Cranberry Bread, 87
Apricot Lamb Chops, 154
Apricot Scones, 86
Artichokes Au Gratin, 78

B

Bacon-Topped Brussels Sprouts, 174
Baked Pears, 139
Banana Apple Muffins, 142
✓Banana Cream Pie, 115
Banana Toffee Cream, 141
Barbecued Beef Brisket, 35
Barbecued Pork Chop Supper, 28
Barbecued Turkey Slices, 40
✓Beef Cabbage Stromboli, 35
Beef Rouladen, 174
Beefy Tomato Rigatoni, 39
Berry Cheesecake Parfaits, 167
Berry Rhubarb Sauce, 131
Black Bean Salsa, 8
Blue Cheese Apple Salad, 62
Blueberry Cream Pies, 112

Bow Tie Turkey Bake, 27
Broccoli Chowder, 54
Broccoli Fettuccine, 144
Broccoli Ham Quiche, 24
Broccoli Noodle Supreme, 76
Broccoli Slaw, 63
Broccoli Supreme, 72
Brownies from Heaven, 96
Buckeyes, 95
Busy Day Beef Stew, 13
Buttermilk Pan Rolls, 89
Buttermilk Scones, 133
Butternut Squash Layer Cake, 117
Buttery Carrots 'n' Onions, 168

C

California Orange Muffins, 83
Candied Sweet Potatoes, 72

Caramel Dumpling Pudding, 135
Caramel Pecan Pound Cake, 116
Carrots and Pineapple, 74
Cheddar Cabbage Casserole, 79
Cheddar Cauliflower, 69
Cheddar Cheese Carrot, 9
Cheddar-Chili Bread Twists, 86
✓Cheese-Stuffed Potatoes, 79
Cheese-Stuffed Pork Roast, 25
Cheesecake Diamonds, 96
Cheesy Chicken Corn Soup, 48
Cheesy Eggplant Bake, 73
Cheesy Potatoes, 138
Cheesy Sausage Nachos, 5
Cheesy Tuna Noodles, 27
✓Cheesy Turkey Burgers, 33
Cheesy Vegetable Soup, 54
Cheesy Zucchini Bake, 34
Cherry Blueberry Pie, 110
Cherry Cappuccino Sundaes, 143
Cherry Swirl Fudge, 103
Chicken Carrot Fried Rice, 33
Chicken Fajita Salad, 55
Chicken French Bread Pizza, 20
✓Chicken Lasagna, 23
Chicken Roll-Ups with Cherry Sauce, 14
Chicken Salad on a Tortilla, 142
Chicken Stir-Fry Bake, 153
Chicken with Peach Stuffing, 172
Chilled Asparagus Salad, 133
Chilled Marinated Asparagus, 51
Chive-Onion Vegetable Dip, 144
Choco-Cloud Brownies, 94
✓Chocolate Cappuccino Cookies, 107
Chocolate Chip Carrot Bread, 85
Chocolate Chip Cheesecake Bars, 95
Chocolate Chunk Shortbread, 105
Chocolate Fudge Mousse, 153
Chocolate Meringues, 100
Chocolate Surprise Cookies, 96
Christmas Gelatin Ring, 48
Cinnamon Snaps, 91
Citrus Grape Drink, 11
Citrus Quencher, 5
Citrusy Avocado Crab Salad, 60
Coconut Pineapple Pie, 113
Colorful Fried Rice, 150
Confetti Carrot Fritters, 70
Cool Cucumber Salad, 59
✓Corn and Peppers, 68
Corn and Sausage Soup, 63
Cornish Hens with Veggies, 26
Cottage Cheese Potato Rolls, 170
Country-Style Ribs, 23
Crab Pasta Salad, 52
Cranberry Apple Cider, 7
Cranberry Cheese Bread, 83
Cranberry Gelatin Mold, 52
Cranberry Orange Vinaigrette, 61
Cranberry Swirl Coffee Cake, 87

Cranberry Walnut Bars, 103
Cream Cheese Chicken Soup, 50
Cream of Potato Soup, 146
Creamy Candy Bar Dessert, 122
Creamy Carrot Parsnip Soup, 53
Creamy Cauliflower Salad, 52
Creamy Citrus Sherbet, 171
Creamy Fettuccine, 29
Creamy Hot Cocoa, 149
Creamy Parmesan Sauce, 68
Crisp Lemon Sugar Cookies, 169
Crispy Butter Cookies, 106
Crispy Potato Pancakes, 143
✓Crustless Pear Pie, 123
✓Curry Carrot Dip, 6

D

Danish Coffee Cake, 165
Dilled Sole with Almonds, 141
Double Chocolate Fudge, 94
✓Down-Home Pot Roast, 15
Dutch Apricot Pie, 128

E

Early-Bird Asparagus Supreme, 77
Easy Macaroons, 104
Easy Rhubarb Dessert, 130
Emerald Isle Dip, 9

F

Fancy Mac 'n' Cheese, 158
Festive Tossed Salad, 51
Fiesta Cheese Ball, 10
Fiesta Vegetable Salad, 61
Flavorful Carrots, 75
Flower Garden Soup, 64
Fluffy Strawberry Meringue Pie, 124
Fourth of July Pizza, 6
French Salad Dressing, 135
French Veal Chops, 138
Fried Green Tomato Sandwiches, 36
Frosty Chocolate Mousse, 121
Fruit 'n' Nut Trail Mix, 11
Fruit-Filled Spritz Cookies, 100
Fruit Kabobs with Citrus Dip, 157
Fruit Punch, 162
Fruit-Stuffed Pork Roast, 27
Fruited Chicken, 29

G

Garden Salsa, 7
Garlic Parmesan Breadsticks, 84
Georgia Pecan Cake, 122
Glazed Blackberry Pie, 112
Glazed Crescent Rolls, 85
Glazed Holiday Pork Roast, 13
Glazed Pineapple Pie, 125
Glazed Pork Tenderloin, 39
Glazed Strawberry Sundaes, 134

Golden Apple Potato Salad, 62
Golden Pancakes, 164
Grandma's Date Bars, 139
Grape and Cabbage Salad, 65
Grape Sherbet, 111
Greens 'n' Grapefruit Salad, 174
Grilled Italian Chicken, 30

H

Ham Loaf with Mustard Sauce, 28
Ham with Vegetables, 45
Hearty Chicken Vegetable Soup, 58
Hearty Vegetable Soup, 47
Herbed Garlic Cheese Spread, 5
Holiday Breakfast Braid, 88
Holiday Fruitcake, 89
Homemade Cajun Seasoning, 69
Honey-Mustard Carrots, 75
Honey-Mustard Tossed Salad, 153
✓Honey Spice Cookies, 95

I

Italian Beef Sandwiches, 20
Italian Potato Salad, 60

J

Jalapeno Grilled Chicken, 22

L

Layered Ham and Spinach Salad, 47
Lemon Basil Carrots, 141
Lemon Pear Pie, 113
Light Candied Fruitcake, 81
Linguine with Garlic Clam Sauce, 44
Loaded Mashed Potatoes, 67
Louisiana Sweet Potato Casserole, 166

M

Macaroni 'n' Cheese for Two, 149
Maple Apple Rings, 76
Maple-Dijon Salad Dressing, 65
Maple Nut Cake, 115
Marinated Beef Tenderloin, 17
Meatball Stroganoff with Noodles, 40
Meaty Chili Lasagna, 42
Mexican Chicken and Rice, 161
Mexican Chicken Manicotti, 37
Microwave Carrot Casserole, 74
Microwave Scalloped Potatoes, 76
Mini Apple Pie, 146
Mini Zucchini Bread, 136
Mint Chocolate Cake, 116
Mint Iced Tea Cooler, 7
Mock Eggnog, 8
Moist Chocolate Cake, 123
Molasses Butterballs, 105

✓*Recipe includes Nutritional Analysis and Diabetic Exchanges*

Mustard Salad Dressing, 172

N

New Haven Clam Pizza, 10
No-Fuss Peanut Butter Cookies, 104
No-Fuss Pork and Sauerkraut, 39
Nutty Carrot Salad, 53

O

Oatmeal Yeast Bread, 82
Okra Medley, 67
Old-Fashioned Chocolate Soda, 133
Onion 'n' Tomato Topped Muffins, 144
Onion Brunch Squares, 164
Open-Faced Tuna Burgers, 162
Orange-Avocado Tossed Salad, 54
Orange Chicken Salad, 133
Orange Drop Cookies, 105
Orange Gelatin Cups, 143
Orange Meringue Pie, 172
Orange Rhubarb Pie, 114
Orange Sweet Potatoes, 78
Orange Truffles, 101
Oven-Roasted Carrots, 73

P

Parmesan Ham Frittata, 138
Pasta Jambalaya, 21
Patchwork Rice Pilaf, 77
Patriotic Pizza, 129
Peach Cream Pie, 125
Peaches 'n' Cream Pie, 109
Peachy Angel Food Cake, 161
Peanut Butter 'n' Jelly Cookies, 105
Peanut Butter Lover's Cake, 120
Peanutty Carrots, 134
Pears in Spiced Raisin Sauce, 150
Peppered Green Beans, 166
Peppermint Candy Cookies, 93
Peppermint Hot Chocolate, 11
Pepperoni Pasta Bake, 43
Pickled Carrots, 50
Picnic Stuffed Eggs, 5
Pineapple Beef Stir-Fry, 26
Popcorn Cookies, 93
Poppy Seed Dressing, 47
Pork Chops with Onions and Apples, 37
Pork Chops with Tomatoes and
    Peppers, 136
✓ Pork Veggie Stir-Fry, 41
Pork with Orange Sauce, 38
Potato Rolls, 88
Puffed Pancakes, 154
Pumpkin Crunch Parfaits, 123
Pumpkin Spice Bars, 102

R

Raspberry-Almond Jelly Roll, 124
✓ Raisin Carrot Cake, 129

✓ Raspberry Cabbage Salad, 49
Raspberry Citrus Bars, 97
Raspberry Meringue Pie, 109
Ravioli with Shrimp Tomato Sauce, 31
Red Raspberry Mousse Dessert, 128
Refreshing Fruit Salad, 136
Reindeer Treats, 103
Rich 'n' Cheesy Macaroni, 69
Roast Beef Sandwich Roll, 24
Roast Pork with Raspberry Sauce, 16
Roasted Veggie Chili, 58
Rosemary-Garlic Chicken and Veggies, 147

S

Salad with Tomato-Green Pepper
    Dressing, 168
Salmon Cheese Spread, 8
Salmon Stuffed Peppers, 14
Santa Sugar Cookies, 102
Saucy Fruit Medley, 164
Saucy Green Bean Bake, 78
Sauteed Carrots, 75
Sauteed Green Beans, 162
Savory Vegetable Beef Stew, 41
Scalloped Carrots, 68
Scalloped Potatoes, 136
Seasoned Beans and Tomatoes, 170
Sesame Dill Fish, 157
Shrimp Dijonnaise, 150
Shrimp Patty Sandwiches, 17
Simply Fudgy Brownies, 141
Skillet Chicken, 134
Slow-Cooked Cabbage Rolls, 29
Slow-Cooked Coffee Pot Roast, 38
Slow-Cooked Rump Roast, 20
Slow-Cooked Tamale Casserole, 33
Slow-Cooker Salmon Loaf, 170
Sour Cream Chocolate Cookies, 91
Sourdough Cheeseburgers, 22
South Liberty Hall Relish, 70
Southwestern Chicken Barley Soup, 55
✓ Southwestern Pork Roast, 25
Spaghetti 'n' Meat Sauce, 146
Spaghetti 'n' Meatballs, 36
Sparkling Melon, 158
Spiced Coffee with Cream, 147
Spicy Chicken Linguine, 32
Spicy Potato Salad, 49
Spicy Tomato Cooler, 139
Spinach Cheese Strata, 44
Spinach Salad with Spicy Honey
    Dressing, 64
Split Pea Soup, 59
Sponge Cake with Blueberry Topping, 120
Squash Rings with Green Beans, 172
Star Sandwich Cookies, 106
Steak Over Potatoes, 168
Strawberry Ice, 116
Strawberry-Nut Pinwheel Cookies, 100
Strawberry Rhubarb Coffee Cake, 81

Strawberry Schaum Torte, 175
Strawberry Sunshine Cake, 131
Stroganoff-Style Pork Chops, 34
Stuffed Pork Tenderloin, 21
Stuffed Turkey Roll, 166
✓ Sugar-Free Chocolate Eclairs, 130
Summer Squash Bake, 144
Sun Kernel Delight, 50
Sunflower Fudge, 93
Sunshine Fruit Salad, 62
Surprise Carrot Cake, 111
Swedish Butter Cookies, 91
Sweet 'n' Sour Pot Roast, 13
Sweet Apple Pie, 125
Sweet Beef Stew, 43
Sweet Potato Bake, 70
Sweetheart Sorbet, 110
Sweet-Sour Beets, 77
Swiss Cheese Potato Pancakes, 72

T

Terrific Toffee, 106
Toffee Malted Cookies, 101
Tomato Bread, 82
Tomato Soup Salad Dressing, 61
Tropical Banana Splits, 149
Tropical Glazed Chicken Strips, 32
Tropical Muffins, 82
Trout Baked in Cream, 44
✓ Turkey 'n' Beef Loaf, 30
Turkey Potpie, 16

U

Upside-Down Raspberry Cake, 114

V

Vegetable Beef Soup, 58
Vegetable Pasta Salad, 62
Vegetable Salad Medley, 64
✓ Vegetarian Lasagna, 31
Veggie French Bread, 158
Veggie Spinach Salad, 154
Very Lemony Meringue Pie, 128

W

Walnut Blintz Torte, 121
Warm Spinach Salad, 150
Western Omelet Sandwich, 149
Whipped Cream Biscuits, 147
White Bean and Pasta Soup, 60
White Chocolate Oatmeal Cookies, 97
Wild Rice Waldorf, 65

Y

Yankee Pot Roast, 42

Z

Zesty Broccoli and Artichokes, 67
Zucchini with Pecans, 135